From
under a
Rock

TAM MACPHEE

From under a Rock
Copyright © 2022 by Tam MacPhee

Tellwell Talent
www.tellwell.ca

ISBN
978-0-2288-7608-3 (Hardcover)
978-0-2288-7607-6 (Paperback)
978-0-2288-7609-0 (eBook)

Table of Contents

My Mom

A s I guide you to the bathroom, there is no rushing you.
We work our way through the process that used to be so easy to do.
Each day is a guess, will she let me help her or must I insist.
It now takes so long to feed you, seems like that's all we try to do.
Trapping you at our table and keeping you by the hand and knee.
Take a bite and open up are now lost, blank commands for you.
Saying your name and finding your gaze, are tricks that seem to work.
I try my best to keep you nourished as you are always on the move.
Adding calories and butter to keep you in the groove.
What's she thinking, where is she drifting, as I say her name, in hopes to see.
Many strive to be so skinny and here you are thin and in good physical health.
Never will you realize you finally got your way.
Fit as a fiddle, and always trying to get away.
I am a voice for seniors,
I have planted many seeds,
I've opened doors with questions
In hopes one day they will listen,
as this disease is growing
and the system is lacking in many ways.
I pray and try to reach out,
for people to come your way.

As waiting for your funeral,
will be a wasted day.
Your life is still here on earth,
your bright blue eyes are proof.
If only people would show you love,
as I believe it is God's way!
I need to see the support,
it warms my heart more than I can say.
As I know you would be there for them,
if there was a way.
Please, please, please visit and give you a little of their day.
Music is your only joy, humming and singing, each and every day.
We love to see you enjoy it, so we leave it on replay.
Many miles you put on, pacing, and roaming back and forth all day.
Searching for things to do with thoughts that never seem to come your way.
Picking things up and carrying them, seems to keep you busy in some ways.
I wish I knew the answers to the few words that you can say.
I search and try to understand, just what might connect your thoughts,
I chat and keep you entertained to try and fill your day.
I can describe it as pure darkness, with a ray of light, now and again,
but never can I really know, the small world you must live within.
Your smile is contagious, your laugh is truly real; your hugs hold the meaning
of life, as we smile and hold you, dear.
A soft kiss good night, I whisper, "see you in the morning."
I say, "Love You Mom. Goodnight!"
A response of, "Love You Too," is my small reward for our day.
I turn out the light, and close the door,
and hope you will sleep your night away.

A poem I wrote while my mother lived with us during 2014–2015.

Preface

My story may not be for everyone, but it is mine. I own what I have lived through to become who I am today.

I pray I help at least one girl to find her strength and become a strong woman by telling my story. Do not allow life's lessons to weaken you. Face them head on and make the choice to become a wiser person. Learn from your life's lessons . . .

No one has the right to put you or any part of your life UNDER A ROCK. I am amazed by the roads that I have travelled in life. I didn't always follow my gut feelings; however, I am learning with years of wisdom, that we should do so every time.

Your inner feelings are true, so embrace them. Take that chance. Change things up. Spread your wings. You never know what will be waiting for you when you do. The universe has so much to offer!

As I read my own story, there are parts that choke me up, and almost feel like it must have been someone else's life. Prepare yourself to experience all kinds of emotions as you follow my story through what the universe has set out before me as my path.

I am not finished my journey yet. The sky is the limit. I plan on following my spiritual path, helping others along the way, enjoying my family, travelling, and exploring the earth.

CHAPTER 1

My Beginning

My life began in Glenwood, Nova Scotia.

I was born July 22, 1974, to Norma Tedford. I was the youngest of four children and my childhood memories are a nightmare. A whirlwind of emotions flows out of me when I think about it; happy is not one of them.

When we woke up every morning, we immediately went into survival mode. Trying to be invisible to avoid being hit, spanked, or kicked was our daily struggle. We never knew if it was going to be a good day, a bad day, or a horrible day.

I hated my ponytail being pulled. Not by my mother, but by my biological father Peter Sinclair. It was nice when he wasn't home.

We lived in a small house that most people would refer to as a shack. We had two bedrooms, a kitchen with a wood stove to cook on, a living room with a small black and white TV that we were hardly ever allowed to watch. We had a pantry and a cold room. I don't remember having a fridge, just a freezer. And a closet for a bathroom. Literally, a bucket with a toilet seat cover, and no running water. There was a small porch next to the so-called bathroom and a back door.

We had a working hand pump some of the time in the kitchen, but mostly we had to dip water out of the well and lug it into the house. The shit bucket was the worst, especially when it would splash up on us. I remember it was primarily my brother who had to empty it, but I do recall lugging it out to be emptied on occasion. It was a horrible experience. You didn't want it to slop down your leg, but if you spilled it there was guaranteed to be a beating as your reward.

In the early years I slept with my sister Sharon, who was one year older than me. We slept in a double bed that had a huge, tall wooden headboard and a footboard.

We were always scared to go to bed.

We often saw the white gowned angels hanging out on the right side of the bed near the bottom. Sometimes two and other times three of these figures would be there. I now know that they were our guardian angels sent to protect us. But at the time we were terrified since we were only about six to eight years old.

In our yard there were two huge maple trees, a pine tree, a cedar tree, and a lilac bush. I love nature. The scent of a lilac still brings me back to standing in our yard by the cedar tree smelling the lilac bush with my beautiful mother. It is one of my cherished memories of us together.

We had huge gardens that we worked in every day all summer long. Currants, blackberries, raspberries, and blueberries all grew close by and around our land. And we had planted strawberries too. The garden was full of root veggies for the cold room, along with peas, corn, beans, and cucumbers. I think we grew most everything. We raised goats for both their milk and meat. We had chickens, ducks, and even a pig at one time or another over the years. We bought very little at the grocery store but somehow Mom managed to feed us and make it work.

My mother was a strong woman, not afraid of hard work and boy did she have to work hard. My biological father controlled everything. We had no phone. We were not allowed to have friends over. He kept us pretty much as prisoners, ones who were barely even allowed to go to school. We were never allowed to go on school outings or to learning events. At school everyone had pen pals, but of course we were not permitted to participate. He wouldn't even let us write a letter to be mailed.

At school we didn't fit in. We lived in "The Shack." We never had money for a treat from the canteen or to buy our meals. We stood out. We were quiet and just plain different.

Our clothing was whatever Mom could find at Frenchy's, a place where you bought used clothing. I don't remember shopping anywhere else. I barely remember going into town. Maybe to Zellers, but only for underwear.

We were poor but still Peter managed to save money and put it in the bank. He was selfish and what he wanted came first. He saved up and paid cash for a new truck when I was nine or ten years old. It was a beautiful red Dodge truck, but I came to hate it. Whenever he would freak out because he had spent his money, he would beat my mom. She took many beatings because of that truck. Mom never had anything to do with it, but he still blamed her. He beat her as it somehow made him feel better.

Before the truck we had a red Rabbit car. And maybe at one time we also had a blue car. But it doesn't really matter because we hardly went anywhere. Ever.

In the yard we did have a pink buoy swing and a wooden rope swing hanging from a tree. I remember playing on the swing, staring up at the blue sky, and dreaming of what life was like for others.

CHAPTER 2

The Terrible Days

From an early age I knew there had to be mental issues at work in my father's brain. I knew he couldn't possibly be normal by the way he was raising us. At one point I even thought that he must be some sort of alien from another world because no real father would ever hurt his children like he did. Day after day.

The brainwashing, the mental, sexual, and physical abuse he subjected us to still to this day blows my mind.

My siblings and I prayed whenever he went somewhere that he would die and never return. We wanted to kill him, but we were always too scared that if we messed up, he would surely kill us. We never talked about killing him, but I assumed my siblings felt and thought the same way I did. I know I wanted him gone.

At the young age of four, I distinctly remember my mother walking us up the road to call her parents to come rescue us. My parents had been in a big fight and Peter had taken off. But he came back before Grampie Tedford got there to get us. I remember my older sister was pulling on my one arm and Peter was pulling on my other arm. However, we did manage to get away from him with the few things we had been able to grab. We went to my grandparents' house, but he stalked us. He sat outside the house and waited for us to come back with him.

He always threatened my mother, saying, "I'll kill your parents if you keep running there," or, "if you leave again, I will find you and kill your kids in front of you."

After a few attempts to escape, she stopped trying to leave him. We all lived in fear and at times he would go off the deep end and beat Mom. He didn't even need alcohol to do it; he would just snap.

He'd spank us for no reason, lining us up in an assembly line. He'd keep us in our room where we could hear him yelling. And hear Mom crying. We never knew if we would emerge to find Mom dead or alive. We watched him choke her on more than one occasion. It felt like we were frozen in time. I saw him choking her, pushed up against our footboard in our bedroom. I thought for sure he was going to kill her.

I was the youngest and I couldn't understand why my older siblings never did anything to stop him. They were scared I know, but I always waited for someone to step up and do something! I always wanted to kill him.

I probably did get some special treatment being the cutest little blonde-haired girl with ringlets and curls bouncing about my head. Maybe it did spare me a little bit, but it likely was more of a curse. I still got swatted and dragged by my hair. How he treated us was disgusting.

Once, we had cleared up some brush and burned a big pile of it on the weekend. The next day everyone went to school and Peter wasn't home either. Playfully, I had a stick and stirred up the ashes. Unfortunately, the wind picked up and the remaining vegetation on the hill caught fire. This put the neighbours' homes at risk, however, the fire department came and put it out. I don't think Mom ever told Peter I was to blame. At least, I don't remember receiving any punishment for the incident. I still tell my children this story, "When I was four . . ."

I remember being the only one home with Mom while my siblings were at school. And yes, at age four I was out helping her weed gardens and do the chores. I loved animals and nature. I loved just being outside; and the land was my friend. I could feel the spiritual pull to the moon and the stars.

We didn't do much to make any happy memories as a family. During my childhood I only remember going for ice cream a handful of times. A few times we did go to Roberts Island to go swimming. But my memory is of

Sharon, and I being dragged out and dunked in the water while screaming our heads off. Peter had each of us in one hand. Of course, after that experience we were scared to try and swim or even to go into the water.

Another time I remember our family getting three orders of clams and chips from the takeout place not far up the road. Peter, being the selfish pig that he was, got a whole order for himself and Mom had to split the other two orders between the five of us.

One summer I was asked what I wanted for my birthday. I replied that I would like to go in the skiff to an island and have a picnic. I loved the ocean.

When the day came there was a thick fog, but we still set out to go as a family on our adventure. I felt special, for a moment. The whole day was to be for me. However, my day soon crashed down around me.

The outboard motor broke down. Peter threw it overboard cursing and freaking out. We had to walk the shoreline instead with the skiff on a rope. Do you know what I remember about that day? I remember everyone's sad, scared faces because the day was a disaster.

I always seemed to have bad weather happen on my birthday and grew to hate my birthday because of this disaster of an outing.

I always longed for the perfect day. But it never happened.

CHAPTER 3

No Happy Memories

Christmas was its own special kind of disaster every year. From trees being thrown out the door before Christmas had even arrived, to all the hollering that took place. Peter was mean and hateful, but he was even more than usual around the holidays.

One year, Mom managed to get us dolls. One was blonde like me, and one was brunette like Sharon. When we opened them Christmas morning, Sharon's doll was damaged. The eye was broken, and she was fussing. We traded and I gave her mine to make her happy. I just wanted to have a happy day. I still have this doll, but I'm not even sure how it managed to survive.

My only other memories of Christmas were of getting a stocking with a big apple and orange in it every year. And the tinsel icicles on our tree.

Our maternal grandparents would bring us gifts and drop them off at the house. They were never welcomed to stay, but those gifts were always exciting. They meant we actually had something under the tree.

Peter always bitched about anyone that would dare come to the house. He was a control freak and we were his prisoners. Occasionally my grandparents would drive down during the summer for a visit. We just stayed outside for their visit. It was always a nice day, and I remember being excited to see them. We knew they were never welcomed, and that Mom had better not tell them anything about what was happening in our home.

Outside on the hill there were several paths. On one side of the paths were birch trees. We played outside under these trees on the steep hill. There was another little hill behind the house covered with spruce trees. That was another spot we could escape from the madness in the house and hideout. While in the spruce grove, we always tried to find some tree gum.

I loved being outside in nature. Beside our land was a lane with a hill. We would go sliding down that hill in the winter. The lane led to a dyke that separated the fresh water from the salt water of the ocean. The dyke was built out of rocks and crossed over to the back end of Roberts Island. It was really high, but we always climbed down over it to stand at the bottom to fish. I couldn't have been very old, and I was scared to death climbing it. On the saltwater side we went blood worming.

Blood worming requires you to walk out into the mud flats at low tide. With your old sneakers tied tight, pantlegs tucked into your socks, along with a special hoe and a bucket. We'd put a little salt water in the bucket, to keep the worms alive. This was back-breaking work, digging and picking up the worms. (A local buyer sold them in the US for sport fishing.) I was eleven to thirteen when I had to do this because I either had to buy my own school clothes, or not get any at all. As I started earning money, I invested in a pair of hip-rubber boots. This was better in the mud than the sneakers.

I remember the excitement of going to a real store. I bought a pink sweater. Boy was I proud of it! It was so freaking hot and sweaty to wear to school and it made me red in the face every time I wore it. I hated being told, "Man, you're red in the face." That comment always made me burning hot with embarrassment. The kids at school didn't care they were being mean. They just laughed at me.

We picked fine rockweed too. We sold this to the worm buyers. They packaged the worms in cooler boxes along with the fine rockweed for them to crawl around in. Then they sent them by plane to their customers. I think when we had the skiff that Peter even went Irish mossing. Locally Irish moss is gathered, sold, dried, and used to make things like ice cream. It is a vegan substitute for gelatin.

Peter was a hired hand on a few different lobster boats. But none of those jobs worked out. When I was younger, he was in a huge fight with the neighbour and never went back to fishing with him. I don't remember the details but ironically, I reconnected with these neighbours later in my adult life. Well, with the kids and the wife, but not with the man my father went fishing with, I barely remember him. My last few years as a pre-teen in Glenwood were spent worming and picking fine rockweed.

Peter would stay home all winter collecting unemployment cheques and terrorizing the family with his free time.

At some point over the years, I did see Mom scraping fur pelts. They were placed on boards inside out and we dried them in the kitchen by the wood stove. I think Peter did some of the trapping for the furs but mainly it was my brother who did that work in the winter. Muskrats, mink, and maybe a fox. They trapped them, dried them, and sold the furs.

My brother and Peter went deer hunting by walking through the woods. I don't think they ever sat in deer stands. My older sister went hunting as well.

My so-called grandfather, Peter's father, would come over, usually drunk. He didn't come often. More like maybe two times a year, despite not living far, perhaps only seven minutes away. He was a mason, building beautiful stone fireplaces and chimneys. I only remember him coming a few times, but he would grab at my mother, and it would always become a hollering match between him and Peter.

There were twelve siblings in Peter's family, four boys and eight girls. In later years I would come to learn his father was a pig too. Some of the girls had moved out when they were very young because Peter's father was very abusive. He beat them and took advantage of his own daughters. Peter's mother even resented some of her own daughters and didn't treat them very well. Most of my aunts had left home at sixteen years of age. Peter's mother died young, so I never met her.

My so-called grandfather was an alcoholic. He abused his wife and his children. When Peter was very young, he was expected to work around the house. If he did something wrong, he was beaten. One day he was hit over the head with a cast iron frying pan and dragged across the lawn. For sure he had a concussion that went untreated. He was backhanded daily, which I'm sure added to the injury. He still had to work, hurt or not.

Growing up in that environment and being beaten himself may provide some explanation for his actions. However, it's no excuse. If you don't like how you are treated, you need to make a choice to change and be different. I believe, on top of it all that he had something wrong with his brain. He must have been chemically imbalanced to act the way he did.

Regardless, he was a sick pig.

CHAPTER 4

A Living Nightmare At Home

The Argyle school was the most amazing place of my childhood. I went to school with the same kids from Primary to Grade 8. Any fond memories I have from my childhood were most likely to be from school.

My sister Sharon was just a grade above me. She went to Saint Anne Du Ruisseau High School. In her Grade 9 year they had a guidance counsellor whom she started to confide in. She never realized what she disclosed would have to be reported because we were being abused.

Social workers soon began to visit me at school to see what I had to say. Sharon had told me what she had done. We were so scared of the truth coming out, our father finding out, and killing us all in his rage. At one point Sharon told the counsellors it was all lies and that she didn't want them to do anything.

But it was too late. I was not backing down when they talked to me. I knew she was scared but we had to keep going to get us out of there. This was our only hope at a real life for us all.

I never wavered from my facts, and I stuck to the truth. Months before, when the social workers had visited Sharon and she had lied, she was simply too scared to tell the truth about what really was going on at home. I remember her coming home upset and telling Mom and Peter about it. I don't think she got in trouble because she had done exactly what he had wanted. She hadn't dared to tell the truth.

As part of my research for writing my book, I requested the social workers' notes. I discovered that many people had reported concerns about our family life. They had tried to investigate. But without a witness or any proof, the lack of evidence forced them to back off. Peter had stormed into the office and had threatened them, stating they had no right to question his kids. At one point in time, the social worker and police had arrived at the house requesting entry. But Peter had never allowed them access and had sent them away. So, they had backed off completely until the counsellor began to report the things Sharon was telling him.

But I recall even before this event, when I was in Grade 6 and 7 that I began to tell my school friends about some of the things I had to live with. My friends Abigail and April constantly and consistently told me that it wasn't normal. Even though I knew of no other life, I continually imagined what my life could be like in different surroundings.

Mom at times would visit the neighbours to use their phones, to try and figure a way out of our nightmare. If she had ever been caught by Peter, the horror she would have faced would have been unimaginable. She was so brave to try.

We had a teacher who lived next door. Mom had been going there to fill jugs with water because they had an artesian well and our well at the time was low. One day, she returned shaking and crying because the teacher had asked her not to come back as she feared for her own family's safety. I have always resented that the only hope Mom had at that time was slammed in her face and she had nowhere else to turn. Why couldn't that woman have helped Mom more? We could have been saved before things got to the point that they did. We were living a nightmare, and everyone was too scared to step up and help get us out of it.

So many facts were kept from us when we were younger, but as I grew older, I began to figure things out. Growing up, I had never been told that my two older siblings had a different father. We were left to figure that discovery out on our own. Mom's first husband had abandoned her at a young age with two little ones. He heard stories about the abuse of course, but never came to rescue his two kids. No one stepped up, everyone was too scared.

She had met Peter in a blueberry field at Argyle Head. They were both twenty-five in 1971 when they met. Peter was tall and handsome, appearing somewhat normal at the time. They married in 1973 after Sharon was born.

At first, they lived in town in an apartment, but they soon bought my mother's aunt's old house in Glenwood. Far away from everyone. I was born the following year in 1974.

As previously mentioned, we had no bathtub. We usually got a bucket with a little warm water in it and did a bit of washing most days. Sunday was the dreaded bath day. Mom had a fish tub and me and my sister were bathed together. Mom would boil water on the stove, and we would have a few inches to sit in while we were scrubbed. The worst part was it was my father who would wash us or dry us off. We were touched and inspected wherever he wanted. Our bodies were never our own from a very young age. I hated it.

We also dreaded kissing him goodnight. Again, he would do whatever he wanted as we would try to escape. I always had to rinse my mouth out and spit after his kisses. It was so revolting. We were forced to say we loved him. Then we would go to bed crying and upset.

Nothing made sense. Why were we even alive? I remember him always grabbing us, and us trying to pull away. This went on for years. It was gradual at first. He had always talked about inappropriate things, but as each year passed his behaviour worsened. He has such a sick mind. I'm sure Mom was mortified asking herself what she had got herself into.

I know my mom wanted to kill him every day; but like us she was scared it would backfire and he'd kill us. The torment my poor mother had to live with, for at least fourteen to fifteen years. Of watching her babies being abused.

My older sister Bev was seven years older than me. My brother was eight years older. My brother graduated high school under these circumstances, but he stayed. I don't think he could leave Mom to do all the work herself. He had been blood worming for years and continued to do that while living with us.

My oldest sister Bev was an amazing student. A's all the way. She was brilliant, but she was forced to quit in Grade 12 because she was pregnant. She was seventeen when she started Grade 12 in September and turned eighteen in November. She wasn't allowed to go back to school after Christmas Break.

So how does a girl who isn't allowed to go anywhere but school get pregnant? I guess she could have become pregnant at school in a closet. Trust me, that would have been better than the darker side of what really happened.

I remember hearing comments at home about waiting until Bev was old enough and could consent. *She will come around* was another statement that I heard a lot. He always ruined every Christmas and had been ranting about how Bev should give him a present. He was obsessed with her being a virgin. Peter often commented about Bev being a virgin, especially when she began to develop. It was all brainwashed into her head for years along with the molestation. It became worse and worse each year as we grew older. This all occurred before I was twelve, so thankfully I didn't understand what it all meant at the time.

You must understand that if you are beaten and scared enough you will freeze. Even when you know what's being done is so wrong. In the abuser's sick mind, they think you're OK with it because you haven't run away. Peter didn't care if we were okay with it or not. We were screaming on the inside and frozen on the outside. Hating every minute of our torture but unable to do anything about it.

My sister knew that if she didn't go along with his sickness he would come after her younger sisters. Probably even more. He didn't go to the extremes with us as he did with Bev, but as we got older things continued to escalate. Bev definitely took the worst of the physical abuse during our whole ordeal. Mom would have been mentally pushed beyond that of any other mother's limits. Mom was physically abused and threatened daily. I describe her life as having a gun to her head non-stop.

We all hated being called into the bedroom because he always grabbed us and grossly kissed us. Every day of our lives with him we were victims of his sickness. I remember on the weekends Bev would be called into the bedroom and Mom would be sent out. God only knows how she managed to feed the rest of us or do her chores while living in the hell she was a prisoner within. My sister's abuse grew worse over the years. Then, when she turned the magical age of sixteen, he basically silently raped her over and over because she was too scared and frozen. She had no way to stop him. Apparently, he believed he was in the clear legally as Bev was sixteen. He also thought she loved him.

We were all forced to say we loved him. Even though in reality we HATED him.

CHAPTER 5

Recounting The Abuse

This book is primarily written from my memories. In the summer of 2019, I turned forty-five and I began to tell people about writing this book. After I talked with my older sister, she expressed her wish to help me with some facts. But I didn't want to make her relive everything like I was while writing this book.

I learned from my conversations with Bev that her abuse was even worse than I had realized. It sent me into a dark place because I had always thought he waited until she was closer to eighteen. Finding out it started when she was sixteen, and possibly even the summer before she turned sixteen, tore into my soul.

That fucking pig. All those years of abuse.

Bev was tortured with sexually verbal harassment for as long as she can remember. She was forced to insert a face cloth until she bled and was no longer a virgin. She remembered how he had tried to rape her in the shack one time but hadn't been successful. But she was raped outside many, many times before she was raped in the shack again. Raped on the ground by the goat pen, or in the woods. Too scared to tell our mother, but I'm sure our mother eventually figured it out.

He never left Bev alone. She never had any peace.

I remember my sisters' bunk beds were taken apart and moved into the master bedroom. She was silently raped for over two years. In July of 1986, she had her baby. A beautiful little girl with blonde ringlets just like mine. I turned twelve in the same month she was born, and I just adored having a baby in the house. Babies at least bring joy to some dark situations.

We were very quiet and didn't ask questions as we never wanted to provoke anything. But it didn't matter. Sharon and I were bought bunk beds and new bikes for the first time. I think that occurred before the baby arrived. I am certain it was a bribe to shut us up about our home life. I was never told my father was the baby's father, but I figured it out. I am both an auntie and sister to my niece. But of course, that was never spoken about.

Mom slept in Bev's single bed, the baby in the crib, and Bev with Peter by this point. I remember seeing this happening but being young I never realized the full extent of what was happening. Mom got up early and took the baby out every day. Mom turned into his maid, I guess. In his mind, he had a new wife and he believed Bev loved him. He was so sick in the head.

I can only describe him as a monster.

Mom lived in a horrific environment, in a trance, with no hope in sight. She never condoned what was happening, but she knew that if she killed him, she would go to jail and her kids would be left alone. But I am certain she wanted to every single day. What could she really do, to save six people? If we left, he would find us, and very likely kill her; or, as he'd promised, he would kill her kids in front of her.

CHAPTER 6

The Big Escape

I was in Grade 8 in 1987. I had just turned thirteen when things changed forever.

The baby was over a year old and that is when the social workers came back. Sharon had started confiding in her school counsellor, as I had previously mentioned.

The social workers were developing a plan to take myself and Sharon from school. We were to be separated and put into foster homes. I would go to the Maple Grove school, and my sister would stay at Saint Anne Du Ruisseau because she wanted to.

The planning went on for months. During the Christmas Break we lived on pins and needles worrying he would somehow find out and kill us.

I believe it was on the twenty-eighth of February when the whole thing went down. A week before the big day we were told to tell our mother of the plan. We were walking in the woods together. I can't remember why but we had Mom to ourselves so that's when we told her. She was scared for our lives but knew it was our only way out.

They wanted her to meet with them, but I explained that would be impossible. She didn't go anywhere alone, and she couldn't call them. But she had time to make a plan of her own; little did we know what she was up to.

We didn't know when we would ever see her again or if she would make it out alive when we went to school that morning. It was extremely hard to leave and much harder to act like nothing was going on.

I took my cat to school with me as I knew Peter would kill her. My beautiful kitty was named Goldie. Peter was abusive to animals. Kicking and beating them if they did anything he didn't like. He'd once brought home a black Lab puppy, but it didn't last long. He killed it. Sharon and I were devastated.

I had six hundred dollars saved from worming, and I took that to school with me too. Mom had promised that she would get us back as quickly as she could. *Just please, God let her make it out alive,* I remember thinking as I left the house that day. Deep down none of us knew if our plan would work but it was time to take a huge chance for the sake of all our futures.

During my research I discovered the social workers had noted that I was very strong and determined to save us and give us a chance at life. I may have been the baby of the family, but I stuck to the plan and never wavered on my facts.

Bev and the baby were at the house on the 28th. I don't know if Mom realized they were going to show up to take the baby too since she was a minor. That part of the plan was kept from Sharon and me. But something tells me Mom must have known because on the big day she convinced Peter to take her somewhere.

Peter and Mom were not at home when the police and social workers showed up to take the baby. Of course, they offered to take my sister as well and they took her to a safe house for abused women. When Mom and Peter arrived back home, my brother informed them of the news. He gave them the papers that explained we had been taken for our protection.

Mom kept her cool and told Peter they needed to go into town to use a pay phone. She said she would find out where the kids were. She must have convinced him that she could get us back, although I don't know how she managed to do that.

When she got to a phone, she called the cops and explained what was happening. They sent six cars to her location at the phone booth. I'm sure they had been notified by the social workers about the threat that Peter represented to everyone. They took Mom to the same safe house where she could be with Bev and the baby.

I'm not sure if Peter was arrested at that time or if that occurred later. At some point the police took Mom back to the house to get some of our belongings, but he had destroyed so much of it before she even got there. She couldn't retrieve much. He had burned the few pictures we had and had trashed the house. My brother had stayed there for about a week after they had taken us, but he finally left and went to live with my grandparents. He managed to save his photo-album, which had the only picture of me I have when I was little.

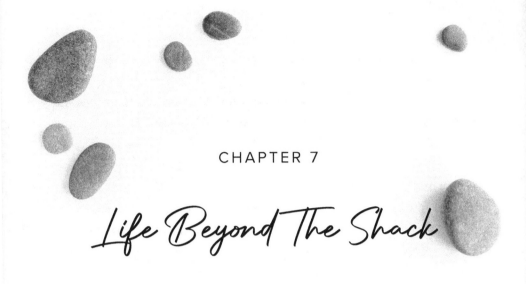

CHAPTER 7

Life Beyond The Shack

We were all safe for the time being.

I was taken to Wellington to live with a family of four. I was to stay in their teenage daughter's room. She wasn't welcoming and it was hard to tell what she thought of me. I had no idea if I was wanted or not.

Likely I was there for the paycheque. I definitely felt like I didn't belong anywhere. But maybe I would have felt that way no matter where I had ended up. There I was, thrown into a big school, with a strange family, and on my own at thirteen.

My mom had an old friend, with a daughter the same age as me. The daughter was asked to help me out around school. Her name was Diane. I was very withdrawn and quiet, but I was so thankful to have her by my side. One of the first people she introduced me to was her friend, Christine, who was in some of my classes. These two individuals became good friends of mine and I have many cherished memories with them.

Diane was very much committed to her studies and worked hard. Christine had an older boyfriend and was pregnant when I met her. Maybe we were drawn to each other because we both didn't fit in with the regular crowd. I don't know, but we spent a lot of time together.

My foster home family went about their life around me. I was just there. Of course, sometimes the mother would ask me to go places with them, but I always felt alone. I remember being left alone one night so I called Mom at the safe house to chat. She must have been concerned because she arranged for someone to bring her to visit with me. I got into trouble for having an unscheduled visit with my mom.

Following that visit, my mom's brother and his wife got expedited for their foster parent clearance so I could go stay with them. That move was better since my grandparents also lived next door. I could see Mom more frequently and have a chance to get to know members of my family that I was never allowed to know before.

I had never experienced real family life where there were happy times, and, of course a few sad times. I didn't understand the dynamics of family because everything was new to me. I was quiet and shy, taking in all that the new world had to offer. Trying to figure things out.

Eventually, Mom got an apartment on Pleasant Street, which would become our new home. Mom had to go to court and prove that she was a fit mother who could provide for her children. Bev and the baby already lived with Mom. Bev decided to resume her studies, getting her GED (General Education Development), and started school in the fall studying forestry.

Mom went to court and was granted custody of myself and my sister Sharon. We moved back in together the first week of July. Once we were settled in the apartment, it meant that I was now living in town. I went from not being allowed to have any friends to having the freedom of walking around town.

Making good choices would prove to be very difficult. I now had so many opportunities available but no previous life experiences to help guide my decisions. It was a dangerous combination.

CHAPTER 8

The Mean Girls

I wasn't a bad kid. I was just lost in my new world.

One Friday night I went to the YMCA to go swimming with my friend Nanette, and I met a boy. He became my first boyfriend, and we hung out a lot that summer.

He came from an alcoholic family, but he was very nice to me. Looking back, I was grateful he was so kind since I could have ended up with someone much worse. He never pressured me to do anything and respected that I wasn't ready. Eventually we went our separate directions as he was a bit older. It was for the best.

No one bothered me while I was hanging out with him but after we parted, things soon made a turn for the worse.

Girls I didn't know were after me just because I was the new blonde in town. My mom had a cousin with a daughter my age named Taralee. Mom thought it would be good for me to get to know her. I remember going over to her apartment where she lived with her parents. She was sorting through baby clothes that had been given to her. She was pregnant at a young age too, just like my friend Christine. We were all turning fourteen that year and I had my birthday on 22nd of July.

One time when I was there visiting, a girl named Tracy called for Taralee to come over. Taralee invited me along, so I went with her. What did I know?

Tracy was mean and had heard about me around town. Tracy even got her sister Shelly involved so that they could whisper and laugh at me all night. I had no idea girls could be that mean. Remember, I never had been to any sleepovers or on any outings with friends during my childhood. But I remember wanting to be swallowed up by a hole in the floor that night.

I stayed quiet, keeping all the hurt inside. Little did I know that what Grade 9 had to offer was going to be so much worse.

There was a bus stop in town for those of us going to the Maple Grove school. This school was where some of the troubled kids from the town school got sent—to the country school. Great. That didn't help me out at all. I could have gone to the school in town but even more of the mean girls I had encountered on the streets would be there. Plus, I didn't feel like starting over at another new school. In fact, I would have given anything to be back with my familiar classmates, at the Argyle school. Just not in my old family life.

Another girl who was awful to me was Jody. She teamed up with Tracy and made me their target for bullying. Now, I was scared at school and around town, for totally different reasons than before. I can't remember all their names, but Tracy, Shelly, Jody, Melinda, and the pregnant Shelly were all nightmares for me. These girls and their friends were nasty. I remember so many hours spent hiding in the bathroom, beet red in face, and sweating bullets.

So much fun. Not.

I was a pretty good student but was having trouble in math. The teacher didn't seem to be very understanding. Instead, he told me that I would never pass Grade 9 math. So, I did a correspondence course and got a great mark. Screw his asshole opinion. Now when I look back, my gut feelings about him were proven right. If only I had known to follow my gut feelings from an early age!

I had Mr. Raymond as a homeroom teacher. Thankfully, he was kind and always nice. The science teacher was also nice in Grade 9. I loved his class. Mr. Comeau was his name. They must have known my background.

I wasn't bad, but trouble followed me. Bullying wasn't talked about back then but that's exactly what was happening to me. Things got really bad around town and at school. I was afraid to go for a walk. I was always being yelled at by these girls.

One girl even tried to be friendly with me and asked if I wanted to go to the Kmart mall one Friday night. Stupidly I went, as I just wanted to fit in. The mean girls used her to lure me there. At the mall they were all waiting for me. They surrounded me and pushed me around. One even connected her ring to my chin causing me to bleed. To this day I still have that scar. I don't remember how I got out of there or got home, but it was a pretty traumatic experience. I'm guessing mall security stepped in, but I've blocked out that part of the memory.

I recall another day when I was walking along the street that a car pulled up beside me. An older girl, the pregnant Shelly, got out and slapped me across the face telling me to stay away from her man. I'm sure the mean girls sent her my way. Her man, Mark, slept with everyone he possibly could, however, I was never on his list. Oh, he tried, but he was gross. Thankfully, I was smart enough to stay away from his fancy car and loud stereo.

How could these strangers be so mean to me after all I had already been through in my life? I just wanted to fit in and have friends. Thankfully, I did have some friends, but they were scared to be around me once I became a target. I remember going to Nanette's house a few times for sleepovers. And I loved her parents. They were what I imagined normal parents to be. Funny and nice.

At one point I was friends with Vicky, who had an older sister that hung out downtown every night. Many girls feared Pebbles, her older sister, as she had a "don't mess with her" aura. I think I was the safest when I was with Vicky. Although, the two of us did seem to always go looking for trouble.

In Grade 9 I often hung out with Christine and sometimes we would have her baby with us while he was in his stroller. Other times we would leave him with Mom and go for a walk. Christine's mother worked at a restaurant in town and would pick her and the baby up after work on her way home. It would be late when she arrived, and it was probably not ideal for a teen in school with a baby.

I also went to Christine's house and stayed overnight while we were in Grade 9. It was her, me, and the baby, who would join us in her waterbed.

When he got up for his bottle, we would fall asleep with him in the bed. We all survived even though we were teenagers. We didn't drink or do drugs. We were just out and about.

I also met Trina, Christine's cousin who looked a lot like her with the same dark hair and a similar face during high school. She was closer to my sister's age, and they went to the same high school together. Little did I know then, but Trina would become a life-long friend. To this day we still have a special bond.

I did end up at a few parties where there was access to drugs and alcohol but that was never my thing. One sip of alcohol would always make my face red. And I couldn't stand being around smoke, let alone weed or hot knifing.

One night feeling defiant, I didn't go home. I was at some Scott guy's house with my so-called friends. I think I called Mom and told her I wasn't coming home. Soon after that call, the cops showed up to take me home. They informed my mom I was hanging out in a place where I would surely get into trouble.

I was occasionally mouthy as most teenagers are sometimes, but Mom was lucky I didn't go down the drinking and drug route. And it would have been easy enough to do. I really wanted to forget where I had come from, what had happened to me at such a young age, and how the mean girls were treating me.

But life is all about choices and where they will lead you. Thankfully, my strong will to survive and conquer the world prevailed.

CHAPTER 9

Going To Court

We had to go to court because of the charges that had been laid against Peter. We weren't allowed to sit inside the courtroom until after we had testified. I believe Mom went first, then Bev, my brother, me, and Sharon.

At one point I remember seeing my oldest sister on the witness stand, so I assume that she was brought back up for additional questions. I remember hearing my sister being questioned and having to testify about the gross kissing. I told the social worker, who was sitting next to me, that the gross kissing had happened to me too. They had never directly asked me, so I must not have told them about it previously.

When Peter was questioned, he sat on the stand and told everyone he had the same plans for me for when I was older. How sick is that? Bev was adopted by him, so she's not his blood. But I am fifty per cent of his damn blood and he was going to do the same thing to me.

I see it now, how he groomed Bev and all of us to go along with his sick plans. He always tried to pull us close, to touch, to kiss, etc. Thankfully, we always got away. Except for Bev.

I have no idea how she recovered from her years of torture. I know what happened to me has affected my life and I wasn't the one raped. Holding these things in, putting them in the closet, does not heal our souls. You must let them out. Work through them. Write it down and burn the pages. Whatever it is that helps you to let them go. Give it over to the universe!

I joke about burning a whole copy of this book; in reality, I may just do it. I may even make it a huge celebration party. Therapy at its best, releasing it from heart, soul, and mind. Sending it out to the universe.

You will never live your life to its fullest potential until you take these steps. You do not have to do it alone, as it is a dark place you must go to. But the other side—once you let go of the hate, resentment, blame, confusion, shame, and embarrassment—is extremely peaceful. Letting go doesn't mean you will ever forget, nor does it mean you forgive, but it will bring you to a place of solitude, where your energies can thrive. I know because I have accomplished that part of my journey. But without doubt I have lots more healing to go through.

That summer before the court appearance had happened, we had to worry about Peter being around town. He would stalk us, follow us, and try to talk to us. We were terrified when we saw him. I remember being so scared on Water Street one evening that a boy I hardly knew offered me a ride to safety on his motorcycle. I was so thankful to be whisked out of there. Other times I would bolt for home when I would see Peter driving up and down the streets looking for us. I guess in some sick way he was trying to get us back, but I always thought he was going to shoot us.

Peter had been charged with rape, child abuse, spousal abuse along with many other charges. The police put a peace bond on him to make him stay away from us prior to the court date. However, we had no idea he would be working at the local fair. It was the first time we were going to be attending the exhibition. My mother, sister, and niece went to kids' day and there he was, working one of the rides. He approached Bev and tried to convince her of his love and that he wanted them back. They were left terrified, and pretty shaken up.

Mom must have called the police because he was arrested and spent the remainder of the time in jail until the court date. Finally, we felt secure to be out in public, not looking over our shoulders constantly.

In preparation for the big court date, the lawyer questioned us in advance. On that day, after we had testified, we were allowed to sit in the courtroom and listen to the proceedings. I remember our counsellors sitting next to us.

As Bev was testifying, I pointed out the things that had also happened to me, but I hadn't been asked about before.

I was mad when some of the charges were dismissed, and by the fact that they only concentrated on the more serious ones. To me they were all serious. He had tortured us for years.

I always felt he got away with too much. He should have had to suffer for just as many years as we did. Instead, he got around twenty-two months when it was all said and done, less the time he had already spent in jail.

It never seemed like it was enough for any of us. But we were safe for a while. We just had to worry about his release.

CHAPTER 10

New Jobs

I had a few babysitting jobs and soon I was babysitting for my friend Crystal. She had a little girl named Samantha. I would get my niece and her together to play. I also tended Aisha for Marlene, who was Crystal's friend, before I ended up working in the fish plant.

The summer of 1989 I was fourteen, but I would be turning fifteen in July. No one bothered me when I was with Crystal or Marlene, and I preferred being around them as I felt safe. They were older than me. I made enough money to buy a huge Kenwood stereo and a queen size waterbed all on my own. I bought a king size comforter for my bed that I still have thirty years later and use in my camper. I was so proud of myself.

That fall I was fifteen and was now travelling to Saint Anne Du Ruisseau for Grade 10. I was too afraid to go to the Yarmouth high school. The anxiety and the sweats were the worst. But school soon became the last thing I was worried about.

Everything got the best of me that year. I hated school. I couldn't concentrate. I didn't feel like I belonged anywhere.

I know now that Mom didn't realize I was being bullied. She had confided in the counsellors that I was getting into trouble and not doing well at school. I wish she had known how scared I was, but I must not have told her. The notes say I refused to go to the town school, but they didn't state why. Mom had made the travel arrangements for me to go to SAR. I had to be driven to catch the school bus.

Mom was doing her best. She had friends, mostly ones she had met while at the safe house. She continued to volunteer there and went out dancing when she could. She dated a few men, but I didn't like any of them. Then she came home with Charlie. He was better, but I still had a chip on my shoulder. I just didn't like men at all.

In my Grade 10 year, I failed Math and English. But school was out, and I was turning sixteen in July of 1990. Mom had bought a little yellow house on King Street. Our first real home. To me it was a mansion.

Mom let Sharon and I have a party before we officially moved in. My brother and his friend were our bouncers. Word got around and we had tons of people scoping out our party. I think it helped my popularity if nothing else. It was fun dancing and seeing everyone have fun.

Mom married Charlie around that same time. It was her third marriage. I was headstrong and swore that I was never getting married.

I decided to work at BB McGees. Other than the fish plant and babysitting, it was my first real job. The place was new and very popular. It was a restaurant during day and a bar at night. I was hired as a dishwasher, but it was only for a short time as I was soon moved up to become a prep cook. I liked that position much better.

As the prep cook, I made deep fried ice cream, got all the salad stuff ready, and did whatever was needed to be done. Renè taught me a lot. He oversaw the kitchen. His father George was a nice man who I still speak with when I see him. I snuck out to use the phone and to get a peek of the bar life, and what I saw was pretty cool.

I met a waitress named Shelly and a cook named Susan. They were older but we had tons of fun together. We have stayed in touch over the years. Susan and I laughed together so much in that kitchen. The chemical salesperson that came quite often had the clearest skin and completion. We nicknamed him the "Makeup Man." He was nice but I'm sure he thought we were crazy.

What's even funnier is later on, although I'm not sure how many years later it was, Susan ended up married to him somehow. They moved to Bridgewater and had a daughter. Shelly and I took a few road trips to visit

Susan. We didn't stay in contact all the time, but we always picked right back up where we left off when we ran into each other.

I didn't go back to school the fall after I turned sixteen. I worked and saved money for a car. I got my licence despite failing the first time. I literally turned right when she said left and left when she said turn right. My nerves got the best of me during the first test.

I still was babysitting a lot for Crystal, and at times hung out with the wrong people. I seemed to be mixing with the older crowd. I even was able to get into the bars a few times at the age of sixteen.

One Halloween Crystal dressed me up and I went with Ray her boyfriend, as his date along with the others to the Clipper Ship. The Clipper was a hard-ass spot. I got into the Red Knight, another bar, quite a few times too. Somehow it was much more exciting to go to them before I was nineteen. Again, I wasn't a drinker. Just the thrill of getting in was fun.

When I was sixteen my mother brought her mother to come live with us. Grammie was silly to me. I loved her laugh. She was suffering from Alzheimer's, hiding things everywhere, and was obsessed with saving food.

Grammie was a lot of work. You really had to watch her. She growled if I tried to use the stove. She was paranoid about everything. Back then, the disease was not well studied. Mom didn't know what to do. She kept her with us for as long as possible.

Finally, Grammie went into a private home, and I remember visiting her. She was tied in a rocking chair.

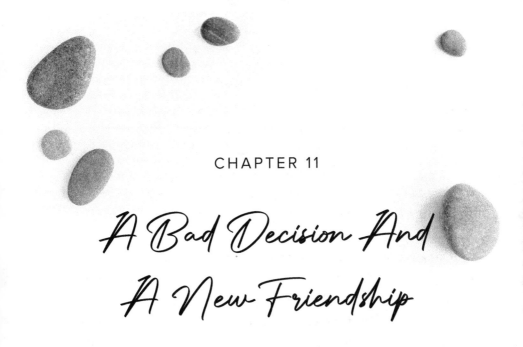

CHAPTER 11

A Bad Decision And A New Friendship

It was one of my biggest bad choices. The day I walked into Cotton Ginny's clothing store, picked up the old-style phone, and wacked a girl upside her head!

I was mad that she was bad mouthing me all around town. I got into a yelling match with her, and I boiled over. I saw the phone there and I don't know if I thought I was in a movie or what. I just did it.

But here's my truth. I was seeing her ex-husband. He was another much-older-than-me guy. I was only sixteen or had barely turned seventeen. Were they completely done? Who knows, but I thought this cute guy was it. My older friend was with his brother. I thought he was single as he referred to her as the ex-wife. Fun and convenient at the time, but it was a short relationship that I'm glad never went anywhere. My life path would not have been as successful if I had stayed on that route.

I was home in my mother's house when the RCMP showed up. A lady cop arrested me, taking me to the station for fingerprints. I went to court and was given community service to complete. I was told my record would not follow me, but that's not entirely true. As my story unfolds you will see how it still haunted me a few times within my life.

I've learned that *CHOICES* are the number one thing that will change your life.

I worked at BB McGees until the woman that was dating my uncle snagged me to go work for her at Kay's Drive In. That was a mistake. She was a terrible woman. All sweet at first then totally different once you knew her.

Josely and Rosie were the two other waitresses who worked there. Sandra and Gladys were the cooks. We all had a good time working there. It was a carhop so we had to go out to the vehicles to get the orders. There was a guy, Johnny, from up the road who always hung out there. He would help if something broke or needed to be done.

One summer's day he and his buddy Brian showed up in a jacked-up Toyota truck, drinking of course, teasing me that I should drive for them. I didn't but Jesus, they shouldn't have been on the roads. They were joking about how Brian was supposed to pick his girlfriend up at 5 p.m. from work but had just left her high and dry. Apparently, it was their Friday ritual to go get loaded after work. Not my thing.

Johnny was nice when he wasn't drinking. I don't like when people drink and totally change their personality. If you wouldn't say or do it sober, then don't when you're drinking. His parents got takeout from the carhop and were very nice people. His sister was different, off in her own world of black and white. His father John had a gentle patience about him that I had never seen before in a man. Not in my life anyways. His mom Shirley went above and beyond helping people and being a social butterfly.

Soon, somehow, I ended up hanging around Johnny. Going to the local car show with him and his family and to other car shows. I enjoyed being around the gentle, kind people they were. To me I was just hanging out and enjoyed being in a safe environment. To Johnny I was the one!

He would do whatever I wanted to do. He never had an opinion or idea, which drove me crazy. Eventually, we went to a car show that involved staying overnight. Our friendship was getting to be too overwhelming. I knew he wasn't the one and I was determined I was never getting married. He was obsessed and I stopped hanging out with him.

I didn't know what love was but hanging out with someone was not it for sure. I was too young. I had turned eighteen that summer and put an end to everything in the fall.

Backing up in the storyline, I only worked at Kay's that one summer; the one in which I turned seventeen.

That winter after I turned seventeen, I took a cooking course through the employment centre. It was held at the Five Corners Restaurant. My friend Marie was in this course. She was a big girl who later went and got her stomach stapled. We were the best of friends. I always tried to help her anyway I could as that is how I'm wired—to help others. Marie haunts my future, and will appear in my upcoming chapters.

I got a job at Harris Seafoods after the course. Some guy called Mike had bought it and Clara Harris was going to help him get it going again. That summer it was fun working with Gladys again. In the fall I went to the Harris Quick-n-Tasty to get enough stamps for my unemployment claim. The seafood restaurant never did well, and it didn't open the following season.

That summer I turned eighteen. I made the hot lobster sandwiches and Seretha was the fry cook. We had fun working together there. I learned lots from Clara Harris, I just loved working for her.

That fall was the one in which I stopped hanging around Johnny. He wouldn't give up, but I was done.

CHAPTER 12

A Big Twist In Life

To my shocking surprise I was pregnant!

We hardly had done anything. How could this be? I never told Johnny, but he found out when I was five months along. He didn't believe it was his. He claimed it must have been one of my other friends who was the father.

He eventually did get used to the fact that he was going to be a father. He tried everything to be with me, but I refused, knowing I didn't love him.

I had everything ready for my baby. The crib was all set up. Mom had a baby shower for me. Shirley also had a baby shower for me. I was talking to Johnny as I figured it was best to be civil.

Then during routine testing the doctor discovered I was not immune to measles. If I got the disease the baby would be deformed. Vaccinations were another thing the school had offered but I was not allowed to have when I was younger. The doctor told me to avoid public places and to stay away from people. I did a lot of walking and had a healthy pregnancy otherwise.

Tristan came into my world at 4:04 a.m. on June 6, 1993.

I had a quick, less than four-hour labour. Intense, with no drugs and a nurse who finally yelled at me to get the job done and to breathe through it. Once I listened to her, it didn't take long, and Tristan was finally here. I loved babies but this one was all mine. He was beautiful and tiny.

Grandpére and Grandmom had their first grandson. They were the best grandparents. Tristan was very lucky to have two sets of amazing grandparents. They all spent time with him and adored him immensely.

I went back to work when Tristan was four weeks old. My mother tended him for me. I usually worked between 4 and 9 p.m. so it wasn't too bad. I was determined to work my seasonal job at Harris's and get enough weeks for unemployment. I accomplished this and being on unemployment meant that I could take upgrading and receive my Grade 12 equivalency. The government would even pay for child care.

My future was important because I now had responsibilities. I was determined to do better for my child than what I had to endure in my own childhood. Never would anyone harm him or mistreat him. I wanted to be able to provide for him in every way.

My personality was getting stronger, although I was still quiet and withdrawn in many ways. Maybe even a little shy. My friend Crystal was marrying Ray. I was in her wedding just weeks after Tristan was born. I also turned nineteen that summer. I still wasn't a drinker, so it didn't matter to me that I was now legal to drink. I was signed up for the GED course that was starting in January of 1994.

If I had a chance to make the decision again of whether to work with Tristan being only four weeks old or getting help from the government's Mothers' Assistance plan, I'd have to say I would have stayed home. I would have wanted to enjoy every moment of my baby's young life.

CHAPTER 13

Meeting Fred

Over the Christmas holidays my school friend Diane was home from Toronto. We were both nineteen and decided to go out to the club for some dancing. Her boyfriend worked as a delivery guy at a local diner downtown. It was just us going out with a plan to visit him after the club closed.

We had fun dancing. I don't think I was drinking at all. Likely I was the one driving. We went to the diner for a snack, and to meet up with her boyfriend.

I was waited on by a Lebanese man who owned the diner and I remember the flirty way he smiled at me as he approached. At the time I never thought much about it. Later, I learned he'd asked Diane's boyfriend who I was, and why he had never seen me before? His exact words to Jamie were, "I have to have that girl."

I was surprised he was interested. I guess I didn't see myself the way others did, especially older men. Turns out he was thirty-one. What the hell was he thinking?

He asked Jamie for my number, called me, and we started spending time together. Soon after our meeting, I started my course downtown, which was close to the diner. I decided to go there once for lunch, which then became a habit.

Fred was always charming, making me something special to eat, and inviting me to come hang out with him. We hung around the restaurant, went for drives, and started going to the club for an hour or two when he could sneak away from the restaurant.

I had never experienced before the way he looked at me. He made me feel special, unique, and worthy of love. No man had ever made me feel that way.

He was smooth, that's for sure. It was like he had reached deep into my soul. Without a doubt we had a deep connection. Why did this guy pick me? I believe our paths were destined to cross as the universe unfolded its plan for us.

Fred had three girls aged four, six, and eight. He adored his children. He told me he was separated from his wife, but she lived in a huge house upstairs while his mother and other family members lived downstairs. He would go to visit his girls for a couple of days and sleep on the couch because he couldn't stand his wife. Fred said from the time they were six months into their marriage that he known it was a mistake. Fred's father also worked at the restaurant and went to Halifax for visits. Halifax was three hours from Yarmouth, where we lived. The family owned a diner in both locations. Yarmouth at the time was a prime location for a family diner.

His father Jake assured me that Fred wasn't with his wife, and that all they did was fight. Fred showed me the separation papers from his lawyers. I had no reason not to believe him. He even told me that because of his culture most of his family believed they were still together, and he was just away working all the time. Their culture meant everything to them, especially how things appeared. Despite whether something was true or not, they went to great lengths to make it appear as if everything was perfect.

I had heard Fred had other girlfriends in Yarmouth, but that none had lasted very long. Fred and I dated during my course. He told me I was different from the other girls. He bought me gifts and sent me flowers. We went to the movies, shows at the Th'YARC (Yarmouth Arts Regional Centre). He cooked special things for me all the time at the restaurant. In fact, we spent a lot of time at the restaurant and soon I fell into the rut of helping him out.

At first it was just little things, but the next thing I knew Jake was showing me how to do everything in the kitchen. Jake said I was a natural and caught on quickly. They said I was not just a stupid Canadian, like most of the other people they had met. I was nineteen, young, and naive. I fell for Fred's charm. He knew exactly what to say.

I had little experience with men. The men in my childhood had betrayed me to my core. Fred knew he could mould me into whatever he wanted me to be. The first thing he taught me was to be confident. I was waiting on customers and developing self-esteem. He believed in me. I learned that dressing so that you knew you look good would give you confidence, and it would flow from you. He loved when I dressed up and enjoyed having me on his arm while others looked on. I was changing so much.

Tristan was still my main priority, and Mom helped me a great deal with his care. Tristan also started going on overnight visits to his grandparents' house and his father's house at around one-years old. All my extra time was spent at the restaurant working; getting paid under the table. That seemed to be the only way for a single mother to get ahead.

I was supposed to go back to work at Harris's that summer, but Fred convinced me to stay at his restaurant and work there. When I had Tristan's birthday party in June, Fred came by the house and dropped off a card and a gift for Tristan. Everything a normal boyfriend would do and then some.

We had a mostly fun summer together. I would bring Tristan for visits at the restaurant, and everyone loved him. Mom and Charlie would come to the restaurant; everyone was getting to know my boyfriend. Jennifer, one of the cooks, said she had never seen Fred this way with any of the other girls. I was different.

I wasn't bothering to be with my friends. I had no time between Tristan, working, and dating Fred. I spent a lot of time with Fred, and his father. We would often only sit down together and eat when the restaurant closed for the night. I stayed at Fred's house a lot, as it was easier than waking everyone up by going home around 12:30 a.m. or later every night. Mom actually preferred me not waking them up as she wouldn't be able to get back to sleep. I tried to be the perfect mom and girlfriend, balancing my home time and my time at Fred's house.

Fred had customers that were also his friends, or that's what he would encourage them to think. They would come to sit at the employee table and have coffee with him. Some would come to borrow his car. Robin Boss worked at the radio station. He was interesting and would go with us for drives sometimes. They made fun of my favourite musical group at the time, Ace of Base—until Robin discovered it was ABBA singing with them. Then he thought they were cool.

I had an old car I had saved for and bought by myself at age seventeen. It was a 1980 AMC Spirit, grey in colour, but I had painted it a deep blue with spray bombs. I loved that car and spent a lot of money fixing it up.

One night at closing Fred offered to bring my car around front for me when we were locking up. That was it! After driving it around front, Fred insisted I get something more dependable and safer for Tristan's sake. He couldn't believe what I was driving. It was old, but it really wasn't that bad.

I had been saving some money and he was impressed when he took me to Doug Thistle Hyundai. Fred had picked out an economical car for me to test drive. It was a 1992 Hyundai Excel. I had eighteen hundred dollars to put down on it and my payments were going to be manageable. Fred was so proud that I was good with money. I always saved for what I needed. I didn't have any credit card debt or crazy bills piled up. He always told me I was not one of the many stupid Canadians. I was different.

We had been going out for about eight months when one beautiful summer's day Tristan and I stopped into the restaurant to see Fred. He wasn't there. They said he was still at home. I was thinking this was odd but went over to his house anyway.

He was living in a duplex in Hebron. When I pulled up there was a Volkswagen van all "hippied" out in the driveway. I recognized it as belonging to a girl who had been in the diner recently. She was visiting from Boston and apparently came up every summer. Apparently, she knew Fred better than I thought she did, from what I saw at the restaurant.

They were on the deck having a picnic. This was the first time he had made me feel this jealous. My mind started spinning. So, it was okay to have lunch with an old friend at your house? He was so possessive over me being just his. What the hell was going on?

It was too late to leave once I pulled into the yard. They had seen me. I might as well get Tristan out and go say hi. I sat on the deck feeling betrayed as they offered Tristan some watermelon. I had to work at 4 p.m. so I didn't stay long. When Fred arrived at work, he said it was a harmless picnic. It wasn't like I had caught them in bed or anything.

But I was hurt. Now I planned to start watching his movements a little closer. The way he talked with lots of our female customers hadn't bothered me too much before since he was always with me. He had always made me feel like I was his. He was very possessive in his charming, manipulative way. Now I felt I had to wonder how many girls he had been friendly with in the past. Fred knew what to say when he wanted me to feel secure. He also knew how to push me away a little and reel me back in.

I was learning a lot from him. I pick up on things quickly. I noticed he told many people different versions of the same story. When I asked why, Fred said it was because no one would ever know the truth if they all had different stories. He never let people really know him. He could be so genuine one minute and such an ass the next.

Fred and Jake were fake with the customers, putting on a good show to their face. I didn't like how they made fun of fat people or less fortunate people. I didn't consider myself skinny. I always had meat on my bones, so to speak. Everyone's money was good enough, but they thought they were superior to the "stupid Canadians." It just wasn't nice how they talked about their customers. I never liked how they treated people behind their backs.

The staff was always underpaid in my opinion, and always had to ask to be paid. And their pay was done all under the table. If someone stayed late, they seldom got paid for the extra time. They were so cheap, trying to make money and took advantage of people all the time. This had always bothered me.

There was a big back room with a pool table. Regular customers didn't go back there, just the workers and acquaintances that Fred allowed back there. On more than one occasion people brought by hot items to sell to Fred for quick money. Then Fred would resell them and make a profit. At the time I didn't realize how serious this was. Sometimes it was computer equipment coming and going, as well as other household items. I remember looking up and seeing things walking through the front door, just like we were a pawn shop.

Then there were times when I was with Fred, and we went to places that had stolen goods. At one point a guy I'll call Paul, was in on a hot computer deal. I didn't know all of what had gone down but many years later I ran into Paul and learned he had been charged, convicted, and had a criminal record all because he hadn't dared to give Fred up. Shit, I was there in the building with the two of them that night. If it had been raided at the time I would have been arrested too. I felt bad for Paul, as he had been on the shitty end of that deal. He was the only one caught with the goods, so he took the fall.

I also somehow ended up on an illegal lobster run. What was I thinking? Fred had done one and had made a lot of money. He asked if I wanted to go with him and said we would be partners with the profit. It was during the off season and at about 4 a.m. when we loaded a flower delivery van full of lobster and headed into the city. At the time I had no idea how serious the charges from this could be. It was a perfect example of how, when you are young, you are stupid and make bad choices.

I was driving and we came over a hill where there was some construction work being done. I just barely got that heavy van stopped in time. Fred had drifted off to sleep but it didn't take him long to wake up. It was a miracle I didn't go off the road. I didn't know the brakes were not great until I needed them. How would we have ever explained that load of lobsters?

When we reached the processing plant, it didn't go as smoothly as the last time either. They were scared to buy the lobsters. If caught they would receive huge fines and charges in addition to us. I was left questioning what the fuck had I got myself into?

They finally did take the lobsters at the second place we visited, but we never made the huge profit promised. All that trouble and I had barely made anything!

Before we left the city, we stopped at the family restaurant in Timberlea. At first, Fred's mother was not happy I was there with him, but he lied to her saying it was for business only. She hugged us, kissed our cheeks, and fed us. Then we were on our way. I absolutely loved her.

But those were just a few of the situations Fred had put me in.

CHAPTER 14

The Relationship Continued

Toward the fall Fred would have weeks where he would tell me he should let me go before we got too close. He would be cold for a couple of days then he would pull me back in with his, "I can't live without you" pleas and passion. Other weeks he would do everything he could to please me and keep me happy. He played mind games constantly and that only seemed to make me try harder. He was getting exactly what he wanted: me wrapped around his little finger.

Fred was clear that he didn't want any more children. He admitted he was not very good to his girls; he never spent much time with them. He longed to have a son but all he had were girls (whom he loved but was never present in their life). He was disgusted with his situation; stuck with his wife on a cultural level. His culture stressed the importance in having sons and he had none. He felt his father was disappointed with him. Apparently in his culture it made them more of a man to have a son.

I was on the pill, so I wasn't worried about having his baby. I still lived with my mom, and I wasn't ready to have any more kids. And I had Tristan to care for. I wanted his life to be really good.

My relationship with Fred was nearing the one-year mark. It had a few minor breakups along the way, but they only ever lasted a day or two. Fred would say he felt guilty that he would never be able to be one hundred per cent with me because of the fake life he had to portray and lie about in Halifax to his family members. He was worried that if his wife knew he had somebody she would take the kids and go back to Lebanon.

In Halifax I was a secret. In Yarmouth we went everywhere and did everything together. He always introduced me as his girlfriend. His father Jake knew everything but his mother, Eveline, would come down sometimes and she didn't know the truth. She thought I was just an employee of the restaurant. She said Jake and Fred both spoke highly of me.

We had dated before I worked there but many assumed it was the other way around. Eveline would teach me how to make Lebanese food and would cook for me all the time. She too would tell me how special I was and that all she had heard about me was good things.

I worked a lot of hours. At times we had to drive three hours to go into the city for supplies as they tried to order only what was needed and worked on a cash only basis. This made us short supplied if we were busier than expected.

I even went to the city to pick up Jake sometimes. Once I even picked up Fred from the big house that they all lived in. Lucien, the wife, was not home the first time and Jake invited me in. I sat at the table with Fred's sister, and we ate the meal Eveline had prepared. Amazing food, all Lebanese of course.

Another time I was there for a meal with all of them, Fred's kids and Lucien included. I was so nervous, but Jake told me not to worry. Fred would say that he had nothing to hide. He would say do you think I would let you go there if I was really with her? Jake would always back him up. In his mind he was not with her but in her mind, well I think she tried pretty hard to make people believe he was. She tried to keep the fake perfect family look going.

One time Fred showed up in Yarmouth with his middle daughter when she was just little. Fred asked me to help take care of her until he could take her back to Halifax.

Another time, Fred went on a business trip to his home country of Lebanon. He had big plans to sell pharmaceuticals overseas. He had a partner, Jamal, who lived in Toronto. Fred always called the restaurant to speak with me when he was away. He claimed to miss me so much. He brought me back gifts, such as a bracelet for Tristan, earrings, hair clips, and tourist stuff—all of it to make me feel special. What girl doesn't like presents?

I was the one who picked him up in Halifax when he was ready to come back to Yarmouth. He wanted me to because he said he couldn't go another day without seeing me. There was such incredible passion between us and at the time I believed it was real. It likely was but not in the healthiest of ways.

He often spoke of wishing he knew me before he was married. With a twelve-year age difference, I'd laugh and say how would that have worked? I would tease him that he was a cradle robber. I was only twenty years old by this time.

Christmas came and went. He was in Halifax, and I was in Yarmouth. He called to wish me all the best. He promised that on New Year's he would be with me. Of course, we were together. It was the busiest day of the year for restaurants, and we worked until 6 a.m. He would sneak me a kiss when we were out of sight by the fridge. All to reel me closer into his tunnel. We had fun working together. But the times he was cold, I hated that I worked there.

He would flip the switch so often to keep me on my toes and trying hard to please him. Mind games were his specialty.

Life continued into 1995. We were always together working or hanging out when I could.

Then, in the spring I realized I was pregnant. I was on the pill but at least twice I had been on prescriptions for infections. I couldn't tell Fred. He didn't want any more kids and I knew he wouldn't want to be part of this child's life. I wanted to run away from it all. I knew he would hate me.

I made this huge plan that I was going to Cape Breton for a week on vacation with Tristan. I have a cousin that lives there, and I had been there before. I scheduled everything and covered things at the restaurant. I wrote down the recipes for the items that I usually made so the other staff could make them instead while I was gone. I figured if they could survive a week without me, they could figure out the rest.

I had actually found an apartment. My friend was moving out of hers and into a house. I had seen it a few times in Coldbrook, and it would be perfect for now. I would be two hours away from Yarmouth, hopefully far enough to live in peace. I had an aunt and cousin who lived in the area so at least I had some support. I arranged to have my stuff brought up there. When I was with Fred, I acted like nothing was going on. After all, he had taught me exactly how to play the very best mind games. For the last few days, I simply wanted to soak up everything just the way it was. The way he smiled at me with his charm before he found out my secret, as I feared it would all turn to hate.

I told no one that I was pregnant. Mom knew and a few days before I left, I went for lunch with an old school friend. I didn't even tell her. Tristan was having his second birthday party and then I was leaving. Fred even brought Tristan a present to my house, but he didn't stay.

I thought I had kept my moving under wraps. Unfortunately, my sister's brother-in-law had found out. I wasn't there at the time, thankfully, when Scott happened to be in the restaurant and asked Fred what was he going to do without me? Losing his best worker and his girlfriend.

Fred stewed over the news. He wondered why I hadn't told him I was moving. I knew when I saw him that he was furious. We had a huge fight in the backroom of the diner, and I left crying. I told him I wanted nothing from him. I was leaving and I wanted to be alone. In fact, I was leaving town the next day.

Fred called in the morning and asked me to come down to talk with him before I left. I saw no point to it, but I went, unsure what I would be facing. The mind games took a new turn. Fred took me over to a booth and sat down while holding my hands. He told me he couldn't be there for this child, but he would help me out financially. He said he loved me and couldn't live without me.

He turned on the charm and talked about how we were meant to be together. He explained he couldn't be a father to the baby, which I already knew. He asked me to consider an abortion. I told him I was already too far along but wouldn't have one anyway. He replied that he was sure he could find someone to do it even at three months or more. He continued to pressure me to consider getting rid of the baby.

I left that morning confused by his response. He would give money but nothing more. Or that I should have an abortion. I never considered having an abortion EVER. He called often and never left me alone. He wanted to see me on the weekends when I would be coming to Yarmouth to bring Tristan for visits. He wanted me to work shifts for extra money to help me out. He poured on the charm and played with my heart and soul.

Fred even planned a trip for us to Bar Harbor. We took the ferry that went from Yarmouth, Nova Scotia to Bar Harbor, Maine in the US. We cruised on the open water, with a beautiful sunset. Hand in hand I felt loved. We toured the town and slept on the boat. It was a package deal.

This was the first time I had ever been out of Canada. We had an amazing time, but there was no talk about the baby.

CHAPTER 15

My Baby's Future

All too soon it was back to reality and Yarmouth.

I had wanted to distance myself from him and never look back. But he insisted on spending time with me, like nothing had changed. One day laying side by side the baby kicked him, and I knew he felt it on his back. I got no response. In that moment I felt that I was very much alone with my baby growing inside of me.

At around the five-month mark, he told me the best plan would be for me to give the baby up for adoption. His main reasons were so the baby would have two parents, not have to live in shame, and not feel left out when Tristan's family would come for visits with him. He insisted I would be stuck depending upon my mother's assistance and would never be able to give my children what they deserved. I only agreed to discuss this with a counsellor. At the time I had no intention of this being my path.

Fred continued to play mind games, telling me if his uncles in the city found out they would never let the baby be born or to disgrace the family name. He told me to be careful driving in case someone tried to run me off the road. He put fear into my life again, but in a different way than what I experienced in my childhood. He didn't want me telling people because it would increase the danger that I might be in. He was worried for my safety and told me I would never be safe again as long as this baby was in the picture. He told me that I should be very concerned.

He told Jake, his father I was just getting fat because I had moved away. He said I wasn't working much and was lazy.

Every time we talked Fred put fear into my mind about my safety, Tristan's safety, and my unborn baby's safety. He pushed the issue of adoption and said it was the only way he wouldn't lose me and be assured the baby would be safe. We could still be together if the baby was adopted by others.

I did believe that we loved each other and had a strong connection. He promised he would take me on a trip, my first plane ride, when this was all over. So many promises he made. He begged me to make the choice that would let us be together. He poured on the charm. He said I was like air, and he could not live without me. He begged me to see things his way so we could be together.

I did talk with a counsellor and, from reading the profiles, even picked out a family that my baby would live with should I decide to go with the adoption possibility. I never said I was going to give the baby up. I just went through the motions and was foggy on what I was really going to do when the time came.

Now that I was starting to show, some of Mom's friends started giving me presents. That was hard for me. I loved her friend Pam. Pam's daughter Kelsey spent every day growing up along with Tristan. And Kelsey's older sister, Dana, came home after school. What would Pam think of me if I gave my baby up?

There was a pastor who came into the restaurant. We knew him quite well as he would always stay around and chat. On one of the weekends when I was in town doing a shift (before I was too big) he came in. He asked where I had been, and noticed I was getting bigger. I told him I had tried to leave and get away, wanting nothing from Fred. Even though he was friends with Fred, he advised me to take him to the cleaners. He told me not to let him get away without paying for his child. I explained how dangerous it would be to back him into that corner. He still insisted I do it.

I had heard many stories of people being taken care of by Fred's acquaintances. I knew Fred would not get his hands dirty, but he led me to believe he had the money to get things taken care of if need be. I was living in fear again. Damn it! After I had escaped my childhood nightmare, I had never thought I would feel this way again.

Around this time, I received word that Tristan's father was taking me to court. He didn't feel Tristan was safe because he had been told by a cop that I had moved to Coldbrook to run Fred's drug business. Now I had to get a lawyer and deal with this issue too.

I was strong enough to leave him and move away. But I loved him and felt our connection strongly. If he only had left me alone . . .

Fred was friends with a big town lawyer, and he took me to see him. I had to eventually tell Tristan's dad why I had moved to stop his foolish accusations. Of course, I was short on the details, I just said I wanted a fresh start. Jesus, I knew Fred was into a lot of illegal things, but never drugs, to my knowledge. Stolen stuff, yes. I had seen that with my own eyes. Selling lobsters out of season, yes that too. Always trying to make extra money anyway he could. But never did I see drugs of any kind go through the restaurant.

Years later, I did learn he had brought some down and sold them in large quantities. But that was way before my time. He likely had become scared and didn't dare do it anymore.

But there was a cop who watched Fred's every move. The cop would stop him, and search through a trunk of pita bread from the city. At one point the cop had sent a young guy to become friends with me at the restaurant, to try to pry out information. This guy was in shit with the law, and if he could get anything useful out of me, they promised to give him a deal. I figured out what was going on, so he never got any information from me. This cop was obsessed with nailing Fred. I heard all about it, through many people.

In June of 1995, Fred was gone on one of his business trips abroad. Eveline was in Yarmouth to help Jake and some of the family had made a trip down to visit. Fred's sister, her husband, along with Fred's brother and his pregnant wife were all there. The brother's pregnant wife was due in September. I was due in December. Two cousins that might never meet.

We sat around talking about being pregnant, dealing with swelling feet, and all that stuff. The funny thing was no one knew I was pregnant. They just thought I was talking about my previous pregnancy with Tristan.

I was suffocating like I was trapped under a rock, living with so many secrets.

CHAPTER 16

Betrayals, Past And Present

I was twenty-one with a two-year-old child and another one on the way. I had found a job near where I had moved to in Coldbrook. My first day was supposed to be Saturday. Fred convinced me to come to Yarmouth instead and I never did go back to that restaurant and explain why I hadn't shown up.

I wish I had followed my plan and was free from Fred and his control. But I just kept letting him lead me back.

I went to Yarmouth but before I got there something happened. My brother had been told Fred was not going to support my child. My brother went to ask Fred why he wouldn't be doing this? They ended up having quite the conversation, which left Fred furious. How he thought he was helping me, has never been clear. I don't know the entire details, but somehow Fred came to believe I was conniving as a child, manipulative, and had probably planned the pregnancy to trap him.

My brother knew nothing about Fred or our relationship. Fred lost his mind, full of anger and went to the bar purposely to find my friend Crystal. He later admitted he wanted to sleep with her to try and hurt me. I don't know how this all took place because I wasn't in town at the time. However, he couldn't find her and went with his Plan B. Only much later would I find out what that plan was.

When I arrived in Yarmouth, Mom told me my brother had been to see Fred. I was not happy. I wasn't exactly close to my brother and if it wasn't for his wife and son, I doubted I would ever see him. He was my half-brother but that was still no excuse for how our relationship was.

I had a good friend, Marie, who worked at the restaurant. We had been through a lot together over the years. I reached out to ask her what was going on, but she had no idea. I walked into the diner to talk with Fred, but he wouldn't even look at me. We hadn't talked in a couple of days because he wouldn't answer the phone and wasn't calling me back. I didn't know why until after I had returned home.

I kept asking him to just talk to me. Asking him what had changed? Finally, he blurted out that I had been conniving as a child, and my own brother even thought that I had planned the pregnancy.

Oh my God! I was blown away. I had tears of anger in my eyes as I responded. I questioned why he would believe a child molesting asshole over what he knew was the real me.

I wasn't the one that had led my sister into the woods and made her hold me in places she shouldn't have to touch. I wasn't the one that had touched his sister inappropriately at a very young age and seemed to enjoy it so much. My God I was young. He was eight years older than me and the things he had made me do. Who had been the conniving child?

I had never told anyone what my brother had done, and here I was twenty-one-years old. Everyone knew what my father had done, but not my brother. When I was little, I remember telling him no. I remember begging him to stop, that Mom would find us, and we would get into trouble. I remember refusing to go hunting with him or into the woods for anything. That didn't stop him. We lived in a tiny shack with two bedrooms, and he still had the nerve to make me do stuff in that bedroom. With only a door between us and the kitchen where Mom was.

I quietly cried, and begged, and was terrified we would be beaten if we were found. Somehow the abuse had stopped. And I did everything in my power to avoid giving him the opportunity of being alone with me to make it start again. My strength came from within, guided by my guardian angels.

I never told my sisters or my mother. This all came flowing out from under a rock when I was twenty-one, pregnant in Jake's Diner talking to Fred, my boyfriend.

I told Mom about it the next day, but I didn't get much of a response. She came back to me later and said she had asked my brother herself. To my surprise he admitted it to her. I wasn't sure if he had told her the details, but he verified I was telling the truth. He had molested his little sister when she was about five or six years old. Mom was so sorry this too had happened to me, and that she hadn't known at the time to be able to protect me. My sisters were asked if anything had ever happened to them. They said nothing had, but he had often made them feel uncomfortable, they had said.

Now it became clear why I had thrown a fit when I was fourteen. I wouldn't allow my brother to take my niece anywhere alone. I would give up my own plans to stay home with her if Mom couldn't. Her mother had been in university. He wouldn't be taking her anywhere if I could help it.

When my sister found out she thanked me for protecting her daughter. Everyone now knew what he had done and apparently, he had talked with the pastor of the church for counselling about this topic. Regardless, I never wanted to see him around any little girls ever again. If Tristan had been a girl, my brother never would have entered my house. That wall was built high. Do not come near me, try to hug me, and don't touch me ever again.

During my teens no one had understood why I was so bitchy around my brother. I did have a nephew and sister-in-law that I wanted in my life. So, I tried to tolerate him for their sake.

But back to Fred. The night I told him about my brother's abuse, he sunk into remorse for listening to my brother. He was so mad at himself for putting me through the memories. Especially when he realized I had never told anyone ever before about what had happened between me and my brother. The restaurant was busy, but he made some time for us and held me while I cried it all out. Fred was back to being my charming boyfriend.

He was bending over backwards trying to make up for being wild at me. The next day it was raining hard, but once he could get away from the restaurant, he wanted us to go for a drive. He said he needed to talk to me.

Fred told me he loved me so much and had to be honest with me. He eventually told me about his plan to hurt me by finding Crystal. He told me she hadn't been there, but he had done something that he deeply regretted. He told me he'd slept with a girl; and they had gone parking.

I was blown away by the hurt. I was a crying mess and just wanted to get away from him. Let me out of this car! I wanted out of the car it had happened in.

We were on Lakeside Drive, and it was raining hard. He wouldn't stop the car to let me out. I was so hurt and disgusted that when he slowed at a stop sign, I jumped out of the moving car and ran off. I didn't want him to find me. He kept calling out and searching for me. But I went into the woods and found a spot to hide. And to cry in the rain.

He said he was going to call the search and rescue department. I was five months pregnant and running around in the torrential rain. I became so cold after awhile and figured he had given up. So, I came out of the woods and started walking back toward the town. But I didn't get far. Fred pulled up, demanding I get in the car. Damn it! I thought after two hours he would have given up. I was cold and numb, so I did get in the car, not saying a word. Betrayed yet again by a man in my life and feeling lost.

Fred took me to his house, got me dry, and put me in his bed. One of the workers had driven Jake home because Fred had never made it back for closing time. I woke up around 4 a.m., snuck away, called a cab, and went home to Mom's. There, I slept and cried.

Fred called but I didn't answer. I wanted to know who the girl was. I was crying on my friend Marie's shoulder, who worked at the restaurant. I had known her for years, and we were close. I was at her apartment. She said she didn't know what had happened and she hadn't seen him with anyone. Marie seemed to feel so sorry for what I was going through. Pregnant by a man who loved me but didn't want the child. Then being cheated on, to top it all off.

Finally, I did talk to Fred and demanded the girl's name. He gave me a fake name and place of work. Like a fool I went to confront her only to learn that no one by that name worked there. I went back to Fred: tell me the truth I demanded. He played games and ran circles around the truth. What he didn't realize was I wasn't about to give up. He had, after all, taught me how to play mind games. Therefore, I would get to the bottom of this.

About a week had gone by before I decided to follow my gut. Something was definitely going on. I walked into the restaurant before Fred arrived and looked at Marie. I told her he had confessed, and I knew everything, just to see what she would say. The look on her face was my answer.

The whole time I had been crying on her shoulder, and it was her. She went parking with her boss, my boyfriend. Granted he had insisted, but she didn't say no. She was supposed to be my friend. I had got her the job. The only reason she could give me for what had happened was, in her exact words, that she had wanted to see why I was so hung up on him.

I wanted to beat her face in. I never did, but oh, I hated her. Betrayed by a good friend in the worst way while pregnant. It was just perfect. Another name to add to my list of people in my life who had betrayed me. We argued at the restaurant and finally she threw her apron on the counter and walked out. It was either her or me.

Fred arrived in the middle of the commotion. I don't remember him saying much. What a mess! Why didn't I just walk away and cut all ties? The drama was too much. But Fred was still trying to win me back and have me wrapped around his finger again.

CHAPTER 17

A Baby Girl Enters The World

Not long after that weekend I was working a morning shift with Jake. A lady from the bank came in for her coffee break and she asked me when I was due in front of Jake. I tried not to answer. Jake finally walked away with a worried look on his face. She was shocked, and he was mad. Jake had thought I was just gaining weight. I had tried to hide it with the apron, but you can only hide so much.

Soon after that event I was done doing shifts. I didn't want to be the fat one on display. When I got really big, about six months along, I no longer went to the diner anymore. Fred continued to visit me in Coldbrook and called me daily. He just wouldn't leave me alone. He was trying to manipulate and control the situation. He was trying to make sure his Halifax family never found out about any of this. Fred's world was spiralling out of his control.

I did have a counsellor in Kentville named Debbie. She was going to be the one to take me to the hospital and to be with me for the birth of the baby. She didn't have a lot of advice to give me; she just basically listened. I was lost, cut off from family and friends and shut down inside my head. I didn't feel anyone would understand; therefore, I didn't talk.

My friend who had previously lived in my apartment tried to convince me to keep the baby. I hadn't said what I was doing for sure. I was in a trance. Day by day was passing me by and I was numb. I developed a rash on my face, and it just kept spreading. I didn't like going out very far. I was big and uncomfortable, and now my face was a mess. They were like little water blisters. Little did I know, this would be a skin problem for life, breaking out once or twice a year, and needing antibiotics each time. Stress was the main factor causing the outbreaks.

The social worker I had to see set everything up. She wanted me to see a lawyer. It was needed in case I decided to sign my baby away. The first man I went to was horrible, asking me if I didn't have any family that I could give my baby to. He told me that once I gave my baby up it was done and I couldn't change my mind. I left his office in tears and my social worker arranged for me to see another lawyer. I don't remember any of the details from the second meeting, so it must have been better.

The first family I picked, when contacted, was pregnant with complications. They couldn't be told someone had picked them. They just thought they were having a routine check.

My social worker had given me so many profiles to read. But in her own way kept coming back to the same couple. She knew this couple and had done their family study. I liked the couple except that it said they were sociable smokers. I was totally against my baby being in a home with smoking and I let her know about my concerns. She investigated and assured me they were not like that at home.

The father was a principal and the mother a teacher. I believe they met while in university. They were older and hadn't had any luck with having a family. I did think maybe they were too old for my baby, but I ended up being drawn to their family's study information. I had to fill out details about myself and the father, but I never gave his full name. Fred didn't know I had given them all the information I knew about him.

I had the opportunity to meet the potential parents before the baby was born. I refused, thinking that I still wasn't sure. I didn't want to have such an emotional meeting. I had chosen the adoption plan where they had to send me pictures every year and, I had requested they keep her name as Natasha. Everything was done and ready now. I just had to decide what I was doing.

I wished Fred would just leave me alone. Damn it! I would never be thinking about adoption and my baby needing two parents if he hadn't been constantly drilling it into my head. I thought I was a good Mom to Tristan. Wasn't I?

He continued to say I would be stuck and depending upon my mother's assistance with two kids. What kind of life could I provide them on my own? He would tell me he couldn't be around me if I kept the baby.

The days went by in a blur. I stayed busy with Tristan. I had never found out if the new baby was a girl or boy. It was going to be a surprise. Fred said a fortune teller told him once that he would only ever have girls. He hated all fortune tellers for that reason.

I was huge, and the baby was healthy. I never talked about adoption. I never said the words.

On the fifth of December, in the wee hours of the morning, I went into labour. I called my cousin to tend Tristan and called Debbie to come and take me to the hospital. I remember the contractions were not too far apart. Debbie needed coffee and asked if she could go through the drive-through. She did and we made it to the hospital. But it's a blur from that point.

I don't remember everything, but it didn't take long. My baby was born at 5:04 a.m. It was a girl, 8 pounds, 4 ounces. She was perfect. I got to see her and hold her. Dark, curly hair, and healthy. I named her Natasha. It pained me to put Sinclair as her last name. No one should be burdened with that name.

The nurses took her to clean her up and after awhile told me I could shower. I remember thinking that's awfully quick, but the hot water felt so good. I kept trying to wash the blood off, but it kept coming and coming. The nurse had left me for a moment, and I remember a lot of yelling. The next thing I knew they were putting an IV in my arm, and I was in a bed. Apparently, I had hemorrhaged. Probably because of the hot water.

They put me in a room and told me to rest. The nurse that had left me was scolded. When I woke around suppertime, I asked for my baby. The nurse said they were tending her at the desk so I could rest. I insisted they bring me my baby so I could tend her myself. I soaked up every minute of taking care of her. I called Fred to let him know and he was glad I was ok. I know despite everything that he wished it had been a boy. In fact, he lied to his father and told him it was a boy.

Would Fred have wanted to hide me if it was a boy, and perhaps keep the baby? Could he have handled giving up something he wanted so badly? Fred said he would come to see me but didn't want to see the baby. I told him If he thought giving her up was what was best, that he had to come and look at her in the face and do it with me. I told him if he didn't want to see both of us, to not come.

I was supposed to get out of the hospital the next day, but because I had hemorrhaged, they kept me an extra night. It was perfect because that gave me more time with Natasha.

Mom called and wanted to come see me. I told her I was fine and to just please tend to Tristan for me. I asked her not to come see me. This still breaks my heart when I think about it. The only visitors I had were Debbie, the social worker, and my cousin Lori.

I enjoyed tending my baby even though the nurses kept trying to take her from me. I bathed her and put on a sweet little pink outfit. I took some pictures. Fred had agreed to see us both and he was coming to bring me home. I wasn't leaving the baby unless he did it with me. He came and held her, gently kissing her forehead, and gave her a blue bead that he had asked his youngest daughter if he could have for someone special. In his culture the blue bead protects children from the evil eye. His daughter didn't know she was giving her sister a very special gift. Maybe one day she will.

When it was time to leave, I was in a trance. I felt like I was floating outside of my body. Fred asked if I could go to the mall to buy Natasha a few outfits to take with her. We went shopping and we got her a few things. Then he took me home. Tristan had gone to Yarmouth. It was the seventh of December. I sat on my couch with a box of tissues and hardly moved. All I remember was crying.

The social worker let me know how things would go and said Natasha had to be in a temporary foster home for several days. She couldn't just go to her new family. In fact, they didn't even know they were going to be parents yet.

I cried for days. Fred called often and at one point, because of all my crying, said to do what I felt I had to do. A few days later Fred came back to check on me. I remember him being pissed that I was in the same position on the couch with my tissues. He said he was worried about my mental health. He wanted me to go to Yarmouth and get Tristan. I guess he thought I would be kept busy and have less time to think about the baby if Tristan was with me.

Fred brought me to Yarmouth and a few days later even drove me and Tristan back to Coldbrook. I was still struggling and in a trance. I told Fred I had to see my baby. So, I made the arrangements, and the foster mother brought her into the social worker's office. I got to hold and feed her and see that she was okay.

Oh my God what was I doing, I asked myself.

CHAPTER 18

My Broken Heart

Fred was worried I was going to bring our baby girl home. I liked making him feel like he wasn't in control. I should have been stronger.

He was relieved to find out she was still with the foster family. I still struggled with the fact that she was with strangers.

I cried and cried every day. Tristan was so cute, hugging me and comforting me. Christmas was coming soon. I had to pull myself together and get his gifts. I don't remember what I got him that year. We would be at Mom's for Christmas and although I should have had a new baby to bring home, I didn't. The chosen parents were going to get the most amazing gift this year. They didn't even know about it until the day before her arrival.

Natasha was being dropped off with them on December 22, 1995. The social worker kept me up-to-date on how everything was going. Tristan and I were at Mom's. I had on a white sweater, and I snuggled with him quietly throughout the holidays. I'm sure Fred kept in close contact. He tried to keep me happy and under his spell.

I had been living in Coldbrook for a while. Between Fred going on business trips, he was trying to convince me to move back to Yarmouth. Fred said he had to take care of me. He insisted on paying for moving expenses and setting me up in an apartment. He found Tristan and I a nice apartment, next to the hospital. I would be working day shifts at the restaurant and would manage everything.

He said he had to know I would be alright before he went on his next big business trip. He promised to take me to Toronto for a week when he would next be needed there. I didn't know when this would be but the trip would be my first time ever on a plane. He had a partner in Toronto, Jamal, and they were going to be selling pharmaceuticals in Saudi Arabia, Syria, Yemen, and Lebanon. He was travelling all around these countries during the first year of Natasha's life. He was home some, working at the diner and then gone again. He brought me home a gold chain and other gifts.

I had turned 22. It was 1996. He was gone for extended periods of time. He kept in close contact with me and sent many postcards and love letters. He talked of bringing me with him and how he couldn't live without me.

Fred would call in the middle of the night and want to talk for hours. The whole month of December was the toughest for me. I got pictures of Natasha and a letter from her parents. This was part of the agreement I had pre-arranged. I also had asked them to keep her name as Natasha. Her parents choose to keep it as her middle name.

Around the time of Natasha's first birthday, or shortly after it, I decided to ask to meet Natasha's parents. I had denied meeting them initially when I was pregnant because I figured it would be too hard. I begged my social worker to ask the parents if they would see me now? She wasn't supposed to, but she helped me. By rights, I wouldn't be able to file anything at the registry to find her until she was eighteen. I knew I couldn't wait. I wanted her to be a part of my life. The pain of not having my baby with me was unbearable. I thought about her every day. Where was she? What did she look like in person?

I looked at every person that walked by with a little girl, especially when I was in Halifax, or other towns in that part of the province. I knew she wasn't in Yarmouth, as I wanted her safe and had picked a family that lived elsewhere. I knew she didn't live in Halifax either, but that didn't stop me from looking at every little girl when I was in the city. It could be possible to run into them anywhere. I didn't know exactly where she was, but I dreamed of finding her.

I told Fred what I had done, and he was one hundred per cent against me looking for her. But I was done listening to Fred. I was following my heart. The request was in, and now I had to wait for their answer.

Fred called me crying one night. It seemed like things were bothering him much more at the one-year mark than when she was born. I had been grieving for a full year, all alone in my head. Like Fred had said, no one had died, but the hurt of missing my baby had never dulled. I was missing a huge piece of my life.

Fred was so upset, saying we were monsters for giving our child away. His father had said only animals got rid of their young. When Natasha was born Fred had called and told his father, Jake, the baby was here, and it was a boy. I don't think he ever told him the truth.

Fred had always wanted to have a son to impress his father. Fred was a mess on the phone, in Yemen I think that time. He was beating himself up, but I had been doing that for the entire past year. Why had it taken him so long? Probably because he was so alone in that strange country and had way too much time to think about her.

As we headed into 1997, Fred was hardly ever around. I started to get the picture he wasn't moving back. Thankfully, I had Tristan to keep me moving forward. I still had to make his life the best I possibly could.

Fred's youngest brother, decided to move to Yarmouth to help his dad and eventually to take over the diner. Fred had told his brother about the baby and me. He told him how much he loved me but wanted to let me move on and have a life. So, I now worked for the brother.

Fred came back occasionally, and it was tough reliving everything. He had sent me so many letters and had made so many phone calls. But he wasn't there and somehow, I was slowly breaking free of him. His visits started meaning less and I knew there was no future with him.

I still wanted to see him and talk about Natasha because I had no one else to talk to. I did talk some to my boss, but he just wanted to put a wall up and not get involved. I never confided in anyone else about Natasha. I stayed pretty much private about the topic of my daughter. Lots of people knew I had been pregnant because they had seen me pregnant. In my mind I thought everyone knew.

To my surprise, I still shock some people when they find out I have a daughter.

CHAPTER 19

Me And The Universe

I did get my trip to Toronto; my first ever flight. It was back in 1996, probably nine to ten months after Natasha was born. But it didn't go as I had pictured it would. We didn't fly together. I flew on my own and visited Diane, my friend from school, for two days. Then Jamal, Fred's partner, picked me up from her apartment, and we went to the airport to pick up Fred together.

Fred immediately put his arms around me and wouldn't let go. He was pouring on the charm. Jamal and Fred would have meetings throughout the day, then we would spend time together in evenings. I was roaming the city, sightseeing, and shopping during day. As Fred needed Jamal's help with me being there, Fred had to explain our situation to Jamal. Jamal even told his wife some of it. Fred said they were very understanding. God knows what he really told them.

Fred had flown in from overseas. He was returning to Halifax with me, after our week in Toronto. But he made sure we were on different flights. His kids would be waiting for him when he arrived. When I left the restaurant for my trip the staff all knew I was going to see Fred. Jake knew it too. Eveline had arrived to help Jake in my absence, and the staff had mentioned where I was going in front of her. To my knowledge that was the first she had heard about our relationship. It had begun in December of 1993. We were now in 1996.

She never mentioned it to me ever. We had spent time together cooking and even during a trip to the city and back. Jake probably had told her a few things, but I don't think she knew about Natasha (or a baby boy).

The highlight of the Toronto trip was of course going to Niagara Falls. We had an amazing view from the revolving restaurant and the best meal. When it was time for me to go home, Fred was in a meeting. I was in the big city, taking a cab to the airport. I was hopeful he would make it back to say goodbye, so I pushed my luck by waiting too long to leave. I missed my flight. I was a mess at the counter trying to rebook. The worker never gave me a hard time; probably because he saw the tears and so he didn't charge me for the new flight.

There were so many reasons for those tears. I missed my baby, my boyfriend, and my unrealistic imaginary life that I thought was going to happen. It was all a mess really.

The one thing I could hold and count on was Tristan. He was my rock, the thing I lived for. I was so thankful I had a reason to live and never give up.

The universe sure had plans for me, but why?

Fred always said I could buy the restaurant when they were ready to sell it. He started saying that long before the baby was conceived. What a joke! Eventually Fred's brother and wife moved to Yarmouth and took over the restaurant. Jake and Eveline stayed in Halifax as Jake was getting too old to work so hard. But he was stubborn. It took a lot of convincing for him to let go.

Fred had confided in his brother and wanted him to look out for me. Fred had promised me I'd always have the management job when he moved me back to Yarmouth. He wanted me to work during the day. I'd be fine. Oh, and when they were ready to sell the restaurant, it would be mine for sure. He'd said that for years! I'd be set for life. That was Fred's plan but not necessarily his brother's.

The place was a gold mine if run properly. Then the middle brother also decided to move his family to Yarmouth. They opened a second location on Starrs road. That diner didn't last long. Next, they decided to buy A-1 Pizza on Main Street. He was going to take it over and leave the name until things got sorted out. I told him to change the name right away. The prior owners had already ruined the old name's brand. People will give you another chance if they think it's totally different. He said I was smart, and that he had never expected that. He also shook his head and made some remarks about what was Fred thinking. I guess the youngest brother had filled him in on a few things.

I know Fred had poured his heart out to one brother. But the new brother in town had just got some of the story, and none of the tears. So, he was a prick to me and had no sympathy.

My boss was the nice one and he was trying to understand. I even showed him pictures of Natasha, which must have hit home. He had a young son, three months older than Natasha. I figure that helped with his compassion toward me. That and he was genuinely a nice guy. He would let me take time off work to go see Fred when he was in town. Then he listened to my meltdowns when Fred would leave again. It was crazy seeing the tears in his eyes over the whole situation.

Most of 1996 was a roller coaster ride. Fred was around for some of the year. Then he was off on his trips. We always had long phone calls and he sent me love letters. Why was I hanging on? Probably because Fred wasn't honest about his future plans. If things worked out for him, maybe he wasn't coming back?

I was hanging onto the idea of Fred, but the relationship was slipping away. I would look forward to his visits. Then crash and be depressed after he would leave. I spent my time with Tristan, hung out with my friend Marilyn, and worked. I never talked to anyone else about Natasha, just Fred.

Mom decided to buy a bigger house. So, I decided to buy the house at 10 King Street from her. I was doing well with my full-time job managing the restaurant. I had upgraded my vehicle to my 1990 Toyota 4Runner. I had just put a brand-new paint job on it. The only payments I had were my mortgage and a side payment to Mom, for her part of the house since she didn't make me take out a mortgage for the entire amount.

Mom and Charlie lived right around the corner. I could pay all my own bills. Tristan's father got away with paying one hundred and twenty-five dollars a month. Boy that did a lot.

I didn't need anyone, and it was the best feeling to be independent. I was evolving and growing into the person I was meant to be. No one would ever stop me now.

The summer of 1997 I was still waiting to hear from Natasha's parents. They had been given all my information and we had both signed the adoption disclosure registry.

I was still receiving phone calls from Fred and lots of letters and postcards. He would come home but not often, and he would act like I was still his. Although sometimes he would beg me to move on with my life. I had told him losing my daughter was the worst thing that had ever happened to me in my life—over all the abuse and pain I had suffered as a child.

But Fred hurt me the most. He was devastated when I said that. He claimed I ripped his heart out comparing him to my monster of a father. But it was true. The pain I felt every single day from missing my baby never went away.

My mind was healing, from Fred's hold on it and our distance was helping me look at what I wanted as a future. I wanted to see my baby and for her to know her brother.

Every time I saw Fred it was an emotional roller coaster. He would show up for a few days and then he would be gone.

I hung out with some of the staff at the restaurant. Some summer nights we would go biking at midnight after work. Marilyn, my friend, would come too. Rob and sometimes Garth, both the delivery guys, would come and off the four of us would go. We even went on the weekends at 3 a.m. It was summertime fun.

One time Marilyn wanted me to hold her handlebar. She was trying to tie her coat around her waist. I couldn't hold it straight and she hit the pavement. I felt so bad. She even had road rash. So sorry for that Marilyn.

Marilyn and I loved to go out dancing too. Her boyfriend worked the door at the Red Knight. I was never a big drinker. I didn't need alcohol to dance and have a good time. I went on our local ferry, to the US with Garth, basically as friends. We toured around the beaches. It was in the fall. I'm sure he was interested but he was even older than the guys I was used to being around. I introduced him to my friend Heather, who worked at the salon behind the restaurant.

Heather had trimmed my hair for years. I adored her. She had long beautiful red curly hair. I had the blonde curls. I guess we were dangerous back in the day. He was fascinated with her. He took her a piece of cake, and they fell head over heels for each other. Before long they were married, and I was happy for them.

CHAPTER 20

Meeting Steve

In the fall of 1997, my mother was running a boarding house. She had some men that were working in the area staying in some of her rooms. She also had a nurse from Newfoundland boarding there. Mom got a call from a young man named Steve that was interested in a hot meal and shower. He was a truck driver that worked nights and had to sleep in Yarmouth before heading out again each night. Apparently, he did the mail run, so he had to pick things up at the post office around 6 p.m.

He would drive to Halifax unload and reload for Yarmouth, arriving in the early mornings. He also dropped off flyers to the Canadian Printers, which ironically is where my brother worked at the time. In a conversation with my brother, Steve had learned about my mother's boarding house and gave her a call.

While the weather was still warm enough to sleep in the truck, Steve enjoyed having a home-cooked meal and a shower for ten dollars a day. Soon Steve started going with Charlie, my mom's husband to Tim Hortons every afternoon around 3 p.m. Steve also got to know Tristan, who was four years old at the time. Tristan would be at Mom's during the day, and I usually picked him up between 5 and 6 p.m.

I met Steve a couple of times at Mom's supper table. Mom had pictures of her four children on the wall. Steve soon fell for the blonde on the wall, who was me. Mom was quick to tell him that I was going to marry a cop, or a man in uniform. Mom also said that I dated older guys and wouldn't look at a younger one.

Even after all that Steve still got up the nerve to phone my work and ask me out. He made the mistake of calling me Tammy. Anyone that knows me knows I hate that. I've never been a Tammy. Mom has never called me that. Mom named me Tam-a-ra. Most people pronounced my name wrong, so she shortened it to Tam. Plain and simple Tam. No Tammy here. Mind you I know tons of people named Tammy. One is Tristan's aunt, and another is a young girl that worked at Jake's who was like a little sister to me.

But back to the phone call from Steve. I didn't respond right away. I was flattered but figured once he knew my story, he wouldn't want to deal with all the baggage. I hated guys in grey jogging pants, with their junk jumping while they walk. There is just no need for that to be seen! Mom informed Steve of this. He would run to put on his one pair of jeans if he knew I was heading over to pick up Tristan. How cute was that?

Charlie teased him about me, and Mom just shook her head, thinking he didn't have a chance. After two weeks, out of the blue, I decided to call Steve back and give him a chance. Just one date. What could that hurt? I had never given a younger guy a chance before. Never in my life. With our work schedules I offered to go on a trip in the truck with him. Staying up all night wasn't that hard. I was used to working crazy hours. I believe this trip took place in early November.

We went down Highway 103, stopping in Bridgewater on the way back for lunch. He probably got fuel; I don't remember. We bought chicken salad sandwiches as our meal on our first date. I hope to never forget that fact. We definitely kissed as I believe the angels were pulling us together. I didn't recognize it at the time but there was unquestionably a higher power showing us the way.

Steve was twenty-two when I met him. Just a coincidence? I think not. I was one year older than Steve. You will see why I like the number twenty-two when you read my special chapter on that topic.

We dated whenever we got the chance, and I joined him at Mom's table for supper when I could. Lots of conversations on the phone. The big brick cell phones that existed way back then.

I told him all about my two children and how I was trying to be able to see my daughter. I warned him not to be with me. I had so much baggage coming along with me. Who would want that? He was single with no children. I felt he deserved better.

I couldn't understand why he wanted to be with me. I was twenty-three with a four-year-old, and an almost two-year-old that I didn't have living with me. I still had a weird relationship with Fred. We still talked all time on phone, and he was still sending me letters.

But I soon told Fred about Steve. He acted happy for me one minute, and the next he was looking forward to getting back to Canada to see me. Talk about confusing, however, I knew there was no future with Fred. In the first eight months of seeing Steve, Fred had made it home for a couple of visits. I wanted to meet with him and talk about Natasha because who else even had an inkling of what I had been though? Once when I found out the day Fred would be in Yarmouth, ironically it was the day that Steve was on an extra work trip to Moncton. I figured a public meal was the best way to go at a restaurant. I will never forget calling Steve to let him know about my meeting with Fred. He was beside himself with jealousy. But I was being honest with him.

Fred was the only other man I had ever had strong feelings for. He knew the basics of the story and what I had been through. Fred wanted to talk to Steve on phone. He literally told Steve that he had better take good care of me or he would break his legs! I was floored. Fred was so possessive of me, and poor Steve was pissed. What gave Fred the right to say that. He gave me back the phone, and I told Steve not to worry, that I was just at supper with Fred. I made sure that was all it was. Steve was pissed as he fully understood that Fred had hurt me the most.

I never did anything with Fred that would tarnish my relationship with Steve. I hoped Steve could understand why I still met with Fred and continued to talk to him. Fred was not impressed that I was looking for Natasha. He begged me not to. He wanted me to leave her new family alone. But I was not listening. I was beginning to follow my gut and my heart. I wasn't looking to take her back, I just wanted to be part of her life.

Just for the record I would have taken her back in a heartbeat. She was my baby. But because of Fred, reuniting in that way would never be possible.

CHAPTER 21

Marriage Plans

I continued to date Steve. He would work all week, then come back down on the weekends. I worked a lot, mainly days, unless I had to stay late. Steve was really jealous of the bar crowd when I worked on the weekends. Oh, my nerves—the night he had a few drinks and I kept kicking him out. Then he'd go around the back, and I'd throw him out that way. Finally, I told him I was going to call the cops, so to just friggin' walk to my house and stay there. That was embarrassing. I made it clear; that was not to happen again.

We went out to the bars a few times together. He danced like a stick man. I was going to have to fix that. I started teaching him in the living room with the music blaring. He did great and to this day spends most of his time on the dance floor when we get the opportunity.

I had big plans of going to Australia for four weeks with Tristan. I saved up the cash to pay for the trip and would be staying with my cousin Twila. We were going in March, and I wasn't staying home because of Steve. I knew it would be a great time to heal and think. And if I missed Steve like crazy then I would know he was the one.

The trip was great. Tristan and I saw lots of tourist sights. We went to see the penguins and majestical underground caves. Her in-laws took us on a tour and a family friend let us stay in the city for a few days. She had a beautiful pool. She took me shopping for the opal ring I wanted as a keepsake. I borrowed Twila's truck and even went exploring a little on our own.

No one was on the beaches, as it was winter there. It was just damp and rainy but on a nice day it was still just as warm as our summers at home. Twila lived on a dairy farm. She worked with her husband. After milking she would take us out to explore the little towns. I bought some handmade pottery at one of the shops. I even got to ride the neighbour's camel. When was I ever going to get that kind of opportunity again?

Steve called a few times missing me like crazy. I'm pretty sure my heart fluttered, and I missed him too. I had no contact with Fred for the entire time I was gone.

Once I returned everything changed. Steve and I decided to get married after only six months of knowing each other. How crazy was that? I had a good feeling this was meant to happen. The angels were at work again. My path, my universe, was pointing me in the right direction.

Tristan started school in September of 1998. We always drove him and picked him up because he was so little. He had Mrs. Noble, and I couldn't have imagined a better teacher. She was great and a family friend of Shirley's, his grandmother. He was an excellent student.

For the wedding, we decided on November, which would be a year from our first date. Were we rushing? Yes! But sometimes things just feel right, and you jump in with both feet.

Steve was picking out a ring in Halifax at Mappins Fine Jewellers. He ended up deciding to have a unique one made with a diamond solitaire. He put a down payment on it.

Our plan was to marry in Cuba, but Steve's mother Charlene didn't like this idea. Steve was her only son. His mother worked in Halifax. She had a very good job as the head secretary for the department of transportation. We met up a few times with her in the city and I even went to lunch with her on my own. She was nice, however, she insisted I call him Stephen. Sorry, that wasn't going to happen. He introduced himself to everyone in Yarmouth as Steve and that's who he was to us.

As time went on, we visited her at her boyfriend Lyndon's house. He was different. She had sold her house and moved in with him, despite Steve not wanting her to. He was left with nowhere to call home but did prefer to be at his Grandfather Miller's anyway.

Steve had nothing when I met him. No furniture, barely any clothing, a huge cell phone bill, and he was taking money from his credit card to pay his truck payment. Wow, how was that working out for him?

I immediately called the phone company to get to the bottom of his bill. I started pointing him in the right direction with his paycheques and soon I had combined his bills onto my Visa so he would have one payment. He eventually sold his Ford truck, which went to pay for my ring. I wanted everything taken care of. I believe the contract for his mail run job was running out soon, so I did his résumé and got him a job at Midland Transportation. This was a good paying job, and he was now local. No more running back and forth to the city every weekend. Our paperwork to be legally married in Cuba was going to cost eight hundred dollars for the translation. So, we decided instead to have a quick wedding in Yarmouth and then redo our vows in Cuba.

The date was set for November 15, 1998. I had a dress made by Kim who was a lady Mom had met while tending her children. She did a very nice job and hand sewed some beads on it too. It was a sleeveless dress with a little fancy topcoat.

We planned to hold a reception at the Manor Inn for all our family and friends. I would get to wear my dress three times, which made me very happy. Everything was falling into place.

Once I told Fred of my plans he started to back off. His postcards were still coming but he now added Steve's name along with mine and Tristan's. He didn't call as often but he still would have breakdowns and call sometimes. I was stubborn and knew I had made up my mind. No one was changing it. One moment he was glad I had met someone and the next he was crying that he missed me.

The last phone call I remember was Fred's plea for me to sell my house, give Tristan to his father, and move overseas with him. Was he crazy? I had my wedding and future planned.

I didn't even consider his option for a moment. I think he was playing mind games again seeing if I was serious. He had talked about this scenario before, but I had never paid much attention. He said I'd have to wear a hijab on my head and always be covered up. Especially in some of those countries surrounding where he now lived.

That was not going to happen. I was now with Steve.

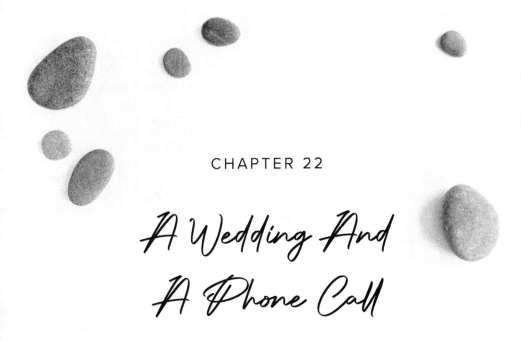

CHAPTER 22

A Wedding And A Phone Call

I was hopeful I would hear from Natasha's family soon. Wouldn't it be wonderful if she could be at the wedding? I had dreams of her being there.

Four weeks before the wedding Steve put his back out at work. I had to go get him and take him to the hospital. The doctor reset it. He was fine after a couple weeks.

Our wedding was simple. We went to the church together. Pastor John married us. My friend Abbi stood with me, and Dwayne stood with Steve. I didn't think I was nervous until it was my turn to speak. I started laughing and then once I realized what I had done I started crying. Then I was mad I had ruined my pictures and had a red face.

Poor Steve was worried I was walking out or not serious. It was just nerves. Finally, I got through it.

We only had Mom, Charlie, Charlene, Lyndon, Tristan, and the photographer at the church. We went home, had some cake, hugged Tristan, and left for our honeymoon. We stayed in Halifax overnight. Then we flew out the next day. It was Steve's first flight as an adult. We had some turbulence, and he was white-knuckled holding onto the armrests. I couldn't stop giggling because he was so funny.

Cuba was hot. Wow, we were not use to the humidity. We arrived in the dark and went to bed. The next morning, we went out to explore our resort. By 11 a.m. Steve was sick—likely dehydrated and back in our room. Chills, diarrhea, and clammy. He spent all that day and part of the next unable to leave the room. He laid shivering in bed.

I came and went. Finally on Day Three he was okay. We met Donna and Gary Malone from Bridgewater. We soon asked them to stand up with us for our Cuban wedding. On Day Five we renewed our vows on our balcony. We went all over taking pictures and the day was fun. The wedding cake was good but had a dairy frosting, which by late evening wasn't sitting well in my belly. I made it through supper but then it was back to the room. By the next day I was fine.

We relaxed, walked the beach, and hung out by the pool.

After the honeymoon was over, we finished planning our reception. The Manor Inn had such beautiful rooms. We had a finger food reception. We danced and stayed there for the night. It was a fun time with, of course, more pictures. With a bronze tan and my hair done in ringlets we had a gorgeous reception filled with family and friends. There were people missing for one reason or another, but the night was still memorable. Right down to the forks in our bed. Thanks to Aunt Thelma and my sister Sharon. They thought it would be funny and apparently it was a tradition of my aunts.

Of course, my boss didn't stop in as he had promised. Not surprising.

Not long after we were married, I received the call I had been waiting two years for. Natasha's mother called me and arranged a meeting for December 13, 1998. Natasha had just turned three.

It was just her parents and me in Digby for the visit. I brought along my new wedding pictures, and they brought lots of pictures of Natasha. We talked for a long time. They wanted the initial meeting to be just the adults. I'm sure it was to check me out before letting me meet Natasha. Everything went well and they said they would be in touch.

My dreams were coming true.

Soon it would be Christmas. December was always hard for me. Memories, regrets, and the "what if" game made it hard. But this year I had a husband. Pretty good for a girl who was never getting married. Amazing how meeting one person can change you so much. We got married but I was clear that I wasn't having any more children. I couldn't bear the thought of replacing Natasha. I told Steve many times not to marry me if he wanted more kids.

On January 1, 1999, Steve had to work. He was not happy being at the bottom of the seniority list. He had to load a huge load of lobsters onto a truck and take it to the airport. Being young, hotheaded and thinking no one could hear him, he was grumbling, complaining, and throwing the boxes onto the truck. Steve came home telling me that he shouldn't have had to do that job alone.

Over the weekend he got a call to come in on Monday and bring his keys. We knew this was not going to be good. He'd lost his job. We were just married. How could this be? Apparently, the secretary had overheard his complaining and had reported him. He hadn't realized anyone could hear him. Now he had to find a new job.

We were in for an interesting year. Steve quickly got a job at West Nova Fuels delivering fuel to houses and boats. For a few months all was good, however, he didn't like fuelling boats on the wharfs by himself. Not the safest job out there. While he worked there his boss had his twenty-fifth wedding anniversary. They had a beautiful party, and we were invited. I pictured us having the same thing in twenty-five years.

Oh, my dreams.

Me, 1976
I was only 2 years old.
The only picture I have of my childhood.

My broken doll that I traded with my sister to make her happy. Mom
made us doll clothes, somehow I still have this doll. ♡

My Mom and her Mom.
My Grammie Tedford on
Mother's Day. - 1989

My Grampie Tedford sitting in
his chair where he could
see over the fields.

My puffy hair at our apartment
on Pleasant Street.
1988

My Grade 9 picture at
Maple Grove School.
1988

My Mom at her parents'
house. This would be
Grampy's view at his
window. The Yellow house
is where I lived for a
few months with my
Aunt and Uncle.

June 1993
My first baby boy
Tristan wrapped in the
blanket I made for him.
♡

Me and Tristan.
5 weeks old.
So much love.

PRECIOUS

NOV 22,93

Tristan
5 months old.
Sweet, sweet boy.

Summer of 1995
Me and Fred, my first love. Cruising to Bar Harbour, Maine, USA.

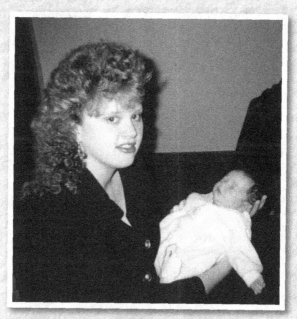

Me and Natasha, 1995
The day I had to see my baby. One more time...

I hope that someday we could go on one of these cruises together without worrying about the rest of the world. someday soon!

pray that everything goes well so that we can go on a trip in february.

FoR Luck

DEAR  :

       Well I'm finally writing you a letter, unlike you it is easier for me to talk to you in person, but here goes. I understand that you have concerns about us and that you have many questions that you would like answered, but things are not that simple the only way to answer all these feelings of doubt that you have is to tell you that I DO LOVE YOU ! Sometime I feel I have no right to feel this way because of the pain that I have brought to you. With my life being so confusing I wonder if I should ever love anyone.I have done so many bad things I wonder whether things could ever be normal. When I hurt you, your pain goes through my bones because that is not what I want, at times i don't even know who I am.The only thing that I know is that I do not want to have another child even though you are carrying that baby right now. The reasons are not only ones of protection for me or you but also for other reasons . I can not be a father anymore no matter how much I love my kids I can't be with them on a dially basis. Also I have this ambition that I have to satisfy because there something more to me than just what I am today, and I can't rest till I find it.

       The way I feel about you is beyond thedescription in which words can be used. When I'm with you every part of my body yearns for you, and when were apart the same parts crave for you. The times that we make love are so passionate that it cannot just be physical but right from the heart it feels that our souls are united at those times in a way that a man and a woman should be united as one .You are now a part of me that I can not do without like I can't do without breathing. The problem that we face is an accident of that passion and we have no right to make it grow up with the regrets that we have because of it's reality. there is an answer to this and you hope that you can see that soon. Maybe I am selfish for not wanting to change these feelings between us but I can't hel it you have become my addiction and I need you on a daily basis to live so please Tam make the decision to come back to me because I need you in every way to achieve what I want in life and I promise to give back to you as much as you give to me.

       I can't write anymore because thinking about you without you being here for me to hold you is to hard. So I am going to tell you that I love and that I always will!!!

see you soon take care of yourself and stop the tears and start the healing.

love always

Fred

Dear Birthmother,

Thank you for reading our letter although our words cannot fully express the feelings we have in our hearts. The prospects of being parents and that this letter may have some impact are both overwhelming concepts. Rather than trying to create an image of what we think you would like to hear, we have decided to do what comes naturally - be honest and open.

Maybe telling you a bit more about ourselves can help you to decide. After twelve years of dating and eight years of marriage, our love for each other continues to grow. During all of this time children have played an important role in our lives. My husband and I are both teachers: I teach elementary and he teaches junior/senior high. We are both very active in extra-curricular activities with young people both at school and within the community.

Family is very important to us. We both were blessed to come from loving homes and keep these bonds dear to us even today through frequent family gatherings which include parents, sisters, brothers, nieces and nephews. The values and morals which our parents taught us have been a good springboard for us throughout our lives. This love that came so freely and the values and morals which gave us a firm base are just a few of the qualities that we want to pass on to a child. Just like all parents we will make mistakes but they will be made out of love.

We hope to be open and truthful with our adopted child about their roots and answer any questions that arise as they grow and become more curious.

Being teachers, we feel strongly about education and believe a child should be encouraged to take full advantage of this opportunity. We believe that a child

needs constant support and guidance and above all, be nurtured in a loving home.

Your decision to offer a childless couple the opportunity to make a dream become a reality is a very courageous one. Selecting which couple must be a very difficult decision. We can only hope that love will continue to be your guide. Whatever your choice we are sure your child will be raised with love and understanding.

Thanks again for taking the time to read our letter.

June 26,1996

Dear Tam,

   I hope your in the best of health when you receive this letter, you and Tristan that is. I am fine working very hard, I hope this pays off because,I don't think I have ever used my head this much. In a way things are very exiting meeting all these new people, but that doesn't stop me from thinking about you and how much I've missed you, also about everything we have been through. I think about Natasha more and more now, I can't explaine why I just do. I thought about you a great deal, but now with Jamal leaving I am sure you will be in my thoughts every night. Don't let anyone give you a hard time, no matter what you hear you should know how I feel about you. We both know about that our relationship is not a normal one, and I can understand when you want to stop thinking about me , believe me, I understand and would never blame you.

   Well the chances of me coming back to Canada in the near future is very small. If I do come to Canada I will probably go to Toronto first for a couple days and I asked Jamal to arrange for you to meet there even for one night it would be great to see you, but I am sure it would more than that, if you want it to.

   Well I have to get some sleep it's 5:35 your time and 11:35 mine, I have to be up at 5:00 AM to take Jamal to the airoport. So good night for now , think of me if you want.

Love you always;

Fred,

Thanks for calling before you left the other day! I wanted to tell you how much I enjoyed you being here and spending time with you. Sorry I always want more than what I get. There will always be anger in my thoughts of you because I will never except that you can love someone so much but walk away from them anyway. I hate the thought that our feelings are so wasted. I figure there is no sense beating myself up this time about being weak so I'm just thinking of how much fun we had.

You are however still wrong for telling Joey. I find him distance from me unless it has to do with work. And no it still makes no sense you said he understood how you could be with me after everything and how you feel about me. But he must not if I couldn't even be in the same room with you. And it cuts to know he sees nothing special about me. The fact he asked you what you saw in me. Nice thought. Telling him caused a lot of tension at work. You said you made it clear how important I am to you. I don't think he sees it. Not the same as you do.

Regardless of my anger, I really wish I could forgive you and find some sort of peace. But there is so much anger and regret for what I have lost and those who are not with me. That I can't find the peace I need.

I will ask you once again to give me the number where you are going to be even if I don't call. If I need to, I can and sometimes I need to more than you know.

I hope you do call before you fly again. And I hope this reaches you in private hands. Sorry I only could get a photo copy of our angel. I have to write them back soon. Its very hard to do.

Please write to me soon and I never want our connection to be broken. At least start keeping that promise I'd always be able to reach you and talk to you.

I will always Love You. Someday you will know you should have been strong enough not to waste it.

بسم الله الرحمن الرحيم

al-mutlaq novotel

Airport Street
P.O. Box 3525 Riyadh 11481
Kingdom of Saudi Arabia
Tel. 4760000 - Fax 4780696
Telex : 405266 HOMTQ SJ

فندق المطلق نوفـوتيل

شارع المطار
ص.ب ٣٥٢٥ الرياض ١١٤٨١
المملكة العربية السعودية
تلفون ٤٧٦٠٠٠٠ ـ تلفكس ٤٧٨٠٦٩٦
تلكس ٤٠٥٢٦٦ هـمتك اس. جي

Jan. 18/97

Dear TAM,

I Am sorry you HAD such A Bad week. Things will get better, Just keep An optimistic ATiTude. Things Here are going well work wise. You know it's Funny I Am doing something I Always WANTed But I don't Even know wHAT HAPPY means. I Had more Fun working with you AT gAke's but that CAN'T be ANYmore. TRISTAN will be O.K. don't worRy, easier said than done. I FeeL Bad about how Things went beTween us when I was in CANADA, BuT I deserved iT and more. I Missed you TAM, but it's better THAT I STAY AWAY. This is beTTer FoR You. I never STop Thinking about you and how your doing, I JUST WANT To punish MYSELF FoR what I did To A girl ThAT Loved me and I Loved and cARed about. TAM I wish you ALL the HAPPiness in The WORLd, I Hope somedAy you can FoRgive Me, and actually FeeL THAT I do CARE About you and will FOReVeR.

I Am Sorry

Fred

NOVOTEL
NOVOTEL AL MUTLAQ

س . ت : ١٠١٠١٠٠٥٣٦ ـ رقم العضويه : ٢٣٦٠٩ ـ المملكة العربية السعودية
License: 1010100536 - Membership Number 23609 - Kingdom of Saudi Arabia

al-mutlaq novotel

Airport Street
P.O. Box 3525 Riyadh 11481
Kingdom of Saudi Arabia
Tel. 4760000 - Fax 4780696
Telex : 405266 HOMTQ SJ

فندق المطلق نوفوتيل

شارع المطار
ص.ب ٣٥٢٥ الرياض ١١٤٨١
المملكة العربية السعودية
تلفون ٤٧٦٠٠٠٠ - تلفكس ٤٧٨٠٦٩٦
تلكس ٤٠٥٢٦٦ هـمتك.اس.جي

Hi TAM!

Yeah twice in one week. I want us to be friends even though you do not like me very much. That's O.K. that makes two of us. Being here in Saudi Arabia gives me a great deal of time to think. About all the things I have done. Boy I am going to hell, I probably will never pass go or collect $200.00. I screwed up real bad. I was thinking about NATASha (I hope I spelled her name right) and had to write to you. I hope someday you can forgive me for what I did, although I can't forgive myself. I am not looking for sympathy, I just want you to know how I feel. I pray things are going better for you and that Tristan is good. (well) Isn't it funny your mother was right I am no good. Well TAM I hope you get this letter before I leave here, Next stop is Iraq and then God knows where. I miss the good times we had together. TAM you are a good person, don't ever let anyone tell you different

Bye!

Fred

License: 1010100536 - Membership Number 23609 - Kingdom of Saudi Arabia

NOVOTEL
NOVOTEL AL MUTLAQ

MAY 11, 1997

فندق تاج سبأ

TAJ SHEBA HOTEL
SANA'A-YEMEN

Hey TAM!

I Hope Things ARE betTER THAN
The Time I TRied to CALL, IN FACT
I AM going to TRY Now. I HAVE MISSed
No MATTER WHAT YOu Think. I THINK
About you a gREAT DEAL. I AM going
to TAKE a bATH Now, I am having pRoblem
calling. I got VERY busy. I TRied to
call but There was No ANSWER it is
SUNDAY AT 2:30 P.M. YOUR Time, YOUR either
WORKing or oUT With TRISTAN. I hope he is
WELL. Though I would send You LiNE to
tellyou ALWAYS think abouTaGREAT DEAL
and you will always be in MY hearT. Have you
Heard ANY news about NATASHA. I Am veRY
NERVOUS but excited AT the sAMe Time

Love Always

Fred

TAJ INTERNATIONAL HOTELS

P.O.Box: 773 - Ali Abdulmoghni Street , Sana'a , Republic of Yemen Phone : 272372 - Telex : 2551 or 2561 SHEBA YE , Cable : Saba Hotel - Fax : 274129

GPG

Generics Pharmaceuticals Group Ltd

Main Office:
PO Box 90209
Riyadh 11613
Saudi Arabia
Tel: 966 1 473-1300
Fax: 966 1 476-6960

Official Office:
CR 187027
PO Box 3151
Road Town
Tortola B.V.I.

22 November 1997

Ms. Tam Sinclair
Yarmouth,
Nova Scotia Canada

Dear Tam,

First I would like to say, I hope I did not do anything to piss you off while I was in Canada, because I am sure you will receive this letter after I have come and gone. Believe I have nothing but the best of intentions for you. I had a very good time speaking with you Thursday, and really miss having these conversations with you in person. Now to talk to you about this guy you are seeing. I hope he is the person that will make you happy. I am sad to see you going to someone else but that is a totally selfish thing on my part. I wish you the most happiness one person God allows. My life for the most part is Ok, there are many variables from day to day. I am always waiting for something from someone else; paper works an OK from the Chairman of the company. But know I could say I am doing what I have always dreamt of. So why am I not happy? When I was at Jake's, although frustrating at times I was happy. Lying next to you was always a good warm feeling. Tam I love you and always will, but because I do love you very much I must say to you go where your heart takes you, and remember you will always be in my prayers and best wishes.

How do you tell someone you want and love to go another person, I can not but please accept my best wishes for your future as that. I hope that when I was in Canada I got a chance to see you and spend some time with you platonically. If we did do anything I am sure I feel great for doing but hope that I did not cause you any pain in the process. I am trying so hard to be different. I hope in my next life I get to meet you before I make any mistakes. What a sappy letter eh?

I hope you like your Christmas gift; I have not bought anything for Natasha, but hope to in the next day or so. I think about her a great deal, you may not believe that but it is true. Tam do not get mad at what I am going to say. Please give her adoptive parents a chance I know you love her but we made a decision that affected all our lives, it is not fair to Natasha or her adoptive parents to give them stress they are trying their best for her. Maintain the contact at the level you have now and play it very easy. Do not do anything that will hurt you or her. Remember you have to think about what is best for her development. Someday she will know everything you want her to know. I say all this because I am worried about you and your future if you keep duelling on the past. Everything will happen in its time.

GPG

Generics Pharmaceuticals Group Ltd

Main Office:
PO Box 90209
Riyadh 11613
Saudi Arabia
Tel: 966 1 473-1300
Fax: 966 1 476-6960

Official Office:
CR 187027
PO Box 3151
Road Town
Tortola B.V.I.

Well I hope I did not piss you off too much. I do love you and wish for our friendship to grow by leaps and bounds. I hope you are having a great Christmas. I hope Tristan is healthy and happy. You deserve good things Tam let them happen to you as you are the one that will control your life. Do not let the past get in the way of the future. If you allow that to happen you will have too many regrets, I am an expert on that now.

Love for always and a day,

Fouad.

المملكة العربية السعودية
منظر ليلي لجسر الخليج
الرياض

KINGDOM OF SAUDI ARABIA
EVENING VIEW OVER RIYADH WITH GULF BRIDGE

TAM!
   Things are going well!
SO FAR, There seem to
be a great of deal of Traveling
in next few months. I am
fine and hope you are too.
I miss you a great deal
can't really tell you
how much. Take care of
Jake
         Love always
              Fred

TAM SINCLAIR
322 MAIN ST.
YARMOUTH NOVA ScoTia

CANADA
B5A 1E4

1996

2 © BY OTE · RIYADH · PHONE 49143 · REPRODUCTION PROHIBITED

Aleppo at night مطهر ليل أبية

HI !
everything is Good
J hope , I missed you
ALL very much, Tell
TAM I said Hi and
I missed her Too! I
Hope everything is good

Ismael.

O.Z

DISTRIBUTOR OMAYA AL ZAIM P.O.BOX 7596 ALEPPO SYRIA

ZAki & Eveline HABiB
322 MAIN ST.
YARMOUTH NOVA SCOTiA
CANADA
B5A 1E4

Photo - Tahar Imyi

1997

Greetings from Saudi Arabia

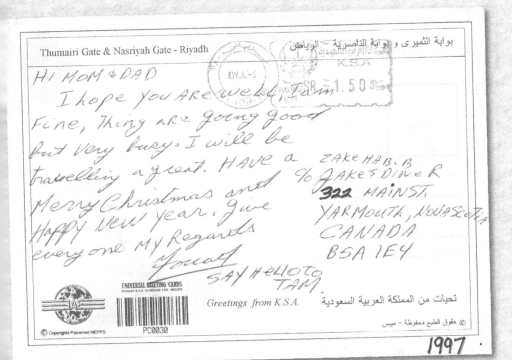

Thumairi Gate & Nasriyah Gate - Riyadh

بوابة الثميرى و بوابة الناصرية - الرياض

HI MOM & DAD
   I hope You ARE well I am
Fine, Thing are going good
but Very busy. I will be
travelling a great. HAVE a
Merry Christmas and
Happy New Year. Give
every one My Regards
                    Yousuf
           SAY HELLO TO
              TAM.

ZAKE HAB.B
% JAKE'S DINER
322 MAINST.
YARMOUTH, NOVAScotia
CANADA
B5A 1E4

K.S.A
SR 1.50

UNIVERSAL GREETING CARDS
Greetings from K.S.A.

تحيات من المملكة العربية السعودية

© Copyrights Reserved MEPPS
PC0030

© حقوق الطبع محفوظة - ميس

1997

HOUSES OF PARLIAMENT

LONDON

Hi TAM!
 As you can see I am
in London. Thought I would
say Hello. Things are Fine
Thanks for the card. Not
what I want to Hug. Very
Nice to Receive it. I hope
you had a good time down
under mate! give My Regards
to Steve
        Always
        Ghost

Photo: Ludovic Cazenave© 622

Demon Inter...
30-day free trial
0800 45 60 3...

5 029322 000005

Published by Images of Britain Ltd. 0181-543 9327

Ms. TAM SINCLAIR
10 KING ST.
YARMOUTH, NOVA SCOTIA
CANADA

B5A 2X8

1998

BY AIR MAIL
par avion
Royal Mail

March 1997

Lindsey Natasha + Parents,

I trust in my heart you all are well. Christmas went by too fast and Now Easter too. Easter is a very important religious holiday for the Orthordox religion. The children are dressed in pure white outfits right down to the shoes. It is Easter by the old calendar not the one as we know it today. Church is an all day celebration and from what I hear a beautiful service is displayed. The children all bring fresh eggs and break them over the cross as gifts to Jesus. I would love to see their service someday.

I love the picture you sent for me. Natasha is so beautiful. She resembles us both in little special ways but I have a picture of myself at 2 or 3 and our faces are so similar. Except I am blonde and a lot lighter. I have sent Tristen's pictures, he is so handsome for such a little guy. He is going to be four on June 8th and already he can rattle off his ABC's and print his name. He sings his ABC's song over + over. Until he gets mixed up. Very independant, he has to dress himself, comb his own hair, do everything for himself just because. He has a beautiful heart he doesn't mind to share his toys a treats to whoever asks. He always helps out when he sees the chance to.

Lindsey Natasha must be so full of energy. Walking and discovering all sorts of new things for herself.

Her birthfather was here in Canada again due to family illness. His father had a very bad heart attack, which lead to a tripple By-pass. He spent about 3½ weeks in the hospital. This was in February. He is now home getting his strength back slowly and recovering well from the whole ordeal. The doctors belive he will feel better and stronger than before with alot less strain on his heart. Anyone who knows him loves him and we all Thank God he is doing so well.

Her birthfather has just finished about 4 weeks work in Saudi Arabia. When he leave Canada again he will be going to Yemen and then Iraq. He prays for all his daughters happyness and health. He told me he hangs all four pictures together in the hotel rooms he calls home during his travels.

Tristan ♥ is a very active happy little boy. He loves his daycare afternoons and is becoming less shy with kids and adults. He fills the fridge at work (pop) and loves to show everybody the good job he has done. Tristan now has his first 2 wheel bike with training wheels. He can't wait to take it out and learn to ride it.

I look forward to your next letter and can't wait to see more of her pictures.

Please give Lindsey Natasha lots of hugs + kisses for us and all our love and prayers.

Love Nan

Monday, 12 January, 1998

Dear Tam,

It was good to hear your voice yesterday it really made my day go better.
I have enclosed the letter to Natasha and her parents. I hope you like it.
The letter was very difficult to write. There is nothing to tell you since
yesterday. I hope you are able to plan your trip to australia on schedule.
Good luck and remember I will always love you no matter where I am.

Kiss for your lips and a kiss for each one of your eyes

Love forever and beyond

Fred

[signature]

P.S. it is freezing here, my hands and
feet are blue from the cold.
you know where I would like to be to
keep warm.

11/01/98

Dear NATASHA, (and her parents)

I have been thinking for one hour how to write the letter, and although I have started I do not know what to say. First I would like to thank your parents for loving you and taking care of you, but that is why you call them mom and dad. From what I have heard they are great parents, I am sure you have given them as much joy as they have given you.

I guess the reason I am writing this letter to you is to let you know that I do think about you and do love you. The last time I saw you, you were two day old. I held you in my arms and kissed you on your head I still remember ~~how~~ your scent ~~smelt~~. I will have that feeling with me the rest of my life walking out of the hospital was the hardest thing I ever did. But I did do it. This is something I will never forgive myself, but the circumstances were very difficult. I wanted to save your mother an myself from a great deal of grief. I felt that I was making the right decision for everyone. I pray every day that you are healthy and happy and that your parents are good to you and you to them. Natasha love your parents, honour them, and above all respect these decisions they have made. They do this out of love and the need to see you healthy and happy. A parents greatest reward to see that happen to their child.

٠٠٠،٢٠٩ رياض ١١٦٦٢ المملكة العربية السعودية سجل تجاري ١٠٠١/٥٨٣٠٠-٥٠٣ هاتف ٤٧٧٢٩٥٢/٤٧١٤٩٦٦ ٠٠-٦

P.O Box 90209, Riyadh 11662, Saudi Arabia CR 1010058300 Tel 00 473 4966 / 472 9952 Fax 01476 1966

I would like to tell you something about your
mother (in case you ask) and myself. The first time I saw her I knew
that I liked her. The more time I spent with her, the more
I loved her. She has a heart of Gold, and I truly love
her with all my heart, but I can not be with her. We
were together for over a year before you were conceived,
and were very much in love. I do not regrette anything
your mother and I had except we could not stay
together and keep you. My life since I left your mother
has gotten worse permanently, but because of obligations
I must condemn with my life the way it is, I swear to you
Natasha you were not conceived out of sex, but I
truly loved your mother.

        Now something about me, Physically I am healthy, a
little on the heavy side. I like sweets especially
chocolate. I enjoy working out and now in my later years
running. I did very well in school, and went to DAL
university in Halifax I Majored in Psycology although
I ended up in Business I rushed everything in my life,
I hope you do not Do the same, enjoy every moment because
it goes by too fast. As you can see right now I am in Saudi
Arabia. I am in charge of New project Development, there is a
great deal of travelling. I do not know where I am going to be
tomorrow. Growing up, I always wanted to be "Blake Carrington"
ask your parents who that is. I hope they know who it is.
By some standards I think I am successful, but it is still
not enough. I am always gambling with my life, tomorrow

I may lose everything and have to start over. I always want more, I am very ambitious and all I want is to be the president of a small country in the Middle East eron! here I go again. The company I am with now, is a Saudi company, it is a Multi national company with offices all over the world I have a five year contract with them, but I am tired of them already.

Natasha, I do not know if we will ever meet but please know this I love you very much, and I always ask about you. You are a beautiful happy girl., whose parents love her very much, all four of them. My advice to you is listen to your (adoptive) parents, they are truly your best friends I wish I could be a parent to you, maybe someday. I hope you enjoyed the presents I sent to you. I hear your parents are wonderful people, and I know they love you very much.

Natasha take care of yourself, study hard in school, and believe in God!

your friend forever
Love
Fred

PS I understand your parents are
Teachers, don't let them check my
Grammar or spelling.

فندق تاج سبـأ **TAJ SHEBA HOTEL**
SANA'A-YEMEN

Jan 22/98

Dear TAM,

You mentioned something yesterday that I have thought, but was said for the first time by you. I was hurt when you asked why I like to hurt you. If you remember in the past, I told you I was going to stop calling you because I feared I was hurting you, but you said No. I ~~now~~ Now that I call you and express my feeling you accuse me of hurting. Maybe you are right it is time to ~~of~~ stop calling, to go on with our individual lives. Maybe it is best to put a stop to our friendship as well, because it is so complicated. As for my relationship with Natasha when the time is right she will call me, If I am still alive, I will answer and make up for the time I lost. As for you go on with your life and I hope you are happy wether it is with Steve or someone else.

TAJ INTERNATIONAL HOTELS

P.O.Box: 773 - Ali Abdulmoghni Street , Sana'a , Republic of Yemen Phone : 272372 - Telex : 2551 or 2561 SHEBA YE , Cable : Saba Hotel - Fax : 274129

فندق تاج سبأ **TAJ SHEBA HOTEL**
SANA'A-YEMEN

Best of luck because this the final letter
I will write. As of today I will stop all
communications with phone, letter, fax whatever
it maybe. My feelings will be mine only. Again
Good Luck & Good Buy.

TAJ INTERNATIONAL HOTELS

P.O.Box: 773 - Ali Abdulmoghni Street , Sana'a , Republic of Yemen Phone : 272372 - Telex : 2551 or 2561 SHEBA YE , Cable : Saba Hotel - Fax : 274129

July 13, 1998

Dear Tam,

By the time you receive this letter I am sure your birthday would be over. I hope you have a nicer birthday than me. I was in Yemen alone. The trip was very good from business point of view. health wise I am fine but a little tired. oh! by the way thank you for the letter and pictures, please, always keep me up to date on what is happening with you. did you get a chance to see Leslie? What happened? I really would like to know. I keep thinking about how your lips feel, is it not crazy that I still feel this? there are some feelings worth hanging on to. Well to ask the usual questions How is steve, work, car, Work. But in a class by himself How is Tristan, is he getting ready to go to school, Yep you are getting old! OH before I forget Happy birthday July 22. did I get the date right. Hopefully I will see you very soon maybe on some island in the Middle of Nowhere. I did not think you would agree. I feel so empty Lately. I Meet so many people and have so Many responsibility but I feel like I am lost. Even when I speak with

RXS

with Natalie, Samantha, Chantal, I
still feel something is missing. In the future, when
you meet Natasha please only tell her the good things
about me. I am sure she will have enough bad feelings
without you adding the bad parts. When I was in Germany
(did you get my postcards) there was a girl in the coarse
named Natasha. When she gave her name at the first
day of the classes, she asked me why I smiled when
she told me her name. I told her, there is someone
I care about very much named Natasha, and it was good
hear the name being said. So am I going crazy? Sometimes
I feel like the song "I don't want to die, I just wish
I was never born." Tam I miss you so much it hurts (don't
say good) but it is my mistake. I hope you are happy, and
if you are it is a ~~illegible~~ a help to me. Does
warnot sure of spelling

steve still know what he has. Don't be too hard on
him, I am sure he loves you.

          take care of yourself
                Love for always
                  ~~signature~~
                     dias Fred

P.S. I will call during my vacation, but I will
      be in Saudi more than you think.

July 1998

Lindsey Natasha & Parents
    Hello!
    I hope you are all having a
wonderful summer. Mine is disappearing
fast mostly at work. March was a
nice month. Tristan and I visited
our cousin in Austrailia. That was
a dream to go some place far away
and relax for 4 weeks. I found
we got a little too lazy and it was
hard to come back to work. My cousin
has a Dairy Farm with 250 cows.
Tristan was quite the little farmer
for awhile. I brought back lots of
souvenirs and a few little things for
Lindsey's Keepsake Trunk.
    In May Tristan and I went
for his introduction morning at
School. He has come so far from
his Mommy I want to stay
with you. Which I didn't get to
see at all. He was second in line
when they took the children to show
them around and only turned back
to give me a little grin. After lunch
and the whole next day he wanted

to know why he couldn't go back to school. I'm sure this fall he will be more than happy to go.

I'm writing because I have not heard anything further from the Adoption Services in Halifax. Nancy from there did let me know she recieved both first forms. Since I filled out and sent my second one a few months ago I have been wondering and waiting for the phone to ring. I understand how worried and concerned you are. I am really worried and nervous about meeting you but I can hardly wait until the day I get the chance to know you. I understand you want the best for Lindsey. I believe I picked the best parents that would be able to give this to her. I also am thinking of her when I say I do not want to be a stranger to her. I know how much you Love and Adore Lindsey. I'm sure she is the center of your world as Tristan is mine.

I just pray our worlds will meet soon. Take Care

Lots of Love

November 1998

Lindsey Natasha & Parents

I hope this reaches you all in good health. I trust you recieved my letter that I sent in the summer. I wonder about it but I have no way of knowing forsure. I think of the three of you everyday and when I do things with Tristan I picture you doing them with Lindsey and it truely gives me such a warm feeling. Tristan is a wonderful child and is doing so very well in school. His teacher sees no weak areas, but insists that I keep working with him at home. Of course I enjoy doing this and we make time every evening after supper.

We recently visited Austrailia in March (we have family there) and stayed for 4 weeks. I purchased Lindsey afur Keepsakes. The puzzle was purchased here in N.S. Tristan loves puzzles. She will have to grow into it. Might be kinda hard right now. Christmas is coming fast and even faster is Lindseys 3rd

Birthday. So hard to grasp that 3 years have passed already.

Tristan's school pictures came out nice but he won't smile for strangers. can't wait to see new pictures of Lindsey. I am anxious and also scared to find out when I will meet you. Please let this day come soon.

I hope to communicate with you soon. Take Care

Love always
Tami

To whom it may concern:

I Tamara MacPhee upon the advise of my doctor, am writing this letter of concern. I was airlifted on December 28th, 2000, from Yarmouth to Halifax. The reason being I was in premature labour. This being my third child I was very concerned with the time issue. My previous two labours lasted only four hours each. My labour started at 11PM on December 27th, When the doctor called for the airlift it was sometime around midnight. She first requested the helicopter, but was informed the weather was too bad for it to fly. Then they said they could send a plane out of Moncton, but it was presently on another call. They were not sure of an arrival time. With my contractions getting stronger the doctor gave me a suppository to relax me and slow my contractions. This seemed to work for the time being. Just before 4AM, I was told the team had arrived. The lady in charge came in and talked with my doctor. We were informed my husband had to drive because there was no room for him in the plane. There was an ambulance team there as well. The nurse in charge checked me. I was 2cm dilated, my doctor said I should have time to get there. We were informed it would take 1½ hours turn around time. I was fine up to this point. This is where I started to be more concerned. I knew I was going to be alone or at least with total strangers, and my doctor assured me the nurses on the flight would be supportive, warm and friendly. She said you will get to know them better on the way. I was sure my husband would not be there for the birth. As it would take him too long to drive.

Finally we were on our way, the ambulance drivers got me on the stretcher and strapped down. I had an IV in my arm, to give the baby and myself antibiotics. I asked for a shot of demerol, to make being strapped down more comfortable. The lady in charge said when we get in the air it would be no problem. We left the hospital 4:10 AM, It was snowing and a bit slippery. The bumps made the ride quite uncomfatable. I had 3 or 4 contractions on the way from the hospital to the airport. I told my nurse I had a really bad feeling about the whole ride and she said I'll check you before we get on the plane to see how far you have progressed. She found I was the same. The pilots informed us they had to have the plane de-iced. This would take some extra time, that I felt we did not have. We had to be on the plane before they could do this. It was more jolting and bumping around for this process. With me strapped to what felt like the hardest back board ever. When I was snapped in I was out flat and being 35 weeks pregnant, in labour this was not a good thing. I asked them to lift my head abit. One of the pilots showed them how to do this. It was a very small change in my comfort level. They told me it would be noisy and alot of bangs when we took off. They did ask if I had ever flown, I had so this did not worry me. I was concerned with the weather and the safety of my baby. The flight itself took only 30 minutes. I was moaning and very uncomfatable when

I would have a contraction, which was about every 3 minutes. Being on an IV and in labour I had to empty my bladder often. But when I asked for a bed pan, they did not have one on the ambulance. They offered to call for one, to be brought to the airport, but I said no, it would take too much time. I thought the plane would have more equipment and I could use one on there. But after we took off I realized the nurses were carrying all their equipment in their bags. There was a respiratory nurse, a paediatric nurse and my nurse. The other two were there for precaution in case the baby was born. They told me they never had a delivery on the plane and I said "I might be the first." For as conversation I was suprised, out of the 3 of them they never really tried to reassure me or confort me during the flight or the contractions. I would turn my head and see them wispering to each other. I felt they were talking about me not to me. Unlike my doctor at the hospital, who was holding my hand and talking to me or my husband who was sitting beside me just so I could see and talk to him. These strangers made me feel even colder and more alone than I actually was.

Shortly after take off, I asked for my shot of demerol. One nurse asked the other for the demerol, and she said oh we don't have that on the flight with us. They had morphine and offered me that but I was not sure if I could have it. They didn't explain the difference. I had only ever heard of it being used for pain, on people who were dying.

I still needed to pee so bad, nothing to take the edge off my pain. No support from the nurses. No idea how my husband was making out on his drive. Being strapped down and in labour, all alone. This was the longest night of my life, or so it seemed.

The thought of my baby being born in this cold dreary plane scared me. The two baby nurses hardly said a word and were seated behind my head. My nurse was beside me but proceeded to do her paper work and glance over every once and awhile, instead of paying attention to my needs. By this time I was begging to empty my bladder. She looked for a bag or something and finally just shoved some blankets or cloths all around and under me. They said to release into that. This was horrifying, and I thought it would be a mess to lay in. During some contractions a few squirts did slip out. I fealt embarased and ashamed of the whole issue. It seemed my nurse didn't understand why I was in so much pain. Landing and being loaded into another ambulance at the Halifax airport took more time. The bumpy drive into the hospital was painful. Still with no bedpan, the bumps took there toll on me. I know I complaind alot. Reaching the hospital, I heard them deaussing how to get to the delivery area. They didn't seem to be sure but finally I'm there at approx 6:40AM. The nurse led me to the bathroom

and I explained I had just held it for 2½ hours,
she was horrified. That nurse was off at 7AM
and I was introduced to another. My pain was
cut in half after my bladder was empty. This
lasted until about 7:05, my contractions got hard
and closer. I asked for the doctor and was
told they were sleeping. I begged her to wake
them up. Finally a sleepy intern entered to check
me and said I was not ready. I said I was and
on that one first push - my baby was in her hands.
They were yelling on the intercom for the
paediatric team, and the doctor who was supposed
to deliver. So 42 minutes after I arrived my baby
was born. Then I knew why I was in so much
pain on the trip to the hospital. I hope the nurses
who seemed to feel I shouldn't be in so
much pain for 2cm, now know just how fast
I went from 2-10 cm and how quick my baby came.
I seriously hope no one else goes through any
of the same problems I endured with Starr flights.
• no bed pan • no demerol • poor bedside manners *
• longer trip than promised.

A page from my journal.

Nov 22/07

I am thankful For

His Hugs, his gift of music,
and his expressions. His beautiful
brown eyes looking up at me.

I am thankful For

Shays many talents + gifts.
his creativity in many, interest
his singing, cleaning, reading
and cuddling.
A Beautiful Child.

I am thankful For

Tristan's handsome height, his
politeness is beautiful. He' is
growing into a nice young man.
He is active and athletic.
I am very proud.

Tristan at Beacon Park.
Mom and I took him there often.
He loved it! - 1997

Tristan at home on King Street.
We lived across from the jail. My
first house I bought.

Mom and Charlie
happy on King Street.
1990

My Mom.
God bless her smile.

Wedding Reception Day - 1998
At the beautiful Manner Inn,
Yarmouth.

Tristan and I heading to the
church, Wedding Day,
November 15th, 1998

Our first dance.
Aerosmith -
"I Don't Want To
Miss A Thing"

Norma (My Mom)
and Charlie on my
Wedding Day.

Me, Steve, Grandad
Miller. He was so proud
of Steve as always.

Cuba Wedding
We took our vows again. Smokin' Hot and beautiful.
November 19th, 1998

2001
Shay and Tristan.
The best big brother.

JJ and Mommy.
My little sweet baby.

JJ and Daddy always
being silly
2003

Natasha loves to hold
and feed Baby JJ
2003

Me ♡ Natasha ♡ Mom and Baby JJ - 2003
So thankful Mom got to meet Natasha a few times over the years.

Shay, Tristan and their little brother JJ - 2003

Natasha meeting her littlest brother JJ.
"So Much Love" - 2003

shay so sweet.

My cute boys.

My family at Aunt Thelma's cottage. We all love it there. 2007

My boys and my favourite flowers.

JJ and Grampy Buck playing in the snow.

Shay and Little Nan.
So much love.

My sweet little boys in my
Heart Garden

Shay, JJ and Natasha
playing in her back yard.
Loved our visits.

Family fun in PEI.
I won 2 nights stay.
We loved it.

My little Sunshine Boys.

Tristan always looking out
for his brothers.

Mommy's 32nd Birthday at home
with the family.
2006

Cuba vacation with Natasha.
"Setting the girls free"
2016

My famous mountain pose on top of
Chamonix-Mont-Blanc France, 2018
with JJ

Breathtaking Atmosphere.
Eiffel Tower, Paris

Me.
Love these flowers.

My Mom at the stone house she
grew up in. She loved the back
beach and visiting this place. - 2014

Me and Mom. Last visit
to her beach - 2014

My beautiful Mother at her
home The Villa in Dayton
2015

Rock formations at Mom's Beach

our love always strong

This man loves me and I gave him my heart

Strolling along the beach with my boys.

Me and my sons. ♡ I love them so much.

My family - 2016. Portmaitland Beach.

Just a girl trying to impress her husband. ♡

Me and my race car, 2018

Steve completely impressed with me driving a
race car and all my checkered flags

20 years later, we are back in Cuba again!

Steve and I, November 1998.

20 years later,
Steve and I on our
Anniversary cruise.
2018

2018 Anniversary Cruise.

Shopping in
St. Thomas,
Rum Punch
fun kinda day.

2018 Anniversary Cruise.

Famous mountain pose.
Mom's Beach
2022

Connecting to the elements. Just Breathe.
2022

CHAPTER 23

Meeting Natasha

One day during the March Break Tristan was in the bathroom with me. He had knocked a candle off a shelf, and he had a little cut on his forehead. The phone was ringing. I managed to grab it and it was Heather, Natasha's mother. They were at the Grand Hotel. She invited us over to meet Natasha.

I was flabbergasted, but unsure if I could get there with Tristan bleeding. It soon stopped however, and we were heading two streets over to where my baby girl was.

I was so thankful to get this opportunity that of course we were going. Tristan got to swim with his sister and Heather was in the pool with them. Bruce sat on the side watching. Steve and I joined him. My niece was visiting us for March Break, so she got to swim too. It was unbelievable. I was seeing Natasha. She was three years old. So beautiful with her curls.

After the swim we all headed to Wendy's where we got to spend more time with her—hugs included, which melted me to my core. I was bursting with thankfulness.

I invited them to visit at our house the next day before they headed home. Natasha held my hand as I led her to play with Tristan's toys. The warmth was shooting through me as we connected. After they left, I sat in a daze, reminiscing about every moment of seeing my baby girl. I was extremely thankful to have had that time with her.

From there I think the plan was we could see them again in the summer.

The year continued with many changes. Steve jumped to Merks, a company in the Valley that hauled to the Toronto area. Steve liked to be home so this was going to be an experience. But he needed to make money and support his new family.

He went on a couple of trips, but he was so homesick. He hated being away. Next, he found a local job hauling rockweed. He barely got trained there when he got a call to go work at Hoggs Trucking, making it five different jobs in the first year we were married.

Delivering for Hoggs was more to his liking. He stayed there, working long hours until the next opportunity arose. I was still managing Jake's Diner, working mostly days. My boss was pretty good to work for, but he rarely was on time. I often had to stay longer than planned and Steve was always annoyed by this.

The other brother was mean to me, bugging me about my so-called father who would go into his restaurant just up the street. He was cruel to me, and even my boss told him to stop terrorizing me. I didn't like him or anything I'd heard about him. As the tension grew it eventually boiled over. The cruel brother insisted to his younger brother, who was my boss to let me go. At the time I was devastated but little did I know it would be the best move ever.

I was done with that family. Finally, and I was free. How dare they treat me like a piece of shit. I was surprised they were not too scared my story would come out from under a rock for making me move on.

I often thought about having everything out in the open. Why should I have to keep everything buried? Well, the most important thing was to keep Natasha safe and that is what kept me under a rock. After I was married, I never saw Fred again. This was for the best. But all his promises to look out for me and that I'd own the restaurant someday had also vanished.

Fred never thought his brothers would move to Yarmouth, let alone stay there. The youngest did well, the middle brother not so well. His wife got a job at my bank and I had to see her often. She was beautiful and very nice. I wondered what she knew, but I assumed it was very little. I felt sorry for her as I heard about the many things her husband was doing that she had no idea about.

Eventually as the news about his activities got hotter around town, he packed up his family and moved back to city. Conveniently before the wife heard how much he was like his older brother. Did he get a cop's daughter pregnant? Did she move away? Why was his truck always at her house? Why was the restaurant staff spreading all these rumours? Maybe the wife did find out. I don't know. I just felt sorry for her and the girl who had to move away. Do they all just do what they want in that family, no matter who gets hurt? Sadly, that's how it seemed.

I couldn't go anywhere without customers telling me how much they missed me, or how things were not as good since I'd left. They claimed I was the best cook down there. I was definitely the cleanest! I missed my customers too, but I immediately got a job at the hospital in the kitchen.

I started working on my apprenticeship papers again as I had completed some of the requirements when I was younger. Harris's counted toward the hours needed, and the hospital would too. I did well there, however, I'm not a morning person. Being at work for 6 a.m. was not fun, but I managed the best I could. Tristan was in school, and Mom helped me when I needed it. Working at the hospital was good for me. I learned lots. I met new people and put my job at Jake's far behind me. My boss at the hospital showed me the emails of praise for how I gave the salad bar a new life. It really came naturally to me as I loved making different creations. Food should not be boring.

In the summer of 1999 Tristan turned six. Steve ran beside Tristan in the field helping him to learn to ride his bike without the training wheels. He was a big boy now and so proud. Steve was great with Tristan. He was more of a buddy but now he had to learn to parent.

We had our obstacles, just like every other family. I have an "if it's broken, fix it" perspective—therefore, we were always learning and growing as parents. One thing I know, is that smart—successful people are always learning new things every day of their lives.

We got to have another visit with Natasha. They invited us over to their house on July 20, 1999. We swam in their pool and had a BBQ. I would have loved to see Natasha more, but I was willing to take whatever time I could get. Tristan had been five-and-a-half when he first got to meet his sister. They mentioned having visits twice a year, but I was hurt. How would Tristan get to know his sister if he only saw her twice a year?

I was always nervous to say or do the wrong thing. If I did, they might not let me have any more visits. I always warned Steve to be on his best behaviour and not to let slip out any swear words. Seriously, it was an anxiety roller coaster trying to make those visits perfect. They did get easier, and I was so thankful for them. Her parents were amazing. The angels had helped me to pick them. I knew higher powers were watching out for her.

CHAPTER 24

Another Baby, Shay's On The Way

During Christmas 1999 I think we got to see Natasha again and started an annual December visit to celebrate her birthday and Christmas. I liked for it to be before Christmas as it completed my heart for the season and made December a bit more bearable.

In 2000, after three visits and feeling that Natasha would be a part of my life, I had a vision. I told Steve early in that year if he wanted to have kids I would, but we were having two boys and that was a fact. The feeling was so strong it just flowed out of me. He was overjoyed but never paid much attention to the fact that I said it would be two boys.

I was determined not to replace Natasha.

As it turned out, the month we decided to get pregnant we did, carefully planning for the baby to be born in January of 2001. The government had changed the child care leave to a full year, effective the first of January of that year.

The pregnancy went well. I stayed active. We had bought our first camper. Tristan's grandfather went with us to inspect the camper. He checked out a couple for us before we settled on this one. I am forever grateful for his presence in our lives. He's a man I have great respect for. We fixed up the camper, making it newer and nicer inside. We did a bit of camping with friends that summer and Tristan loved going.

This year was to be full of surprises. In September Steve got a call. A local guy that drove a straight truck for Day & Ross told him they were looking to hire another broker. You were required to buy your own truck and follow their rules. Steve had no down payment and he was working for nine dollars an hour at Hoggs. I had the house and my Toyota 4Runner. The Toyota was paid for, with a brand-new paint job on it. I planned to keep it and I loved it.

This was an awesome opportunity, and my gut was saying we had to do this. So, we traded my Toyota for an older straight truck. We found it on a lot in Coldbrook, which was in the same block where I had lived when I was trying to get away from Fred. Small world but that's where we bought our first truck.

We got everything in order and Steve started his new job in October as an owner and operator for Day & Ross. The amazing thing with Steve and I, was it was all about building a future together. We never gave up or quit. We just always tried to do better for our family. I always say Steve has a negative personality, and I have a positive one. We balance each other out.

He is a lot of work, because I always must show him the other side of things. I have the ability to look at things from every angle. He sees things in a straight line, until I soften it for him. So, working with another guy proved difficult sometimes. The other guy had more experience, and he knew what freight he wanted. Steve got stuck with the shittier stuff, and sometimes he would get heated up. Basically, they shared the town freight, and then each had a route to do in afternoons. However, the better paying stops always ended up on the other guy's truck. So, they would end up arguing.

The job paid well, but Steve had his hands full. There were three of them working out of the same warehouse. A married couple and Steve. Most times it was two against one. Even though the wife did a courier town job, she would still stick up for her husband.

I have a rule not to hate people as it will eat up your peace of mind. However, I strongly disagreed and disliked how they operated. I want to say that my heart breaks for their girls as both parents lost their lives to illness at an early age. Sincerely, may they rest in peace. Life is so unfair.

But it was time to be on our own. We named our new company TST Trucking. At the time it stood for Tam, Steve, Tristan. During this time, I was pregnant. Christmas was coming and so was another visit with Natasha. She sat on my lap and tried to feel the baby kick. We were at Roo's Playhouse in Greenwood. There were lots of things for Natasha and Tristan to do there, so we spent the afternoon.

Going home was always emotional, especially not knowing exactly when I would see my baby again, which made it so hard to leave. I cherished every minute I spent with her.

Christmas was good. I was getting big and was due on the twenty-nineth of January. Steve's mother was down and planned to leave on the twenty-eighth of December. However, on the evening of the twenty-seventh of December, as I was heading to bed, my water started leaking.

How could this be since I still had another five-and-a-half weeks to go?

We got ready and went to hospital. As they say each baby comes quicker and my first two labours had been around four hours total. My doctor arrived and informed me that I had to go by ambulance to the IWK children's hospital, which was three hours away. They didn't deliver babies in Yarmouth unless you were over the thirty-six week mark. I was frantic because of my quick labours and was afraid of not making it there in time. The doctor tried to get the helicopter; however, it was out on another call. Oh, did I mention there was a snow and ice storm happening at that time? They decided on a chartered plane and sent for that.

My doctor gave me a suppository that was supposed to relax me and slow down the labour. What a hassle. I had to go in an ambulance to our airport. I immediately asked for a bedpan on the way. I was told they didn't have one. How could an ambulance not have one? I asked for a shot of something. I was told when I got on the plane, they would give me something. Well, here I was strapped down on a backboard and put onto this old plane. Then the plane had to be sent to be de-iced before takeoff. Everything was taking so long.

Three nurses were there with me, talking about how tired they were because this was their second trip of the night. I was just so scared that I was going to have this baby in this cold plane. Plus, I needed to pee so badly.

I thought the plane would have had more equipment; but nope it was a charter, so I asked for my Demerol shot. They only had morphine. I didn't think I could have that, and they didn't explain that I could. I thought it was just for people who were dying. I have never felt more alone than I did on that plane.

The three nurses talked about me more than they talked to me. They rolled their eyes over my worries of having the baby on the plane. Finally, they shoved some blankets under me and said to pee into them. Strapped to a backboard I couldn't but every time I had a contraction some squirted out. No one held my hand or told me everything would be okay. I was so alone and worried.

Steve was grabbing some stuff and driving in the storm to meet me in Halifax. I arrived at the Halifax airport and then had to go in an ambulance to the IWK, which took about thirty more minutes. They used the sirens at my request, but the roads were not great. I finally got checked-in and immediately asked to go pee. The nurse was shocked at how long I peed. I walked back to get on the bed, called Steve, told him all was good and hopefully he would make it before the baby came. I hung up the phone and the nurse looked at me stating that it looked like I was going to push. Within seconds I did push, and she screamed on the PA for help as the team hadn't arrived yet.

Everyone came running in to help. The baby was fine, and I got to hold him after he was delivered. But within a few minutes he began to have some laboured breathing. They took him to the incubator and gave him oxygen.

Steve arrived and I couldn't believe that he hadn't seen the baby in the hall. Everything had happened so fast as soon as the pee was out of the way. Thank God they didn't have a bedpan on any of the ambulances or the plane after all. I know Shay would have been born mid-air somewhere if they'd had. I got the nurse to go find the ambulance attendants to let them know that I wasn't crazy. He was born twenty minutes after I arrived at the IWK. His birth time was 7:22 a.m.

My guardian angels were at work once again.

We spent a week at IWK where the nurses were fantastic. Daddy only got to stay a couple days while his friend covered his run for him. Then he had to leave. Steve cried so hard and felt so bad leaving us there. When you own your own truck and business this would be just one of the many times that life would be unfair.

During our stay in the IWK, Fred Fredericks passed away. He was Steve's Little Nan's husband. I had met him a couple times. He'd had a stroke in the previous years, and he had kept her busy. They say he was controlling and abusive. He was never a grandfather to Steve. In fact, he would rather stay in the bedroom instead of visiting with Steve and his mother. All of this had happened before my time.

When we had Shay, she dived into our lives with her new freedom. I loved her immensely. She was genuinely an angel, born in 1922. We instantly connected. The poor soul never raised Steve's father. Her husband, Carl, died when their baby was six weeks old. It was a tragic accident where he was crushed by a truck. She was young and so she lived with her sister for help and support. So instead of raising Gary, Steve's father he had stayed with his Aunt Roxie and Uncle Keith. Pansy, or Little Nan, had went to school. She eventually met Fred and remarried. Fred was not interested in being a father figure to Gary. And Gary preferred to stay with Keith and Roxie. They raised him like he was their own. Bless them for being such wonderful people. To Steve they were his Nan Roxie and Granddad Miller. However, he often shortened that name and mostly called Keith, Dad.

I found it interesting and amazing to hear Pansy's stories. She and Carl had served in the war. She was overseas and I have her medals and a picture of her in Europe. Gary was born in 1946, after the war had ended in 1945. They must have been married just after the war ended. I was never sure where they had met.

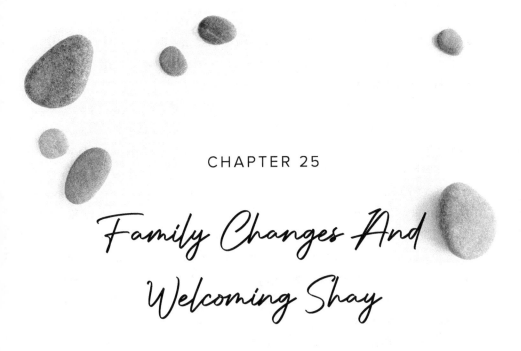

CHAPTER 25

Family Changes And Welcoming Shay

Back at the IWK, I tried to breastfeed. But I couldn't seem to make enough milk and we had to do both—bottle and breastfeed—for Shay to gain any weight. Steve's mother ended up driving us home. I didn't know about her driving record at that time.

We stopped at Aunt Thelma's on the way. My grandmother was bedridden and in need of full-time care living there. I always went there to visit. I took pictures of Shay with her. I felt deep down that she knew we were there. She was just stuck in a body that no longer worked. Shay was too sleepy to eat much. Therefore, we had to continue on our way home.

Tristan was so happy to meet his baby brother. Grandmom and Grandpére were also waiting for us. Shay was the best baby for sleeping. In no time he was sleeping through the night and napping well during the day. Just like Tristan. I struggled with breastfeeding, trying to pump and had many visits from the health nurse to help. I never did produce enough milk. I tried many things, but nothing worked. I gave up at around seven months.

Shay and I put a ton of miles on his jogging stroller. Mostly walking but we loved being outside. Spring was beautiful and brought us a new business adventure. A broker from the city called and made an offer to us to purchase a truck that ran wild. Basically, the driver would call dispatch and be sent where they needed him to go, never knowing where until he made the phone call. This was a learning experience for us.

At six months old Shay got his first trucking trip. We went with Daddy to take a load to North Sydney. Shay could play in the bunk. He had a blast. We tried a few different drivers, but nobody had the drive to work hard enough to make this truck successful.

Due to some unpredictable circumstances, we got another business opportunity. The broker Steve worked with had been fired. Day & Ross immediately called us to take over the run. We traded in the truck we had for a brand-new straight truck and hired Roger Crowell. Steve and Roger worked well together, and things ran pretty smoothly. Shay was now seven months old. He was so much fun. Tristan couldn't wait to get home from school to play with him.

Steve's mother and Little Nan made a few trips to our house. Little Nan was a natural with children. However, Steve's mother always expected the kids to come to her. She wouldn't get down on the floor and play with them. Kids just don't take to that.

As time went on, I learned just how uncomfortable my kids were with Steve's mother. They struggled to hug her, and nowadays you don't force kids to hug. I wish I had realized that back then. They were great with my mother, and perfectly comfortable with Little Nan.

My relationship with Steve's mother was on a downhill slide. She would never respect my parenting choices; she always went against what I would ask her to do. Why did she have to make things so difficult? We did give her a chance, and I really did try. We even let her babysit one weekend.

Before I went back to work, we decided to take a long weekend and go away, just the two of us. We had Steve's mother babysit, and my mother came over to help her out. We enjoyed our time, but Steve got homesick and decided we should cut the trip short. We arrived home, and everything seemed well.

Steve has quite a soft side and loves just being at home. I took three extra months off. I went back to the hospital to work when Shay was nine months old. One of the babysitters I got, left me hopeless. I was so torn to leave Shay with her. That one didn't last long. I then hired my neighbour Linda, and she was amazing. At least I felt good to be at work. We were busy balancing everything.

I was trying to find the time to work on my apprenticeship cooking papers. I did manage to complete two-thirds of the bookwork. Previously, I had gone for two, six-week sessions at the Burridge campus. It was hands-on training. How was I going to get this done?

I did the bookwork for our business, worked at the hospital, plus had Tristan and Shay to raise. I tried, but the kids and the trucks just got busier.

My neighbour and babysitter, Linda, became a grandma to twins. She decided to stay home with them. So, I started taking Shay to my friend Kim's place. She had offered to start tending Shay in her home. It was always nice to have in-home child care, but this would give me a chance to get errands and things around the house done.

Steve insisted we needed a new camper trailer. He picked out a new pop-up tent trailer. He thought it would be a great investment. Tons of family fun to be had. I had no idea how much I would grow to resent this trailer. I mean, it was great once it was set up. Lots of room and was brand new. We never had anything brand new before. We loved camping with friends. South Mountain was our favourite spot to go at this time.

When Shay was born, we had started going to the Wesleyan Church. My Aunt Debbie went there, and I loved being there and especially loved the singing. I wanted my children to have some knowledge about God and Heaven, probably because I didn't have any church background. I had always wanted better for them. Somehow, I still knew and believed in God and Heaven.

CHAPTER 26

Meeting JJ

Steve and I wanted to have our children two years apart. So, it was time to get pregnant with the next one. I would be able to have the full year off this time for my child care leave. Once again, we conceived quickly. I continued to work. I was at the four-month mark, when disaster struck on a Friday. I experienced heavy bleeding and was in bed for two days. I spoke with friends, which confirmed my fear that I was likely having a miscarriage. Heartbroken I had to wait until Monday to see the doctor. She sent me for an ultrasound, just to confirm. Never in my wildest dreams did I expect to hear the words, *I see a strong heartbeat!*

The doctor explained I likely had a twin in there, which had settled in a spot that could not be sustained full term for some reason. I had always wanted twins, but I didn't dwell on it. I concentrated on taking care of the baby I was still carrying. We were overjoyed the baby was healthy. But saddened as well by the fact that our other twin had not made it.

The doctor took me off work. Perfect, I was on sick leave. More time to spend with Tristan and Shay. Then it would be switched over to child care leave for a year once the baby was born. I loved being home, being a mom, and being a wife.

At one point I slipped getting out of the shower at home. I didn't realize I had pulled the ligaments in my groin. I was blaming the camper for being uncomfortable, but the pain persisted. I went to the doctor, and she asked me if I had experienced any falls? I told her about my leg slipping and we figured it must have been what had caused my injury.

The pressure of the baby sitting on my pelvis with pulled groin ligaments was intense. I couldn't get any relief. As you know your bones soften for pregnancy to allow birthing. Other than that episode, I had a great pregnancy—despite waiting every day in the last eight weeks of pregnancy to go early.

I was at high risk due to Shay's early delivery. It was hard on the brain, wondering if everything was going to go smoothly for this one. Also, at five months I went to the Valley Hospital for my ultrasound and to find out the sex of the baby. My friend Michelle was there to videotape it. They tried hard to see the sex; however, the baby was not co-operating. The technician told me she was eighty to ninety per cent sure I was having a girl.

That was awesome but if you remember I had stated I would only have two boys when I decided to have more babies. Therefore, I never ran out and bought a ton of girl clothes. I did buy stuff at Frenchy's knowing I could pass it on if need be. I never believed it was a girl. Because of my high risk, I had another ultrasound around seven months. The technicians in Yarmouth were not allowed to disclose the sex of the baby. I told her about the previous ultrasound, and she was surprised. I could tell she wanted to tell me something. She even went and got her supervisor who walked in, looked at me for a moment, and said that was nice about having a girl and left the room. The technician was so frustrated but could not openly tell me the baby's sex. I told her not to worry. I had believed long before conception it was meant to be a boy. So, I gave away the girl clothes.

I went full term. In fact, a day after my due date as I stood up at 8 a.m. my water broke. Tristan needed to get off to school and Shay needed to get to the babysitters. I told Steve that I guessed he wasn't going to work. So, we got ready and headed to hospital. I tried to tell them at nurses' station that I normally don't take very long to deliver, and I need a room fast. They didn't have any rooms available and had to make a storage room into one for me.

Finally, I was in a bed but not for long. I was sent right over to the delivery room. Tammy, Tristan's Aunt, was videotaping for us. Steve had missed Shay being born, so there was no way was he missing anything this time.

Dr. Webster was to perform the delivery. But this baby was not going to be as easy as Shay, who was small and out on the first push. I had a harder time, but it was very quick.

I pushed the head out and the doctor told me to stop. I didn't know what was happening. I later found out the cord was wrapped around the baby numerous times. The baby's shoulders were stuck, and the doctor later admitted he wasn't sure how he was getting him out. He managed to work him free and unwrapped the cord so it wouldn't strangle the baby. The relief on the doctor's face was all I needed to see. I also said, "Man that was a big baby."

JJ was here and wasn't a girl. JJ weighed in at 9 pounds, 5.5 ounces. My water had broken at 8 a.m., and he was born at 10 a.m. I tried to tell them I moved fast.

Kim, the babysitter, brought Shay to meet his little brother and Tammy went to get Tristan from school. By 11 a.m., Steve was off to work. I was in my makeshift room trying to breastfeed. With Tristan, I had tried. I did manage to for a while, but he needed formula when I worked. Now I knew it hadn't been working well back then either. He likely hadn't been getting enough without the formula.

With Shay they said I had difficulty breastfeeding because he was a preemie. I had tried everything and had many visits from the health nurse. I gave up around seven months. I had high hopes it would all work out with JJ, but no such luck. I tried and tried but could never make enough to satisfy him. I did both bottle and breastfeeding for six to seven months before giving up. Why was it so easy for others? My sisters never had a problem. I blamed some of it on the abuse I grew up with. Hating parts of your body and being violated stays in the back of your mind for a lifetime.

I was adjusting to having a new baby. The first three months are always the hardest. JJ was not going to follow in Tristan's or Shay's footsteps. They spoiled me by having good naps. With JJ, I was lucky to get thirty minutes. He slept well at night but just wanted short little naps during day. The car had to be moving or he didn't like it at all.

I guess the saying no two babies are the same, is somewhat true. Although Tristan and Shay did mirror each other. JJ taught me lots of new things.

With little time for myself, my weight climbed higher than when I was pregnant. My husband never commented on my weight, and in fact he insisted I was beautiful at every stage throughout our marriage. I used to tell him he was crazy, but he loved every inch of me. He is better at it than me because I see every flaw and every pound.

My sister-in-law was going to Curves, a new gym craze. I decided if she could do it maybe I could too. JJ was six months old. I stole an hour for myself in the evenings and joined. It was the best thing I ever did. I lost some weight, had more energy, and started eating better.

This was the beginning of my everyday struggle, to stay at a comfortable, healthy weight. For some, this comes easy, for me I can't drop the ball or it creeps back up. I walked a lot. I even got a double stroller. Again, keep it moving or JJ wasn't happy. We went on lots of camping trips. Ellenwood, South Mountain, and a Digby campground were the most frequent. Tristan loved to fish, swim, and play with Shay. He was the best big brother.

Backing up for a moment: some information about our new house.

We considered building onto our house in town. However, the estimates were ridiculous, and we still didn't have much room for our yard, or the business. As much as I was attached to that little yellow house, we agreed we needed to expand for our family.

Back in 2002 we decided we were going to find our dream piece of land and build a house. We looked all over. We looked at houses for sale, as well as land. We continued to come back to a spot on Tinkham Road. The man that owed it was deceased.

We found out his sister was in charge of his estate. I got ahold of her in Ontario. We were one hundred per cent sure we wanted the twenty-six acres. She had many pieces of land for sale. Before that, a realtor had talked her into listing them all. Damn. We called her immediately and she said she was so sorry, but it turned out she had been pressured into it. We spoke for our land, however, a local businessperson was trying to get the land first, to clear the logs off it. He had no use for it after that, so he showed up at the house with a proposal for us to buy the land. He would clear it with the intent to sell it to us ASAP. Basically, it was just a promise.

At that time, we had the baby on the way and wanted to be in our new house quickly. So, we agreed to the terms. He would clear the land and then we would buy it from him. Crazy as this sounds, we asked to start building before the land was even in our names. March 17, 2003, we dug the basement. The twenty-seventh of March JJ was born.

Steve was always working. But I went every day, JJ in tow, to see the progress and answer questions. Shay would be with me too, or at Kim's to play with other kids. Tristan was in school, and we drove him to the Central School. He had gone there all his life. We would also go back some evenings to see how things were progressing with the build.

Our builder went right at it, and we were to move in on the July long weekend, but not before we had lived in Wedgeport for three months. My first house at 10 King Street sold within two days. I put a higher price on it than the realtor had suggested, which gave us a good down payment. Plus, Little Nan had gifted us our land.

Don't be mistaken. Both of us had come from nothing, and we were damn proud of where we were going. Hard work does pay off and we were very thankful to sweet Little Nan. The only one in our lives that ever truly helped us financially.

My mom helped us incredibly, in more ways than I can explain. However, she never had any money to offer, just her precious time.

Packing up King Street, and moving to Wedgeport, twenty minutes outside of town was a lot of work. JJ was a newborn and Steve had no extra days off. No wonder I was stressed out, gaining weight.

We moved into the new house on the first of July. The work never stopped and there was lots to do. I'd take the baby monitor and go outside to do yard work. I never got very far with JJ's short naps. Shay even helped me. What kid didn't like being outside, getting dirty. Tristan would help too when he was home.

My kids were all outdoor kids. I didn't believe in buying video games. Any fun money we spent was on outside activities. My dream was to have a pool. We had a ten-foot inflatable one to start. We all loved playing in that.

Shay loved his baby brother. He always said, "Hi baby, hi baby, hi baby!" He played with him like he was a little doll.

In the spring of 2004, we hired an excavating company to make our huge lawn. We were fortunate enough to have tons of topsoil on our property. They screened over fifty loads, spreading them mainly out front. They dug a hole out back and this would water the lawn. They supplied the pump and sprinklers. All the hours we had spent trying to do it ourselves were for nothing. The lawn was huge, and it turned out beautifully. We were happy with it. On top of that, we had more loads of soil to sell. This paid for our lawn, which we were so thankful for. Everything was coming together nicely.

Our boys either were playing outside, or they were building forts in the house. They were never bored. They had quite the imaginations.

CHAPTER 27

Being With And Without My Kids

The kids were little when I decided to take Tristan to Disney. Spending one-on-one time was important to me. My friend Trina and her daughter Megan went with us. I cried all the way to the airport, but I knew I was doing a good thing for my son Tristan. Leaving little ones behind is never easy, but you should do it for "the greater good."

They were fine with my mother and their father Steve. And I don't believe they even remember me deserting them.

We had a good time. The water park was probably the most fun for Tristan. He liked the Shrek 4-D movie clip as well. Staying with girls in the room was interesting, with clothes and shoes everywhere. Tristan had never seen anything like that before, lol.

It was my friend Trina's first flight. She was so funny asking me what it was like to takeoff. I told her she would be sucked back in her seat, like a rocket ship. Her eyes were as big as saucers. I got her hooked-on travelling. She's addicted to going to Florida.

One day I left Steve's mother to tend Shay. I was only going to be gone for an hour to go to the warehouse to help. When I returned my baby was standing at the door completely soaked in snot and crying pretty hard. Steve's mother was on the phone with a boyfriend! She was ignoring Shay. I was furious. She wasn't even trying to calm him down and when I questioned her about it her response was that he hadn't wanted her, that he had wanted me. I responded that it was no wonder, since she didn't think he was very important and she was on the phone. I felt like a bad mother, for leaving him with her.

I already didn't let her drive them anywhere since she was a terrible driver. She had lots of accidents. The negative energy that she brought to my family was draining.

My kids were always outside. I'd be working in the garden, and they would have their dump trucks playing in the dirt. One time I ran a hose up to made them a mud run. Boy, did they ever run, pushing their trucks through that. I can still hear their giggles.

Their clothes had to be thrown out sometimes, but it was worth every minute.

Then there were the pool days. They lived in their swimsuits. JJ had a wetsuit and when he was smaller, he had a built-in floaty ring, so I didn't have to worry. In and out all day. No video games in our house. I didn't believe in too much screen time. They had video players in the vehicles for our long drives, and iPads when they were older for travelling. But never gaming systems. I gladly put my money into outdoor things.

They did watch movies and I believe we wore out The Wizard of Oz, Cars, and the fire station dog one. Shay would use a line out of The Wizard of Oz and call me "My Pretty." He loved how I lit up with a smile, hearing it. When Tristan was little, he always watched the Littlefoot Dinosaur movies, Pooh Bear, and later The Ninja Turtles. Tristan also had gaming systems at his father's, as I couldn't control what went on there. Even though I tried.

Geesh, I didn't know about the junk cupboard until he was like twenty. Imagine his confusion, going from one extreme to the other. I always tried to feed them healthy. I had strict rules. Fries only once a week, no pop except for special occasions, and never dark pop. It was either water at sit down restaurants, or milk. Treats should be once a week, not every time you go to town, or in a store.

When I was a kid, we were lucky to get three treats a year.

Every summer we tried to take the kids to Aunt Thelma's cottage. One particular time I hauled the camper. Steve was meeting me there after work on Friday. There was family there to help us unhook, and pop it up. Well, I was on a little slant when they started unhooking the trailer. There is a huge cliff, just beyond the lawn. No one thought the trailer would roll, or they simply were not communicating with each other. The guy at my hitch unhooked just as I yelled for Tristan to put a stick of wood under the wheel.

Within seconds, my life flashed before my eyes. Tristan could have been knocked down by the runaway trailer. It was so close to being a disaster. Tristan could have been seriously hurt and the trailer could have been totally destroyed. I know my angels were watching over us that day. I am so thankful.

Grade 8 was the last time Tristan wanted to sleep over at his father's. He was content at our house and with just visiting with his dad's side. I tried to encourage him, and we talked. He broke down saying he didn't want that lifestyle anymore. So young to make a brave decision in his own best interest. I respected his decision and that was it.

Tristan joined a basketball team. It was the best thing for him. He was getting a good workout and he sprouted to become six feet tall. It totally changed him for the better. The boys loved going to watch their brother play. Tristan was a great student, hardly studied and still had good marks. The principal told me they wished more students were just like Tristan. All his teachers and principals loved him.

Steve and I took Shay and JJ to Florida in 2005. We were there when JJ turned two. That was the trip when I found my beautiful cross that I still wear on a discount table at the jewellery store. I have received so many compliments about my cross over the years.

We stayed at Nanette's, a friend from my childhood, for a night and then headed out touring around. We went to some water parks and beaches. I loved the warm weather.

The business was doing okay but we had to be careful how we spent our money. We couldn't afford trips every year. Just occasionally. We were fortunate enough to not have to worry about how much I spent on groceries. To me that was a huge blessing. I always shopped smart though, and sales do matter. Stock up, so you pay less overall.

Life was busy. After JJ I never went back to work at the hospital. Our business had grown. I debated that decision immensely, but I did resign.

When we decided to put the pool in, oh what a job it was! We hired a neighbour. He had done his own. This was in 2006. He had a backhoe to dig the lawn out of the section needed. Then the weather didn't co-operate. We had the sand all levelled out and a torrential rainstorm washed it away. Back to square one with rented equipment to try again.

Finally, after much frustration, we were putting up the sides. The liner was next. We had to spread it out as the freezing cold water was going in. We managed to do a pretty good job. It was a little off in just the one spot. The neighbour built us a platform and ladder. Tristan loved the pool. Shay with his water wings and JJ following right behind with a tube and wings of his own. They each had wetsuits. JJ still had the whole suit with the built-in floaties.

I had never learned to swim. I didn't like people near me in the water. But the kids helped me with that problem. As a mom I didn't have a choice.

I eventually learned to swim alone in the pool. I would only let go and try by myself, as strange as that might sound. I still don't like to be grabbed in the water, which followed me from childhood trauma. But I will go out swimming anywhere with a pool noodle for comfort. Deepness doesn't matter. But I never overcame my fear of putting my head under water. I guess I couldn't win them all.

I don't think the pool was ready in time for Tristan's birthday. For his thirteenth birthday Tristan had a skating party with all his friends.

All the boys played soccer and baseball. We were always a busy family. That summer we made it to the Yogi Bear Campground. They especially loved being there, as it had so much for the kids to do.

In 2006 I won a couple nights' stay at a Rodd Resort. We took the boys and went to PEI when they were three, five, and thirteen. We had so much fun exploring. Definitely, it was one of the favourite family trips that sticks out in my mind.

We always went to Natasha's in the summer or met them at Upper Clements Park. It was a beautiful theme park, and the flume, roller coaster, and bumper boats were always the favourites. In the fall we took our camper to Camp Peniel, a Christian summer camp. They had fun family weekends. Tristan attended camp there for a week on his own, and we all went together in September. I loved being there. Meals were supplied in the big hall, so I got lots of time with the family, doing all the fun events.

More Family Time

Shay started school, which was hard to believe. But I was looking forward to having some one-on-one time with JJ. Both parenting them as a family and solo time was very important. I always gave one hundred and ten per cent, and this was no different.

For sure, I was the strictest one between Steve and me. Not only that, but I was the structural one as well. Steve was a hands-on dad. He hated when guys would say they were babysitting their own kids. How is that even possible? You are raising your own damn kids. They don't just belong to the wife.

Little Nan turned eighty-five in December. I loved her spunky personality and her laugh. She was the cutest little human I have ever known.

For Christmas we searched high and low for a toy backhoe for JJ. Mom's cousin Fred ended up finding one on eBay and managed to snag it for us. He was so excited getting that backhoe.

Shay got a guitar, and Tristan got the keys to the four-wheeler. The only problem with that was Tristan was timid on the four-wheeler. His father had put him on one a few years earlier, with no training. He had run it into a tree. We were hopeful he would become more comfortable on his own at our house.

Overall, the boys had a great Christmas.

Easter always meant a huge egg hunt. The kids each had a chocolate bunny all to themselves. But not JJ, he didn't like chocolate. And there was lots of outdoor play stuff. Bikes, when they needed them, helmets, soccer balls, and baseball equipment. It was our spring is here, excitement time.

A huge highlight was when Natasha came to Yarmouth for her skating competition. Every year it was held in a different part of Nova Scotia. This year the Yarmouth Skating Club held the event. I had never seen her skate before. She was so beautiful. She placed second in one event and took home a silver medal. Seeing her on the podium, melted my heart. She actually had a cousin on the ice with her and didn't even know it. Fred's brother's daughter was in the skating club. At this time, they still lived in Yarmouth. Little did they know who I was there watching—their niece, my daughter with Fred.

It was another moment when I wanted to scream it from the rooftops, but I remained under a rock.

Steve decided he wanted a dog. Somehow, he heard about an eight-week-old Cocker Spaniel; the owners had split up and the dog needed a home. Steve went to get him. It was going to be his dog, to go in the truck with him every day. He named him Hunter.

It all started out fine; however, as Hunter got older, he didn't enjoy the truck as much. He ducked when the truck came to overpasses; he was scared. I ended up keeping him at home. He was such a beautiful dog. I taught him to sit, roll over, shake his paw, high-five, and to walk with me nicely. He did bark every time someone came in the house, or yard. I always said he was just doing his job.

During 2007, we continued to improve our property. We put in a basketball court for Tristan. He had joined the basketball team at Maple Grove. We loved going to watch his games, even though he didn't always get to play much. I even have pictures of Mom out shooting hoops with Tristan.

Then we built a garage with the help of Mom's cousin Fred, John the neighbour, and others. I wasn't scared of manual work. In fact, I cut all the boards for the roof and handed them up to Fred, who nailed them down.

Steve worked long hours, so he had no interest coming home and working all night on the garage. He was also no carpenter, as I would learn every time that I asked him to do a project. I didn't mind building the garage. Things are always more rewarding when you're hands-on. The cement work was even fun.

One year, John built me a privacy wall between the driveway and the pool. Another year we put in a cement retaining wall behind the pool. Then finally we started the construction of a huge deck all around the pool in 2008. We made custom balusters. John showed me how to cut them and I just kept cutting. I actually loved doing all the outdoor projects!

I am not sure which year I started the garden, but that was a lot of work too. I enjoyed growing things to feed the family. We also planted maple trees, and different bushes. Steve always told me I was "a make-work project." He just needed to embrace my creative side.

I traded a load of topsoil to a guy down the road, who built me a heart shaped stonewall around my garden, on the front lawn. I loved hearts, and it was so beautiful.

I then built myself a stonewalled garden in front of the garage; we had lots of rocks in the back field. There's nothing you can't do if you put your mind to it. And I can be pretty stubborn. I have always loved the physical labour of working outside, in the fresh air and sunshine. There's nothing better and it's my happy drug.

That year Tristan had a pool party. June was still chilly, but they were teenage boys, so they had a blast.

With Tristan, things were not always perfect. We had our trials and tests. Raising another man's child is never easy. You must think before you speak and show them a lot of love, as should all parents. Tristan was used to having me all to himself, then Steve came along, and then the brothers came along. So, there were a lot of adjustments.

As with any child, there are times of arguments and conflicts. Steve was naive thinking that his kids would never struggle with their mother and rules like Tristan did. I assured him he was wrong, and that all kids struggle with rules and conflicts and don't want to listen at times. And yes, even the best kids can show hatred toward their parents' rules and boundaries.

We did, however, seek professional advice and saw a counsellor, which all parents should do when there are issues. It helped us tremendously. The biggest thing I remember was being told it should only ever be one parent, who is trying to parent at a time, unless it's a major situation. Then if needed, the first parent should ask the second parent for help. It should never be the two parents who are ganging up on the one child. That will spiral into a complete yelling match. Steve began to relax and let me do most of the parenting with Tristan without interrupting or getting involved. I assured him he would face the same struggles with his children, and how they would speak to their mother and him.

You must remember that every child has their own personality. They are not going to say and do exactly what you want them to. You also must let them grow in their own ways. This is hard, especially on the first child. You are stricter, and you have all these expectations of teaching them your ways. Trust me, you relax with the second child, and with the third, things are even easier.

I can't change that fact for Tristan; he was our first and he did get the stricter end of things. He was held in a straighter line then Shay, and for JJ his line got pretty crooked because he was a totally different personality. Unlike anything I was used to.

JJ was our spitfire. If he saw a teacher across the parking lot, he was yelling at them, "Hi! Mrs. so-and-so." Whereas Tristan and Shay would be hiding their heads hoping they weren't noticed. They were not as outgoing.

Shay mirrored Tristan, but JJ changed everything in our house. We love them all equally, but with that being said they were all different. With different interests and needs. I didn't always add things up to make sure everything was perfectly equal. I never believed in doing that. Christmas presents were of course close, but even then, I considered their different interests.

CHAPTER 29

Continuing Life Adjustments

Back when I traded my Toyota 4Runner to start our business, I swore I would have another one. Instead, I chose a white Dodge Durango as my deal for sacrificing my Toyota. I loved my Durango. I liked keeping things and getting your money out of them, while Steve has the fever to upgrade, get better, and newer all the time. My upbringing taught me to take care of your stuff and appreciate what you have. That way it will last. Plus, I didn't always want to have the payments. Live within your means is the way to prosper.

The company was doing ok, but I ran a tight ship to make that happen. We didn't chrome up the trucks, despite Steve wanting to. Looks don't pay the bills. We had to be careful setting our baselines. I didn't have to worry about how much I spent on groceries, but I did have to be careful where the rest of the money was going. At one point they were building huge stores in our area. Steve had the idea of buying a dump truck. I quickly diminished that idea as we live in a seasonal province. There is not work all year long but there would still be payments every month. Plus, who wants to spend the entire season working seven days a week to make it worthwhile having a dump truck. Not me and thankfully I am the financial brains of our operation.

Going to Aunt Thelma's cottage was a treat. Beach walking, hiking, swimming if you're brave, enjoying the thunder and lightning shows, and playing with the family. My boys all loved it there.

We managed a trip per summer, usually. One summer we were there with a lot of my cousins and their families. Mom loved it there too. It was the first place she took us the summer we were free from my father's nightmare. We continued to go there each summer, until we had our own slice of heaven.

All Tristan wanted for his mid-teen birthday was a trip to Aunt Thelma's camp. We took Ryan, his friend with us. The boys brought all their fishing gear and were planning to hike up the brook. These boys were always up for an adventure. There was trout in the ponds farther up the brook. They were gone for most of the day.

I had always had knee problems. My knees pop right out of place, which if my weight is on it at the time stretches all the ligaments. Apparently, I have no ligaments on the one side, and too many on the other. After seeing a specialist, I decided to have a lateral release done. He felt it would help for at least ten years. I did it, but unfortunately, I had some complications. It bled under the kneecap and my two-week recovery ended up being more like eight weeks. I even went to Tristan's Grade 9 graduation and prom on crutches. Junior high proms are nice but not as fancy as high school proms. Basically, just a chance to say goodbye to middle school and move on to high school. I was thankful to be able to hobble along to these events.

I am not one to sit around. Summer was coming, and I was on crutches. I gained a bit of weight back, which was depressing for me. The operation did work in the way it was supposed to in that my knee didn't pop of joint for at least another ten years. However, I was supposed to have both done, and I never did the second one. I didn't want to chance another bad recovery. I just had to keep telling myself, no running. Biking and walking were my best bet.

Our summers mirrored each other. The boys were in baseball, soccer, and they loved to swim. We had fires in the backyard. JJ learned to ride his bike with no training wheels. Lots of family fun times together. Steve can take all the credit of running beside all three of our boys and teaching them to ride their bikes.

We didn't go back to Aunt Thelma's cottage that summer of 2008. Instead, we had everyone come to our house. We had a big baseball game on our front lawn. Everyone got into the game. I believe all the cousins were there, and as time went on this was getting harder and harder to manage. Some of the cousins were getting older and would be working at their summer jobs. I can still hear everyone cheering and see everyone trying their hardest to win.

We went on our annual summer trip to Natasha's. The kids all played soccer in her backyard together. I remember her telling me how at school she would get into arguments with the other kids. They would tell her that she didn't have any brothers and she would tell them that she had three! She had once asked her mother if she had grown in her belly. Her mother had told her no, that she had grown in Tam's belly. I was thankful they were so open and honest with her. My children were always told about their sister. I had her picture on my nightstand and we had another picture of her in our living room. Natasha was not a secret to my boys, or anyone that entered our home. I loved seeing all four of my babies together. It was the icing on my cake, so to speak.

We went to Camp Peniel once again with our camper. The memories spent there are some of the best. Shay climbed the wall, there was a huge bouncy inflatable in the water, there was a slip and slide, archery, field games, concerts on the grass, lovely meals cooked for us, a variety show in front of the fire, a fishing boat for their imagination, and tons of crafts and games.

When it was time to go back to school, Tristan was heading into Grade 10 at the high school. Shay was in Grade 2 and JJ was in the Primary Grade. My baby was going to school. They sure were growing up fast. They continued their Music for Young Children program, however, all that practising and none of them picked up on playing any musical instruments. Oh well, it was fun to see their accomplishments as always.

Mom and I travelled to Kentville for a couple of years while a doctor made notes about Mom's abilities to communicate. He felt she qualified for a study and decided to enrol her. All she had to do was answer ten questions. It was approximately 2008 and she was about sixty-two. She failed to answer any of the questions and the doctor apologized for getting our hopes up. He realized Mom looked well on the outside—bright and cheerful—but her brain was failing on the inside quicker than he'd thought. She did not qualify for the study.

There was not much point in continuing our visits. Usually, he said the life expectancy is no longer than ten years from a diagnosis of Alzheimer's. But Mom was diagnosed early because as a family we saw the same signs as we did with my grandmother. We knew when she was about fifty-eight or fifty-nine. The doctor confirmed it at sixty. Nothing can prepare you for the road ahead; the disease is also unpredictable in the same way that people are all different.

Christmas was beautiful of course, and this year the boys got dune buggies, and Tristan got an iPod. Here comes the crazy technology phase! I had no idea just how crazy this was going to get. But I had held my kids off longer than the majority of kids when it came to getting phones.

CHAPTER 30

Through The Years: 2009

The years seem to go by so quickly. As you get older every year seems to be faster and faster. During 2009, Steve and I managed a trip to Cuba in April. Life is short, and goes by fast, so my motto is to enjoy it while you can. I've been on many trips, as you'll read. Sometimes by paying out of pocket, other times through the benefit of Air Miles.

In June we put in a beautiful hot tub. I cashed in my old life insurance policy. I wanted to spend the money on something for the whole family.

We had bought new life insurance policies. One that covered more of the important years. But if we lived a really long time, we could end up with nothing. We felt buying the life insurance was the right thing to do. So, I put in a cement slab to set the hot tub on. A little bit of luxury for the backyard.

Tristan turned sixteen in June. He got his beginners driver's licence, and he did his driver's education program.

Steve, I, and Tristan's father chipped in on a Volkswagen Jetta for him. I thought the car would last him through his high school years. Tristan fixed it up, his father painted it, and we bought him the car parts that he needed and wanted for it.

After all that work, Tristan had other ideas. I learned a parenting lesson through this for the next boys. I should have laid down the law that selling it or trading would not be allowed. However, I didn't see that scenario coming until it was too late. Tristan had all these plans, and it became quite the argument. Hard to watch, but he made his own decisions concerning the car.

Tristan had always worked hard; therefore, he had some money, and decided to trade-in his vehicle. I knew it wasn't the best financial choice, but he went ahead and did it. I learned at this age I can give the best advice, but it doesn't mean they will listen. They need to make their own choices and deal with the consequences.

Later in June my sister Sharon got married to Wayne after many years of being together. It was nice to have the whole family together for her celebration. They got married in the Eastern Passage on the beach, surrounded by a beautiful meadow.

The boys were busy in music classes, and my friend Jennifer taught them. I loved it when they performed. I practised with them and learned many things. Piano really does take a lot of practice but when they worked on a song, they were able to learn it pretty good.

I thought it would be neat if they brought their portable piano to Natasha's house so they could perform for us all during our Christmas visit. We had a nice time with Natasha and her parents, and once again it completed my Christmas season to spend time with her.

Mom loved to decorate cookies with the kids. It was a traditional, yearly thing. I will treasure that memory of my mother dearly. I have many fond pictures and memories of this activity.

For the boys' performance I think this was one of those things where I insisted that they do it. But they didn't necessarily really want to do it. I didn't fight and scream with them, but I did convince them that it would be nice for them to do this.

I was hard on my kids in the way that often I did make them do things. Whether they wanted to or not. Because life isn't fair, and they're going to have to do things for their bosses that they don't want to do. Giving a child too many choices all the time does not set them up for a realistic future. Sometimes they need to do things just because it's a good thing to do. Or it just must be done. It's hard to explain until you lived life and see just how much this will happen. Age truly is wisdom.

Raising my kids, I often said at thirty or forty years old I have this many more years' experience on earth than you. You learn every day of your life and usually older people's advice is very good. I hear your opinion but try to understand mine too.

I was very good at seeing both sides to every situation. Steve would often call from work, complaining about one thing or another. I would always show him both sides and try to get him to understand there's always more to every circumstance. Being open minded is a very good trait to have. He would sometimes get frustrated with me and say I always took the other side, but that's not what I was doing. I would just show him that there's always two sides to everything. I did this with my kids as well.

My kids loved being outside. The boys like playing in the hot tub, especially when their friends would come over, or Jordie, my cousin. When it's snowing it's especially fun. One day JJ was building a snowman, and of course mommy was helping him. We had some really nice kits to dress them up with. We made a big one and a small one. When I asked JJ who the big one was, he said Grampy Buck. The two of them together were Grampy and him. I have no doubt that Grampy Buck was there in spirit with us. Steve's father was always with my children and Steve, watching over them. I felt his presence and when I took the picture there was an angel orb in the picture. I felt his energy and it was real.

That Christmas Little Nan and Steve's mother were with us, along with my mother so we called them the Golden Girls. Steve had got the boys cheap little four-wheelers from Canadian Tire. We had quite a bit of snow, but they drove them up and down the driveway all day. It was quite entertaining.

I had no intentions of getting another puppy as we had Hunter. However, I saw a picture of a little girl puppy during the Christmas holidays online at a local breeder's house. She was Hunter's half-sister and looked exactly like him. I fell in love with her picture and decided that I needed another female in the house for balance!

CHAPTER 31

Through The Years: 2010

In 2010 we found our lake lot in Springdale. We obtained a line of credit and bought it, as it was perfect for us. It was cleared enough to park our camper on, and we would go from there. It really felt like the right property; it was speaking to me.

We also took a trip to Toronto to buy my antique car. I had been talking to a guy online for the past two years. He finally dropped the price enough for me to say let's go get it. I guess I was drawn to it because it was unique. It was the same car I had bought as my first car when I was sixteen. This one was souped-up and a little nicer, with big pipes running down the sides of it, and a new paint job in cherry black. My 1980 AMC SPIRIT.

Steve and I camped in my Durango on the way to Toronto. We stopped to see friends Julie and Rob along the way. We got the car loaded and made our way home in time for Shay's baseball game. We went directly to the game. While we were at the game, we got a phone call that Steve's Little Nan had passed away. I was heartbroken. I was so very close to her. She called me almost every day to see how my children were. I was guilty of sometimes being too busy to chat for as long as she wanted to. But I loved her immensely.

The kids were young, life was busy, but don't let that be your regret—that you don't take enough time for those phone calls. These people will not always be there in your life.

My kids very much loved their Little Nan. She was so sweet, and she loved to play with them. I can still hear her laughter from when she rolled around on the floor with Shay. At times I had to step in because they would ask her to do the silliest things, and she would do them, even at her age. We were all going to miss her dearly.

Years before she passed, Little Nan had put Steve's name on the deed for her house. She didn't want him to have any problems when it came time for her will to be actioned. A year before she died, she also added his name as one of the executors, along with her two nieces. The nieces were unaware of this, so when she died, they immediately started doing things.

To their surprise they found out they should have waited until the will was read. Steve was her only living immediate family member and everything was left to him, except for some jewellery that was specified as to who was to get it. They shouldn't have even been in the house without Steve there. I wanted to respect her wishes and make sure the people specified got her jewellery. The law was that all bills had to be paid before anything was given out. I overruled this and made sure everyone got their jewellery.

No one knew that Little Nan had a loan that she had taken out at the bank. The bank hadn't realized that Steve's name was on the deed when they had given her that loan. Short version of the story, the bank ended up losing out, as there was no money to pay her bills from her estate. The house no longer counted as her estate because it now belonged to Steve. Unfortunate for the bank, but she would not have wanted us to pay that bill. And we were not obligated to pay it.

I was also surprised by people thinking they should be able to come in and pick out what they wanted of Little Nan's at her house. These people were some of the ones I made sure got their special piece of jewellery. They still made me feel bad by asking for other stuff. Steve and the kids were her only immediate blood relatives. From my knowledge of her, she would have wanted them to have everything.

Steve drove her car for a while, but we did end up selling it. We sold the house as well, as it was too far away from where we lived, and we didn't want to rent it out. This was a huge problem for Steve's mother who felt that she deserved to live there for free. She always showed her true colours and she was not Little Nan's daughter. She and I never connected as I would have liked for us to, at least for Steve's sake. She was always jealous of Steve, but this was pretty hurtful; her thinking that she deserved the house over him.

Why do people think they deserve stuff when someone passes away? Material things are overrated, and not as important as these people think. I would love just to hear her voice one more time. But she is with the angels, and that was comforting for me.

CHAPTER 32

Through The Years: 2011

Early in 2011 we went on a family trip to Edmonton to see my friend Julie and her family. It was very cold, but we did manage to get to the West Edmonton Mall and have some fun. It was a short trip. My niece was pregnant at the time. Unexpectedly pregnant, so she wasn't sure what she wanted to do.

Her parents didn't think she was mother material and told her she couldn't bring the baby home. If she kept the baby, then she needed to get herself an apartment. I believe it was their way of making her be responsible. She was twenty-five years old and had graduated from university. However, she still didn't know what she wanted to do in life. She had huge amounts of debt from school. Oh, she had dreams, but she didn't have the determination to make them happen.

I'm very close to my niece. I did offer her the choice of keeping the baby and coming to stay with us. I never told her what she should or shouldn't do; I simply gave her an option. The choice was all hers. Helping her was hard, as I had been down this road myself. She was considering adoption, just like me, right up to the last day of being in the hospital. She wasn't sure what she should do. In fact, when I drove to the IWK I didn't know if I was bringing her and the baby home, or just her. I simply tried to be supportive and let her talk with the professional counsellors to decide.

Late in the day, she made her decision. On the fourteenth of February I drove them both home to Yarmouth. My sister wasn't mad, but I did get the feeling that she wished I hadn't intervened. But I believe everyone should have options, and not be forced into things, with somebody else making their decisions.

My niece has a very quiet personality. It's hard to know what she's thinking or feeling. I helped her as much as I could, and they ended up staying with us for about six months. I loved spending time with baby Luke. Babies were my thing. I have the touch.

He was a good baby, and we enjoyed helping him out with his beginning. My niece had lots to learn, as does every new parent. Toward the end of their stay, the situation was a bit stressed. Our personalities are immensely different. Mine being, I do whatever needs to be done at one hundred and ten per cent. Hers is hard to describe; she's unique.

I don't think there was enough communication between us, and we certainly didn't understand each other. I shed many tears in my gardens that spring. I didn't know what else to do. I am a fixer, and a teacher if you are willing to learn, but at some point, there was no more that I could do. My niece ended up going home to her parents' house. They welcomed her, and her mother helped her with the baby. It was for the best. I did what I could to help my niece and her new baby, and I planned to keep the communication open and be there whenever she needed me.

I never charged her anything for living with us. I always believe if you have more than enough, you should help others and that's exactly what I did. Some will say that I give too much, but I think we were meant to give. I consider my generosity as a gift. Anytime I give I'm not looking for rewards. It just feels right to me.

This was the year my first son graduated high school. I was so proud of him. He was off to university thinking he wanted to be a teacher. But probably not sure what he really wanted to do. None the less it would be a learning year for him to figure it out. He was in a three-year relationship with his girlfriend, which always plays a factor in their decisions at this age.

I have often had spiritual readings done. I thrived off the energy and they ignite the energy within me. The readers told me lots of things they would have had no way of knowing. Deep personal stuff. One thing that always stood out was I was always told how much my husband cherished me. He was the one I was supposed to be with, and we fit together. It was meant to be. I felt that way too. Thirteen years married and stronger every day. I always counted my blessings.

In November we lost Steve's GrandDad Miller. He was a huge volunteer in his community, and very well loved by all.

CHAPTER 33

Through The Years: 2012

In 2012 we got out of our comfort zone. Friends were going on a cruise in January. This was not an ideal time for us to travel as storms, winter conditions, and work problems were at peak season. But we decided to go, despite it being a stressful time to leave. We had a mostly great time. We did our own thing most of the time, meeting up with the group for dinners and evening shows.

We had some work issues that I could only deal with when we were in ports as we had no service out on the sea. I just did the best I could. It would all be waiting for us when we arrived back home.

Mom was living in her own seniors' apartment. She was able to take care of herself, even driving until about 2012. I started stopping in more often. The bank let me know that when she would come in with my brother that she would get very flustered and upset as she could not remember what she had to do. Mom asked me to be her power of attorney so we went to see a lawyer.

There were so many family things that filled up our 2012. Shay was becoming really good with his cooking techniques. This child would read cookbooks for his school homework reading requirements. He would ask for ingredients to make some neat dishes. He could follow the recipe exactly, and he cared how the presentation looked. I was bursting with pride every time he cooked.

I had a dream to go to New York, so I took Shay as we were so compatible. He wanted to go to Carlos' famous bakery in New Jersey, so we did. No regrets, it was amazing. We loved eating off the food trucks; the flavours were exceptional. Shay swears he had the best pizza ever in New York. He still raves about it.

We visited the park where the movie *Home Alone* was shot, the memorials for 9/11, and walked so many miles. We took in a Christmas show at Radio City Music Hall and went on a Christmas lights tour. We made the best memories together, and he was old enough to remember them. He was almost twelve.

Shay was also participating in a run club at school. I am not a runner but wanted to try it out. We did a bit of training, but it was tough. I was heavier than I should have been. However, Shay and I ran with the other participants in the kid's Bluenose Race in Halifax. I must say, despite it being only three kilometres long, crossing the finishing line was memorable. I was so proud of Shay and myself for completing it. Steve and JJ were at the finish line to meet us. I can still hear them cheering us on.

I got running fever in my head. So, I decided to join a run club of my own, with my long-time friend Trina. We had so much fun. We worked our way up to 5 km, even running up a few hills. It was summer and I'm pretty sure the night we ran 5 km without stopping it was close to midnight. We even entered in a Run the Lake race. I finished it, but 6.6 km later I thought I would die. Lots of hills. I did a lot of walk-running of course. Accomplishments are the stepping stones of life. The more things you complete, the better your life will feel.

That year, Steve and I went to our first ever concert. Pitbull was playing in Halifax. We had never been to anything like it. I couldn't stay seated; I love to dance too much. The music moves me. Steve thought it was too loud. I don't know what he was expecting! We drove home directly afterwards, something about work, I'm sure. Making plans never went as smoothly as it should have. Our company, drivers, and truck problems always changed our plans.

JJ was busy with his spring hockey league. He was playing for the Sharks. He had the best coaches that year, Devan, and Derrick. We travelled a lot with this team. It was not local, and we lived three hours from a major city so to be able to be a part of extra sports we had to drive. Practices were close to two hours away. Games were three to five hours away.

JJ also liked to fish. We took his fishing stuff on day trips where he had breaks in-between games. One day he told the coach he was going to catch him a fish. Well, we tried all afternoon and just as we had to head back to the rink, there it was. A big fish for Derrick. JJ brought that fish in and slapped it into the sink, right in the dressing room. The whole team was excited, however, the proud sparkle in my son's eyes will always be etched in my memory. He was bursting with pride. Derrick promised he was going to eat the fish for supper. Priceless memories. I was so thankful we finally caught that fish. He was so determined.

Natasha managed to make it to two of JJ's hockey games in Kentville. I loved it when she could be there watching her little brother. And it did my heart a world of good to see her.

Steve won a special Driver of the Year award, along with winning the provincials at the truck driving competition that year. Nationals would be in Moncton in the fall; it was our turn to host for the Atlantic provinces. I was always super proud of him; he was exceptionally good with manoeuvring big rigs. I won the spousal competition for an obstacle course in an SUV. It was a great feeling beating twenty or so ladies and being number one! I guess we are both competitive.

This was also the year Steve finally got his little procedure done. Mind you he had to be drugged up to finally get it done. I believe that with all women must endure giving birth, it is the smallest gesture for the man to have this done. Steve had many prior appointments for a vasectomy, but never went through with it. In his defence the doctor had said there's probably six or eight people out of the thousands that he had perform the procedure on who were as sensitive.

Steve was special alright. He feels pain like nobody else does. Every little thing is major to him. Super sensitive, I say. I've never seen anyone like him. I tease him about it all the time. He once cut himself. After sitting for a long time at the emergency department for his turn to see the doctor, the doctor told him to go home and put a bandage on it. Well to Steve's perspective, his finger was ready to fall off. I can't help but laugh when he has these moments.

I'm huge on family photos. In June we had a session done at our camp. We tried to get some in front of the lake and in the forest. We also sat on the road, under the trees. Everyone mostly co-operated, as they knew if they did, it would be over quicker.

Tristan was home from university with the intention of going back I thought. However, that changed, and he decided to stay home, work at our local hospital, and take a carpentry course. You must let them figure it out, but boy it's hard to watch when you have the knowledge from having been on earth longer and having gone through shit. The truth is you want to, but you can't make their decisions for them.

In the summer we took the boys to a hockey school in PEI. Great memories were made there, and we got to visit my cousin Nancy, and her twins. Driving there we stumbled across some tractor pulls, and they were pretty amazing. The kids were in awe, watching the beefed up tractors. Sometimes the unplanned events are the most memorable. We were always on the go with one thing or another. Sometimes I would say our life was in fast forward. We needed to slow it down and enjoy it more.

We did make time for Steve and me to take the Sea-Doo up the Annapolis River. That was fun, just exploring. As we came around one corner there were lots of cows standing in the river. We just zipped up between them. As the river got narrower, I told Steve to stay away from the ripples. He asked why? I couldn't believe that he didn't know why! There are rocks in those areas; what do you think causes the ripples? Apparently, I had put my life in the hands of an inexperienced boater. I should have clued in, as previously he had chewed the propeller off an old speedboat he'd bought to play with in the lake.

In August we lost another great man, Grandpere. One thing I know is how much he loved his grandkids. My boys were close with him. Especially Tristan, when he came home from university all he wanted was his birthday supper to include Grandpere. Of course we did and that was the last fun family time we had with him.

Steve was always looking for new opportunities. He somehow ended up driving a local tour bus just for fun. He did wine tours and trips to Peggy's Cove. He had never been to Peggy's Cove, nor had I. Therefore, our kids had never seen it either. The lighthouse sits on a cliff of huge rocks. Steve ended up doing a tour on his birthday, so I took the opportunity to meet him there with the kids. It was beautiful. We ate in the restaurant and walked around. On the way home I stopped at the Flight 111 site where a terrible accident had occurred. A plane went down and everybody on it perished. We read all the plaques. It was quite an eerie feeling to be at the monuments. How we had never taken a drive down to Peggy's Cove before, I'm not sure. This little gem of a tourist attraction was right under our nose. All these years of driving the main highway and we'd always went right by it.

In October I took Mom to Newfoundland. The water was beautiful on all our sightseeing excursions. Melanie was so happy to have us visit. She was the one I mentioned earlier that had stayed at Mom's boarding house. We rented a car and squeezed in as much as possible. Just seeing Mom's smile was worth the trip.

November brought the World Junior A Challenge hockey tournament to our little town. Our boys got to carry the flags in one of the opening games. They are huge hockey fans so this was a memory they will cherish for a lifetime. It was pretty neat having people from all over the world in our little town!

Christmas of course was always special. That year Shay and I had been to New York (as mentioned above and more information about this trip in my travel chapter), which put me in a special magical place. Sharon and her daughter Rebecca decided to spend Christmas with us. We just didn't know how many more Christmas seasons Mom would have with us. Especially where she could talk and be her silly self. Her Alzheimer's was definitely changing her, but she kept a good sense of humour.

Tristan and his girlfriend Hannah were with us too. We had a great time. I'm all about the presents under the tree; however, I usually can't tell you what they were. I just like everyone opening stuff and having stuff to open. We didn't have that in my childhood, so I've loved doing presents since it's been in my control. I did get my first robotic vacuum, which I loved and immediately knew I'd always have one or two around the house. News flash though: women do not want household items as gifts. It's a huge no-no! How is an appliance, which benefits everyone in the house, a personal gift? Come on people, buy your spouse a thoughtful, personally picked gift just for them. As it should be.

CHAPTER 34

Through The Years: 2013

Steve had coached JJ's hockey team for years. I was the team manager and often did the off-ice training. We volunteered a lot of time to hockey over the years. Since Steve drove the tour bus, he was able to take the whole team and most of the parents on a few road games. These were always fun, except for the hour and half drive in the worst snowstorm ever. I was thankful everyone arrived home safe and sound that night.

That year Shay and Steve went skiing with the school. Steve loved this as he'd skied a lot in his school years. Spending time with Shay doing the same thing brought back great memories for him.

We planned a trip to Boston. We explored the city with the kids and watched a couple of hockey games.

School was busy. The boys did huge projects on Day & Ross (the company we had contracts with), and JJ also picked Peggy's Cove (the place we had visited on Steve's birthday). They did a great job, and it was fun to help them with these. When I was a kid, projects were my favourite thing in school to do. I loved being creative.

Call me crazy, but I decided to get some pet goats. I had them when I was kid, so why not? When people would ask me why I wanted goats, I would tell them so my kids could learn how to shovel shit because life is not easy. Also, so they could take care of living animals and learn how to treat them. They wanted to bunk out with them the one night. They only made it to about midnight before wanting to go into the house to their beds. It was a great little adventure for a few hours. So cute.

I took on a joint account with Mom and did everything for her so she wouldn't have to worry. I arranged for an assessment to see what benefits Mom might be qualified for. The very first one was in 2012 and she didn't qualify for anything. During the second one in 2013 we began to wonder if she was ready to be put on the list for long-term care. Despite my brother stopping in, I arranged for my aunt to do some suppertime visits and cook, with myself doing every lunchtime.

The biggest thing I learned in that assessment was how alone my mom felt. She cried and told the lady she was always alone.

I often picked her up and brought her to my house for the day. She often spent overnights visits with us. I hadn't realized the minute we left her that she would forget we were ever there. She would sit in her apartment alone. She would walk the halls but the minute the conversation was over with a neighbour she would forget that she had seen someone.

In her mind she was alone 24/7 and no one was visiting.

I cried for her, heartbroken that she felt so alone.

Apparently because she could still dress herself, find something to eat, and do her laundry she was okay to live alone. She did qualify for some home care and if nothing else it brought a visitor in. I arranged for her to have home care. Mom was outgoing and I thought she would enjoy having someone to talk to for one hour a day. They would let me know if anything was wrong on a daily basis too.

Home care was there while she had her bath. She didn't need help, but they were there just in case. I would ask Mom about the visits, but she couldn't tell me much about them. I still felt better knowing she had more people stopping in. Things continued like this for most of 2013. Mom could still call me. It was only later when she lost that ability that I would realize how important it was.

Mom still went for walks on her own and could find her way back home. But later in 2013 things changed. Mom stopped using her stove, and we unplugged it. She could still eat stuff from her fridge and cupboards. I called for another assessment. This time she qualified for going on "The List," which at the time we were told it could be up to a year.

With careful monitoring I was hopeful she could stay in her apartment. I would say I was naive. I should have brought her to live with me that fall. The winter was scary because she got locked out so often. If you called and said a time you were coming to get her, she couldn't remember, so she would get ready and wait for hours in the entryway wondering when we were coming. Some of the neighbours distanced themselves from her because she was acting differently.

At one point I got a call from the RCMP who had taken her to the outpatient's department because she couldn't remember where she was going and wasn't dressed properly. Another time I got a call to come get her for the same reasons; she couldn't find her way home.

I was constantly worried about her. If I wasn't too busy, I just took her with me whenever I could.

Things were getting dangerous, so I called the assessment people again. She was now on the list but how long it would take to find her a bed was a mystery.

For Shay's Grade 6 graduation Steve was stuck working. For some reason we were too stupid to park our trucks back then for special occasions. One of those things if I had it to do it over I would have parked the damn truck when it was a special event. Steve should have been there. He was too stubborn to park them back then. At the time I thought it was okay, but over the years I began to realize how it really wasn't okay. You do not get those moments back.

Shay was still cooking up a storm. He entered dishes in the annual exhibition in a few different categories. He won lots of ribbons and some were first place.

Mom camped with us that summer. She loved being at the lake. Nancy my cousin and her twins enjoyed their annual visit, as well as Krysta and Dawson who were regulars for our summer adventures at camp. Tubing was a highlight, but not my favourite thing to do. I just liked a calm ride on the lake. Floating around on a hot day is also amazing.

JJ was into hunting and was told, "if you kill it, you eat it," so they had squirrel and frog legs over the campfire. They knew I was serious after that experience.

We dug a pond in the backyard. JJ was determined to have trout in it. Oh, the things we did for our kids.

JJ, Shay, and his friend Charlie decided to swim in the pond. Didn't matter that we had a pool, the pond was new. Boys will be boys, that's for sure. Especially if you let them! I definitely did, mud and all.

On the tenth of July, Shay got to cook with Laura Muise. She is a local chef. I followed her cooking journey, and she was inspired by Shay's young creativity. They made a delicious meal, which I got to be a guest to enjoy. This was during the renovation stages of The Hatfield House—an amazing restaurant Laura poured her soul into establishing.

Unfortunately, that year a friend of mine developed breast cancer. I learned lots from her about how sugar feeds diseases of all kinds. I will never understand why we poison ourselves with preservatives, sugars, and things that aren't even really food. If you can't pronounce the ingredients, it's probably not good for you.

Natural, real foods from the earth and the animals are how it was meant to be, not packaged junk. The things we put on and in our body are not how we should have evolved. But then again, I don't understand smoking and putting toxins into our lungs either.

I'm not saying I'm perfect, because I'm certainly not. But knowledge is power. I have the knowledge to know that we should be putting real foods into our bodies, and using real products on our bodies, not chemicals. Sounds pretty simple. I guess there is way too much available at our fingertips for people to realize how we are slowly killing ourselves.

My friend survived her cancer, and she still follows a healthy lifestyle. I just want to give her a personal shout out and let her know how much I love her. Hockey mom friendships are some of the best!

Luke visited in the fall and little did we know that one of the pictures we took of Mom and the family would end up being Mom's obituary picture. The picture was taking on November 22, 2013. We were simply playing with the goats and snapping a lot of family photos at the time.

In December we did a family outing on the tracks with the four-wheelers. We'd always go get a real tree in the woods, cut it down, and drag it home. Ever since Little Nan had died, I enjoyed getting a real tree and decorating it with her antique ornaments. This was special to me and just felt right. Like she is smiling down on us.

You could tell by this time that Mom had Alzheimer's, but she was still able to do things with us and go places with us. She was pretty funny doing the Christmas cookies with the boys that year, making faces while I was trying to take pictures, just like the boys were.

The boys assisted in making the apple pies. It was always Mom's job, but I had to take it over this year. It was just Grandmom sleeping over that year for Christmas, and the traditional big Christmas dinner where my brother, Tina, and CJ were present. I signed us up for the Boxing Day Turkey Run. My sons were not impressed, but I was! Tristan ran the whole thing, Shay and JJ finished, and Steve and I did a combination of walking and running. We have the pictures and medals to prove it.

CHAPTER 35

Natasha Comes To Town

As Natasha got older, she began to ask more and more questions. When she turned eighteen, she and I went on a shopping trip to Halifax. I brought all of Fred's love letters and pictures to show her. I didn't realize I hadn't told her his last name, Habib. Therefore, she had never been able to search on Facebook, or other social media, for him or his family.

That all changed that night as we snooped through everybody she was related to. I was able to explain who everybody was: her sisters, cousins, aunts, and uncles. It was information overload.

She had every right to be curious. Anybody would have been. I probably would have told her his last name sooner. If she had asked me earlier, I would have. But I seriously didn't realize that she didn't know. Facebook wasn't around for all my life. It was something new and I had only joined maybe in 2008.

We were in Halifax when she was eighteen, I believe it was December 29, 2013. I had found my peaceful place: with Natasha. We had a great relationship. I was excited that she wanted to spend time with me. It was great. We shopped and had fun, but I knew her mind was heavy with all the family members she had viewed—not knowing if she would ever meet them. I had mixed feelings about whether she should reach out. I always heard Fred's warnings in my head.

We kept in close contact into 2014. In fact, Natasha came to Yarmouth in August of 2014. We went to an exercise class together taught by my friend Jessica. It was a warm summer night. We also went for a run in the warm rain showers. We loved it and she'd stayed overnight.

On the fifteenth of August, we went into downtown Yarmouth. I was trying to find the right moment to take her into Jake's restaurant to meet her uncle. I didn't know how he would respond, but I had to try. I warned her I wasn't sure how things would go. Would he be mad? Would he be happy? Who knew? Soon, we were walking along on Main Street. At first, we walked right past. I couldn't go in. I never went there, as I wanted to leave the past in the past. But I had to do this for Natasha. Several deep breaths later and I knew I was ready, so we headed back.

As we got to the block where the restaurant was located, we had to cross at the crosswalk. Who was sitting there to let us cross? Her uncle, my old boss. As we approached his truck a funny thing happened; seagulls were flying all around and they splattered shit on us. I guess that's supposed to be good luck.

We reached his window, and I said that I wanted him to meet Natasha. He looked at me like he didn't know what I was talking about. So, I just kept repeating myself. This is her. This is Natasha.

He finally got the point and was so worked up that he parked the truck and jumped out to hug her and see her. He invited us into the restaurant to have something to eat. Even though he was on his way to an appointment, he made a few moments for her—taking her number, which he said he would relay to Fred. There were tears, and he was excited.

He said he couldn't wait to tell his son, about his beautiful cousin. He kept saying, "Oh my God. You're so beautiful," to Natasha. She was overwhelmed. I was thankful for his reception of her.

I kept repeating that I had brought her because it was not her fault. Fred and I were to blame, but not her. He agreed and was very sympathetic. I was surprised that he said he was going to tell his son about her. I wondered if he actually would because she was still a secret to the entire family, except for the brothers and maybe their wives. Or at least, as far as I knew. If they didn't know, they likely found out that day when he came home with his story of meeting her. Natasha was very happy with his reaction.

We headed out to camp for the rest of the day. We stopped at the house for a little bit, where I took the most beautiful picture of Natasha with her grandmother Norma, my mother. But she kept wondering when she would get a phone call from Fred. And so, did I. Would he be mad that I had taken her there? I didn't care. She was eighteen and had waited long enough to have her connection with his side of the family.

I never dreamed that the phone call would be on the same day, but after we had hung out and had supper, her phone rang. It was Fred. She cried and cried as she tried to talk to him in the chalet.

I tried to be there for her, but I really didn't know what to say. She was very overwhelmed as it had been quite an emotional day. First talking to her uncle, and then talking to her biological father Fred. It was way more than we had thought was possible for one day.

I spoke to Fred for a moment on the phone, but I don't remember what was said. I know he was compassionate on the phone. Fred and Natasha made plans to meet during Christmas when he would be back in Canada. I really didn't want her to leave and drive that day by herself. She was pretty emotional. But after a while she did head out for her parents' place in the Valley.

Well, that was that. She had made her connection with Fred. We still texted and talked a lot about the whole family. She was looking forward to finally getting to meet him.

I was shocked that when they finally did meet that he showed up empty-handed. Not even the smallest gift for her. Her birthday had just passed, Christmas was coming, and he had never met his daughter. How could he not bring her a memorable gift? I thought that was odd for him since he had always brought me stuff.

Natasha was heading for university in Toronto to attend a very prestigious university. I was so proud of her for being confident enough to move away and do this on her own. I always felt Fred was thankful that she was not going to university in Halifax, where she could run into other family members. He contacted her some, but not as much as she'd expected. He wasn't living up to the person she had imagined him to be in her mind.

I offered to meet Natasha in Toronto, figuring we could have some girl time and continue building our relationship. I was so happy with where we were. I felt such great relief knowing that our secret was out from under the rock. It was freeing.

I booked an amazing hotel at an amazing price. The perfect location. Ironically, it was brand new, but the same hotel chain Fred and I had stayed at while in Toronto. It was even more amazing when we ended up on the twenty-second floor, as if I had requested it, which I had not.

We toured the city, and she taught me how to use the subway. The aquarium was close by, so we checked that out and went shopping. Unfortunately, Natasha ended up with a cold and didn't feel like doing anything toward the end of our trip. Sometimes when you take time for a rest, that's when viruses will take over your body. Regardless, I loved the trip and spending time with her.

In the spring I was at a local aesthetic salon. I always had conversations about life with the lady who did my appointments. This particular day I had told her about Natasha meeting her uncle. Since it's a small town everyone knows everyone. This lady's sister had worked previously at Jake's, so she knew all about their family. Basically, we were gossiping. She didn't remember Fred. So, she asked to see a picture of him. I looked him up and showed her what he looked like. She didn't recognize him. I also showed her pictures of mine and Natasha's trip, thinking that I wasn't doing anything wrong. I wasn't! It actually felt great to talk about Natasha. She was eighteen. I saw no harm in being free from what I had kept under a rock for all these years.

I left there not thinking much about the conversation; I was just excited that Natasha had been in Yarmouth. And by the fact that she was finally getting to meet some of her extended family. Unknowingly, the same lady mentioned something to Natasha's uncles' wife, when she was in her shop.

She had no idea it would cause so much turmoil.

I guess he didn't go home to tell his son all about Natasha after all. His wife was furious that I had dared to show someone pictures of my daughter. Really? It's my life. I am proud of Natasha. She is eighteen and I wasn't ashamed to talk about her, or about my past relationship with Fred. It was a part of my life previously and I got to choose who I talked to about it—to keep her safe while she was growing up. Surely there was no reason to continue protecting her, now that she was an adult. They would just have to deal with her existence.

Shit soon hit the fan.

I was in South Carolina with JJ when I got a message from Natasha saying that Fred would appreciate it if I didn't show any more pictures of him or Natasha around town. He didn't want anybody's family getting hurt. I took that as a threat. He had no right to tell me what I could do anymore, or ever. I was furious. How dare he threaten me and use Natasha to give me the message. That was low, even for him. The bastard.

I played that comment over and over in my mind. He didn't want anybody's family to get hurt. Was he insinuating he was going to hurt mine? My peacefulness that I had felt concerning Natasha soon fell apart. She was hurt by how Fred was acting and that he still wanted her to be a secret for his own sake. It was my turn to be furious. How dare he? He was still trying to control my life. Natasha withdrew from both of us to take some time to figure things out. She really didn't know what to think and I was very hurt.

Around this time, I went for another spiritual reading with Kelley. I remember one of the things she told me was that our relationship had crumbled, but that it would build itself back up. Natasha would see her truths and we would start again. This took some time, as she just wanted to concentrate on her studies.

I was so hurt and felt like I'd lost her again.

She eventually came around and we slowly started working on our relationship again. In fact, she moved back home and decided to take her second year at Dalhousie University. Fred had let her know that he did not think that was a good idea and that she should stay in Toronto. I wonder how much of that was for his own selfish reasons.

Fred became a touchy subject. We didn't talk about him as much anymore. Fred also moved home from overseas, coincidently around the same time that Natasha moved home. He was in Halifax for a while. Then he decided to move to Newfoundland where his sister lived and had a restaurant. I'm guessing his pharmaceutical dream business did not work out since he was back working at his sister's restaurant. His marriage was officially over too, he was divorced.

I'm not sure exactly when it happened, but Natasha did tell me how much he'd hurt her when he had her meet him at a coffee shop. Which ended up being a coffee shop that his daughter either owned or worked at. Natalie her flesh and blood sister, Fred's daughter was there that day. Natasha had thankfully brought a friend along with her because she said she had no idea how she would have got through that meeting without her friend. Fred had the balls to introduced her to her sister as his "good friend's daughter." What a terrible thing to do. She was so torn up.

She texted me one day and said that Fred did not end up being the man she thought he would be. He had thoroughly disappointed her in many ways. He had hardly contacted her, and he didn't seem to be too interested in building a closer relationship. His loss because she is an amazing person.

I cherished every moment I got to be with her. I'd lost three-and-a-half years, but at least I got to see her grow up, even if it was from a bit of a distance. She's beautiful and she has an amazing, manifested, purpose in this universe. I love watching her grow and I know that she's going to do miraculous things.

A few years later Natasha started talking about writing a letter and giving it to one of her sisters. She had dated a Lebanese guy who was friends with her youngest sister's husband-to-be. They were still friends and he'd offered to help her out with her request. We often talked about it. I wanted her to wait until this book came out. It would take the pressure off her.

I had mixed emotions about her approaching them. I didn't think it would go over as well as when we'd approached her uncle. Unfortunately, my book was taking longer than I had planned. Ironically, that is exactly what Kelley told me in a reading in 2019. My book would take longer than I planned, but it would happen.

At the time I finished writing my book in February of 2021, Natasha had still not approached her sisters. She wanted to, very much, and maybe she will when the time is right. I will support and stand behind her, no matter what she decides to do. I believe I've communicated this to her well, and I've always offered my help if I could be of any assistance.

For the record, my book would not be published until 2022. There was still a lot of editing to be done. Plus, I couldn't possibly choose any other year to do so. It just wouldn't feel right.

CHAPTER 36

Through The Years: 2014

Miami here I come—with Jessica my cousin—for a short trip to start the year. We were still volunteering with hockey; in fact, I was managing both kids' teams.

Steve and I also took Shay and JJ to Mexico for some fun in the sun. Then in May I treated myself to a trip in Cuba with my friend Tanya since this was the year in which I was turning forty. We had an amazing trip. I love Cuba's beaches and the people are so genuine.

Natasha graduated that year. Tristan and I made the trip to watch her graduation. I hadn't raised her but that didn't stop me from being immensely proud of her accomplishments.

By February 2014, Mom had been out in the cold numerous times, and was thinking her neighbours were stealing from her. She was scared of the wind outside her windows and I knew we couldn't wait. It was time for a change. I found a private home willing to take her. We cleaned out her apartment and moved her in. She was upstairs in a nice big room. The move confused Mom even more and she had troubles taking care of herself. She started not knowing how to get to the bathroom or what to do if she did make it. She was into everything, even if it didn't belong to her. I visited often and the stories of what she was doing grew. Mom really needed one-on-one care and unless you are wealthy that's just not going to happen.

Mom also started having seizures that were serious, lasting up to twenty minutes. An ambulance was called for the first few. The doctor put her on Dilantin, however, she was acting way too drugged up for me to accept the need for the medication. There was a high risk of falls with her being so out of it. We adjusted the dosage many times and I'm not sure if it ever helped. After two months the home called and said Mom had to be moved out by the end of the month. She wasn't adjusting and was way busier than they could have imagined.

On the first of June Mom came to live with my family. The only other choice was to put her on an extended list for the first bed available in Nova Scotia. She could have gone anywhere. I couldn't do that to her. I couldn't send her off to be alone.

Mom kept me busy, and I adjusted to bringing her everywhere with me. My husband took over some of my business obligations and supported my decision to have Mom in our home. My kids showed her so much compassion it melted my heart.

Mom qualified for one hour a day of home care, and I got a few hours per week of respite care where I could leave her in the mornings. Often it was new workers, so I was constantly leaving her with strangers. Not to mention having strangers in my home. But I made it work.

That summer we took Mom to the camp a lot because she loved being with us. Thankfully, we made so many memories. I had been told by her case worker in June that Mom should have a placement by the end of the year, probably in the fall. Fall came and school and hockey all started. I hired private workers to care for Mom while I was travelling for hockey. The year Mom lived with us was probably my busiest ever. Two boys in hockey and I was the manager of both their teams, with a busy business to run, while still being a mom, wife, and running the house. Time flew by.

She must have gone for a respite stay in the summer because the five of us went to a hockey school in New Hampshire. We had a great trip—once we got there. The bus trip itself to New Hampshire was not fun. The bus broke down, before we'd even left Canada. The spare bus we ended up with was not much better. We had to stop twice to fix things along the way. Steve and a couple other parents fixed it enough to get us to a shop. We arrived close to 5 p.m. as they were getting ready to close. Steve knew what the bus needed, and after a case of beer, and some cash (that I supplied), we were back on the road and several hours later we finally arrived at our destination.

The trip home was no better. The bus developed new problems. The AC unit stopped working. We were baking in the bus. We finally tied the emergency windows open, for a breeze at least. When we stopped at a store, everyone was putting cold drinks in their shirts. Shay was sitting right in the ice freezer. We were all a sweaty mess. What a road trip to remember. I'm glad the stay in the mountains was memorable because the driving was not. We all said the next year we would be bringing our own vehicles.

The border crossing coming back into Canada was tricky. We were a busload and they picked me and another dad to take in the backroom for extra questioning. The look on the kids' faces showed they were scared for their mom. I seem to always get questioned because of being arrested back in the day when I hit that girl with a phone. It still haunts me when they ask if I had ever been to court? Had I ever been arrested? I must answer yes and explain why. I shouldn't have to because I was so young, and it wasn't supposed to follow me. But bad choices always follow you, and that's why I can't stress it enough to always make good choices.

The next year we did drive ourselves. We arrived a day earlier before the hockey camp started and stayed at a motel. We were in a heavily forested area—it was the mountains, after all. We were late in the evening checking in, just us and a couple other families. I sent Steve to the office to ask for more bedding.

We were outside chatting when we heard Steve screaming. He came running toward us, arms up in the air, yelling "Get the fuck in your rooms! There's a bear! Hurry up, get in your rooms!"

He was not being chased, but he had seen a bear when he went around the corner of the building. A huge bear apparently. He was flipping out, screaming. He didn't like the fact that I wanted to go see if I could get a picture.

None of us raced to our rooms since nothing was chasing him. But if you could have seen him, running, and screaming, you would have thought a whole family of bears were chasing him. This tale is always a must-tell story; we enjoy telling it quite often. It is shared with my 11:11 friend Tina, who was there.

I loved when Tristan would come with us on trips. It made my heart almost complete. He didn't always like to travel as much as we did, and I always felt he was missing out. I was glad he'd made this trip.

He was now twenty-one with his whole life ahead of him. In his teens he'd had a girlfriend for three years. I really liked her. She was a nice girl. They were young and I didn't think it was forever, but when you're young you assume it is. I'm pretty sure that's why he didn't do lots with us back then because he didn't want to leave her. Most teenagers are like that. It's okay, it's a learning curve that everybody goes through.

But this time, he was single, and enjoying life.

Tristan was soon heading off to PEI to take a course he had picked: Sheriff and Officer of the Courts. I was so proud he was finding his way in life. Good things happen when you work hard.

JJ went deer hunting with the neighbour that year. He was there when the neighbour shot a big one. Our neighbour is like a grandfather to my boys. He was always teaching them stuff and was always there when they needed something.

JJ started snaring rabbits, as he was too young to shoot them. I had snared rabbits as a kid, but I didn't have a choice as we'd needed the food. JJ got involved with hunting for the sport and the challenge, but he definitely enjoyed putting food in the freezer.

Hockey and hockey tournaments were a huge part of our life. We were always on the go with Shay and JJ playing at two different levels. I needed outside care for Mom to be able to be that many places. It was a struggle, but I did the best I could.

Mom lived with us, so she was there for Christmas. Tristan was home from PEI. We had a lovely Christmas. Shay got a dirt bike. JJ got a scooter. Shay was responsible so Steve wanted him to have the bike. JJ not so much, and we didn't dare get him one. Another example of how different interests, personalities, and wants always contributed to what we gifted our children. Tristan usually asked for car parts as he was forever changing vehicles.

We did our best. Others can do as they choose. Counting dollars and being even wasn't what we dwelled upon. Life's not fairly divided, but everything and everyone is different. Different views, styles, and rules. To each their own. Not passing judgment should be everyone's priority.

Parents teach your kids to not judge others. You can definitely have an opinion, but judgments are harsh. We are all individually created.

CHAPTER 37

Through The Years: 2015

February of 2015 was when my trip to Toronto to meet up with Natasha occurred and a chance to do some sightseeing. I was also super proud to go to Tristan's graduation in PEI. He graduated with high recommendations and a new outlook on life. He thanked me for always pushing him to do his best, for keeping a clean house, and for teaching him how to eat and be healthy.

I was never prouder of the man he had become.

Finding your way in life is not easy, and it's never going to be easy. And it never gets any easier. Hard work and determination are the only things that get you through. Tristan has some of these traits, like me. I also have a "never give up" attitude. I hope all my children develop that one as well. Life is hard, and they will need it to get through.

These times are different, especially when raising kids. Everything is evolving constantly. Things were so much easier before technology started taking over the world. Makes one wonder what the future holds.

Shay graduated from Grade 8 and JJ from Grade 6. They were both doing well in school; however, they could have been doing phenomenal if they studied more. But my boys wanted to be outside playing. They didn't want to be in the house, and I couldn't blame them. I loved being outside until dark as well.

Tristan was in Halifax working at the shipyard. He was actively looking for a full-time job in his field of choice. After a few months, the opportunity arose. A job in Thompson, Manitoba in a city policing pilot project was available. He applied and the next thing we knew, Steve was driving with him across the country. Steve went as far as Winnipeg and flew home, leaving Tristan to drive the last eight hours on his own. How could this be, my baby off conquering the world all alone. The city was terrible, but he did meet some great friends.

While Mom was living with us, I had a past and present moment collision. One morning the home care girls arrived for my three hours of free time. Mom required two nurses for her level of care. This day they each brought a trainee with them. I was in the kitchen when they came in. When I looked up and I saw the last girl coming through the door, I was shocked. On my porch stood one of my teen bullies.

Tracy came in praising me for taking care of my mother. She was going on and on about how she'd loved reading the story in the newspaper about Mom and me. I was baffled by her obvious fake behaviour. I was put on the spot. No way would I ever leave my mother with such a cruel person. Her bullying of me in Grade 9 still cuts deeply in my memories. I will never forget how she treated me.

I listened to her praise for a moment, then I found my voice and told her exactly what I thought. I told the other ladies that she needed to get out of my house. I could not be expected to have her caring for my mother. It wasn't happening!

I asked her if she remembered what she had put me through? She denied it all. Maybe bullies really are that stupid. She didn't remember putting me and other people through hell. I believe she knew but chose to act like it hadn't happened. I don't know, but I did know she had to go.

Her trainer took her back to the office. The other nurse stayed with her trainee. I was shaking. I felt so empowered to have thrown Tracy out of my home. She was never getting the best of me, ever again.

I had overcome all my bullies years ago and when I see them in my adulthood, I have no fear of them. I guess I can thank them for making me as strong as I am today. Despite never being in a fist fight ever in my life. I am told I have a "don't mess with me aura." I will take that as a compliment because as you have read, my road getting to that accomplishment was a long one.

I do believe in speaking up for yourself. No one else has your back, so you must have it for yourself. I believe you shouldn't let people walk all over you. Also, don't be afraid to ask for something. You have two choices: ask for it and possibly get it, or don't ask, and you will never know. You will get further in life by asking for help, things, and opportunities.

I am known to always ask for a good deal, and I usually get it. Often my deals are massive, and I love to barter. Even if it's a savings of ten dollars, it's better to have it in your own pocket than theirs.

By May of 2015, I was tired. They could not tell me how much longer before Mom got a bed. Mom's condition had progressed, and they changed her paperwork to needing a lockdown unit. They recommended I change her options and to add Caledonia to her choices. With it being two hours away it was a hard decision. In June, I did add it as an option and within two weeks she got a call to be placed, with the condition she would get a bed closer to home as soon as one became open. For three months I travelled to Caledonia. I couldn't go there everyday as it was four hours just in driving time. Mom was losing weight as it was hard to get her to sit still to eat. She just walked and walked. I would take her outside for fresh air when I was there. I really wasn't there enough. Three months passed and I got the call that Mom could go to Meteghan. Thankfully it was closer, but every move was hard on Mom and took so much from her.

This was the year that Steve started racing. I knew the previous year when he took the kids to watch numerous races that I was in trouble. What most people don't know is he had sold all his racing stuff before he met me. I had never seen any of it. He had never talked about doing it again either. I had no idea what was in store for us.

As it turns out it is quite an expensive sport, especially when you need something new every time you turn around, or something gets broken.

His first ever race he didn't even have a chance. There was another car on the track that lost their brakes and took him out. He hit the wall, hard. He got out of the car complaining about his back and laid on the ground waiting for the ambulance in front of all the spectators. The kids were at the fence very worried about their dad. My heart was ripped in a million pieces—my husband was laying on the ground and my kids were at the fence with tears in their eyes. What was I doing here with my children? That was what I kept asking myself.

Some of the people racing didn't seem to have much in life but boy, they had a beat-up old race car on the track. I feel it's a sport where people do not have their priorities in line. Things completely blew up when I stated my opinion about somebody going on the track, knowing full well that they didn't have any brakes. Were they seriously trying to kill somebody?

Of course, this statement didn't make me very popular not knowing very many people at the racetrack. Especially since the man that took Steve out was very well known. He was a veteran at the track. Regardless, I'm entitled to my opinion and the accident should not have happened.

His daughter and his girlfriend ended up being quite the challenge for me to be around. They didn't scare me off, but I did not want to be a part of their drama. Steve was okay and managed to get the car fixed for the next race weekend three weeks later, against my wishes. Little did I realize that this was going to be the main topic of our arguments for many years to come. The racer that caused Steve's crash did publicly apologize to Steve and our family for the distress he'd caused.

Many people believe that I wear the pants in our relationship, but I will tell you, there would be no race cars and no money spent on racing in our home if that were the case. I don't get to make every decision. Yes, I am definitely headstrong and don't back down, but this is one thing Steve always did against my wishes and better judgment. I saw it as a money pit. He saw it as an amazing opportunity for himself. He loved it. Who was I to take it away from him?

I just prayed that the novelty would wear off and he would realize this was not where we should be spending all our hard-earned money. Not to mention every spring, summer, and fall was being consumed with only racing and repairing race cars. What about taking the kids to the beach and doing other things with them that got lost in the confusion?

We did always manage a hockey school trip, thankfully. We went to Waterville Valley in New Hampshire, in the mountains. That was the year JJ and I stayed for two weeks. We went to Boston for a tournament on the first weekend. We even managed to squeeze in a ball game at Fenway Park. Then Steve and Shay met up with us for the second week. It was a mix of hockey and family fun. There was swimming, biking, hiking, golf, games rooms, and a beautiful town square. The parents had just as much fun as the kids. We went there for a few summers.

Later that August I flew to the Dominican Republic for my cousin Jessica's wedding. I'm not a fan of flying in the summertime. There is so much to do around home, but I felt I should go. I had babysat her when she was a little girl. I was close to her mom and the whole family—the only ones from my father's side of the family that I have anything to do with.

That fall, the Nationals for the trucking competition were held in Regina. Steve placed second in his division, which was a huge accomplishment when you are competing against the best in the country. We always enjoyed our trips to the Nationals. Expenses paid, meeting new people, and exploring new places. Afterwards we drove across the province to Tristan's place in Thompson, Manitoba. I wasn't going to be that close to my son and not travel the extra miles to see him.

Thompson was a terrible place to live. It is in the middle of nowhere. Very lonely and isolated. Tristan was in the city policing unit. He dealt with difficult people every day. I didn't realize until years later how this would negatively affect him. Tristan showed us all around but there really wasn't much to see. He had been there since June after getting his full-time job.

Steve turned forty on the twenty-fifth of September. I believe everyone should celebrate milestone birthdays. So, I hired a band to play music at our camp and I planned a huge surprise for him! Everything went great, but it was a tad bit chilly for an outdoor party. We were all wrapped up in blankets. The band, however, was great.

While Mom had lived with us for a time, eventually she did have to go into a long-term care facility. As stated previously she had started out in Caledonia. But now she had to change care facilities from Caledonia to Meteghan. This timeframe was a huge adjustment for me and her. I had this nagging need to take care of her and this move would mean that I could do so more often.

Mom was in Meteghan for two weeks before disaster struck. I was going to miss a day seeing her to get ready for Thanksgiving and to bring her home for an overnight visit. I got a call from the home that she had likely broken her hip. I met the ambulance at the hospital where Mom reached out for me; she was in so much pain. I will never forget the look on her face.

The doctor on call took me aside and because I am the POA asked me what my decision would be. Did I want her to have the operation, or did I want to leave her as is, where she would eventually get pneumonia and die. I had no idea it was even a question. I assumed she would get the operation. I hadn't realized I'd have to choose her fate. Shortening her life? Of course, I wasn't going to leave her in that amount of pain for an unknown length of time to eventually die.

She was transferred to Kentville for surgery. Thanksgiving was put on hold. I wasn't leaving Mom. I stayed by her side for two days as she waited for the surgery. When she finally came out, she was wired, trying to get out of bed, and not understanding why she couldn't. I went to bat for Mom at that time. I pushed for one-on-one care because if she didn't get it and fell out of bed or tried to walk, she could rip her titanium hip right out of place and ruin the results of the operation. Somehow it got approved and Mom recovered for six weeks in Meteghan, with the extra care.

Despite the physiotherapy recommendations, Mom got very little time spent with her. I tried to do the range of motion exercises for her as often as I could. Then I got the best news ever. Mom was coming home to the Villa in Dayton where she would be just five minutes away from me.

Finally, I could be there with her every day again.

She was now in a chair, but the rehabilitation offered at the Villa in Dayton would be better for Mom. She would have her own room again, get to sleep undisturbed, and be in a better environment.

In December, Steve was playing hockey with the gentlemen's league. I received a phone call from one of the arena workers. He started off by saying, "Steve's okay, but something has happened," which, of course, makes you think the worst. My mind was racing. Why hadn't Steve called me? Apparently, he was in too much pain, laying on the ice. He had snapped his ankle.

He ended up needing surgery in Kentville, and the injury would not be capable of weight-bearing for quite some time. He was used to being active, not to mention working every day, so this was a big change. The first two weeks he sat around moping, and not taking care of himself. He paid the price for that choice because he developed blood clots and needed to go on blood thinners for the second time in his life. All because he let himself get so dehydrated. He couldn't be bothered to use the crutches to go to the washroom, so he thought it was easier just to not drink anything. I did notice he paid a lot more attention to drinking water daily after this happened the second time. I often say, *some people need to learn the hard way.* Steve was definitely one of those people.

It was in December of 2015 when Norma spent her first week at her new forever home and the struggles were real.

We gave Mom lots to drink during the day, as it was good for her and helped with her constipation. But she wasn't being taken to the bathroom often enough. So unfortunately, she would soak through her clothes and chair. I understood she was time-consuming, and I didn't know when everyone's breaks were, but I was hopeful that she could be taken more frequently. Also, when I was there, I didn't mind being the second or third set of hands to help with her. If she was sound asleep it was okay to let her sleep and take her when she woke up, like right before lunch or supper. Still, it didn't always seem to work out.

Regarding her bath I was told so many different things. I said from Day One I wanted her to try the whirlpool. I also kept asking to make sure that I could be present to talk her through it and to help. On Sunday they said they couldn't give me a specific time, but it wouldn't be in the morning. When I arrived, they advised me that she had been given a full sponge bath in her room that morning, and did I want her to go to the hairdresser? Yes, at some point, but I thought she was going to try the whirlpool today. The nurse advised me she didn't think the whirlpool would work for her. I still insisted we try it sometime. The nurse finally said we could try it at 2 p.m. She was sleepy but physio always got her going and she loved the bath. I could be there on Mondays at this time, and I wanted to be there to help.

Little did I know this particular nurse would be very difficult to work with in the future. She often had different opinions than what the family wanted, and she frequently tried to get the other nurses to side with her. I never backed down, but I also knew I had to be careful about what I said since these nurses were all that Mom had for help when I couldn't be there.

I found her toileting schedule that I had requested was not being followed or even given a fair chance. The system is so broken for providing seniors with dignity. The ones who can toilet themselves do OK, along with those who can ask, ring a buzzer, and wait their turn. But the ones with no voice are the ones overflowing their diapers and sitting in it until they get their turn.

Also, Mom needed to be talked to. I'd hold her hands and talk about trying to pee and poop. She needed at least fifteen minutes sometimes, especially if trying for a BM, and she might need longer. I did not find that some of the nurses were willing to talk her through things as I had noted she needed. I found some went about the job of changing her and assisting her without saying much. Mom was time-consuming. But does that mean she had to give up her dignity of being able to use the toilet and instead go in her Depends?

I noticed when a nurse was excellent with her and talked with her. Not all residents needed this, but Mom did. It was easy to make her laugh if you kept the air lighthearted and friendly. Roseanne was one of the nurses who Mom responded well to; Mom loved her bubbly voice and was all smiles and laughing.

Her hands needed to be held out of the way for toileting, getting her dressed, etc. On her busy days I held her hands while feeding her. The nurses mentioned her hands were always in the way too. Yes, they were, and that's why they needed to be gently controlled!

On the eighth day I didn't feel she was provided with sufficient fluids to drink, but it is true that she does drink better when I was there. The nurses mentioned she had no luck on the commode that day. So many seniors get a minimal number of drinks in the day, and they are likely dehydrated.

Christmas was always my favourite time of year. The Christmas lights, pretty decorations, the music, the hustle, and atmosphere are all things I love. I especially loved the family getting together for an amazing meal. I took over this job when Mom could no longer do it, but I did enjoy doing it. Feeding people is my thing.

I never minded cooking extra when the kids had friends over, or if family stopped by. It was never a problem for me. We brought Mom to our house for Christmas Day that year as I couldn't imagine Christmas without her present. I remember her watching me do some of the cooking. I parked her in her wheelchair where she could watch.

I also loved the gifts under the tree since I never had that as a child. It didn't matter how much things cost, as long as there were boxes under there for everyone to open. The excitement of opening gifts, especially when they are little, was priceless.

CHAPTER 38

Through The Years: 2016

M om was settling into the Villa nicely. It was so nice having her close. A few people that used to visit her could see her again. My friend Tammy was one of them. She loved Mom as if she was her own mother. I was so tired after having had Mom live with me for the year. I decided to do a solo trip to Cuba so I could just lay on the beach, read books, and just rest. Tammy was there for Mom while I was gone, and this was really comforting for me. I hated for Mom to be alone as she couldn't speak for herself. Life is just so unfair.

Steve understood, to a point, but he never liked me to be away. I always took everyone's feelings into consideration, but sometimes I still took the time for myself, even though I felt guilty for doing it. Only later in life would I learn that I should have done more for myself. (Just as everyone reading this book should also do.) People should not feel guilty for taking care of themselves. You cannot take care of other people unless you take care of yourself. I have always said that, and I know it's true. But it is still a hard thing to do.

I also found yoga and it proved to be a saving grace for me, especially during my time tending my mother. An hour to be away from your phone and the responsibilities. To just breathe and flow through the movements.

Heavenly really, and we were so lucky to have our own little yoga studio in our little town.

I came home recharged from my Cuban trip and submersed myself back into taking care of everyone. I did have an Air Miles trip planned for the four of us to go to Jamaica, however, with Steve's slow recovery after breaking his ankle he did not feel stable enough to go. Our sweet Shay decided to stay home and keep his dad company. So, it was just JJ and I off to explore Jamaica.

When I returned, I decided to get a tattoo. I had always said I would never want a tattoo, but something within me changed. I wanted a blue bird on my ankle with a heart in its mouth. This bird would represent Mom, and the heart would represent Mom holding my heart. I also wanted an open fancy heart on the back of my neck, as I feel I have a lot of love to give unconditionally and openly.

I decided to go to Cuba again, one more time; just five nights this time. My daughter was completing her second year of university and I really wanted to spend some time with her. I would do anything to spend time with her. I loved being with her and we had a nice trip. She always had questions about her father's family, and I tried to answer them the best I could.

We were both hopeful that one day she might meet her three sisters, despite the fact they still didn't know she existed. She wanted to reach out to them. She was an adult now and she could do what she wanted. But I wasn't sure what to tell her. I was still frightened by some of the threats Fred had always told me existed for her. He was a coward not to tell his daughters they had another sister. At times Natasha and I wanted to scream it from the rooftops.

As I've said before, nobody has the right to keep any part of your life under a rock. This book tells my story for the whole world to know. I'm not ashamed; my path was set out for me, and I had to take it. It has made me who I am and I'm proud to be where I am today. There are no mistakes, just life lessons. If you look at it that way you will be more positive in life.

Steve picked me up in Halifax from the airport after my trip and we returned home the following day to discover one of the biggest surprises in my life. Despite being asked if I wanted to race in the women's races at Lake Doucette and answering "No!"—I was fine just watching my husband race—Steve had taken it upon himself to buy me a race car and fix it all up. The kids had even helped to paint it.

I believe it took me two whole weeks of biting my tongue, and the kids saying, "Mom, are you even going to try it?" before I said I would try it.

Did I want to race? No.

Did I decide to race? Yes.

I often told people the only reason I decided to race was to impress my husband. That is the only reason I raced. Sure, I loved it when I won. But the drama at that track was not my cup of tea. Now I was going to be racing with two of the girls who absolutely hated me because I had spoken my mind. How did that sound like fun to my husband? Let's get my wife a race car. I've never understood why but somehow, he thought it was a good idea at the time.

Shay had moved on from doing a lot of cooking to finding projects in the garage to work on. It broke my heart that cooking wasn't his thing anymore. He was almost embarrassed that people knew how good a cook he was, even though there was nothing to be embarrassed about. Most people would love to be able to cook like he could. Regardless, he was now building a souped-up lawn mower from parts that he had collected. It turned out to be pretty cool.

Shay was very proud of his accomplishment as he had put a lot of hard work and many hours into making his project come to life. He had a couple of older friends that convinced him to enter it into the local car show. There was a category for young people. His lawn mower won first prize and I will never forget the look on his face while receiving his trophy. These were the best memories.

Our pet goats had baby goats of their own. Which meant lots of work for me because I had decided to milk the moms to make yogurt and cheese. Not sure how I thought I had the time to do the milking, but I didn't let that stop me.

Mom had done it when I was younger, so for some reason I thought I needed to try it too. My roots and where I came from weren't very good, but I still held onto some of the things I had learned from those early years.

I guess I'm a sentimental type of person. I hold on to things that mean something to me. Good memories are at the top of my list.

Tristan took three weeks of vacation in June and came home to see everyone. While home, he was going to the YMCA where he had met a girl that he couldn't stop talking about. He kept saying there was no sense in asking her out because he was leaving. Well as it turned out, she was telling her friend the same thing. She was heading over to Thailand to teach, but they both were interested in each other. Finally, Tristan got his nerve up to ask her on a date.

When I met Sam, I immediately liked her. She's smart, cute, sweet, and a hard worker. She was into a healthy lifestyle, working out and didn't do drugs, and only occasionally drank. She was much better than the last girl Tristan had brought home. That one—that he was trying to save—had turned out to be a nightmare. Little did he know that one actually must want to save oneself before one will give up the bad lifestyle. I was never more thankful than when that relationship ended.

I remember saying to Sam, "You just never know. If this is meant to be it will work out. You won't know unless you try."

She went out to see where Tristan lived and worked up north before her placement in Thailand started. Soon after, Tristan began making plans to spend his Christmas Break in Thailand since she would be teaching there. It was quite the trip and vacation for him. We missed him at Christmas, but I was glad he was with Sam. That's the story of their beginning.

As for the rest of my 2016, we enjoyed our time at the camp. The kids had a fun water mat in the lake and the sunsets were always beautiful. It was definitely my happy place.

JJ and I went to Debbie's wedding, (my neighbour from when I was a child). It's funny how your lives cross paths again. She married Dave, who is a friend of my husband Steve. One of those small world things.

We took part in the summer car show on Yarmouth's Main Street. Shay with his lawn mower, Steve with his blue Camaro, and me with my AMC Spirit. Dave and Debbie had cars too. In fact, we have lots of friends that had cars in that show, which made for a good day.

That year's Nationals were held in Ontario. Steve and I went a few days early to explore Niagara Falls and enjoy our time together. Steve had his highest score ever at Nationals that year. He had an awesome day. But there was a young guy who had never taken part in a trucking competition before who came in and swept it all. We had never seen anyone with scores that high before.

So once again Steve placed second at Nationals, even though in my books he had definitely won. I was always proud of him. He knows what he's doing when it comes to the trucking competitions.

I believe that fall was the first time JJ got a deer, which was a big accomplishment. JJ was good at anything he set his mind to. The kid would watch YouTube videos on how to hunt better, how to fish to catch the big ones, and he absorbed it like a sponge. Too bad he didn't do that with his school work.

JJ was playing hockey in Shelburne, which was an hour away since he hadn't been picked for the rep team in our hometown. Anyone with a child that plays hockey knows how important it is to be on the top teams. We might have had to drive a little bit more that year, but JJ was definitely on the best team ever. They won everything all year. We knew some of the families on the team from playing spring hockey, but we made even more new friends. It's funny how things work out sometimes. It really was for the best.

At our house I turned Tristan's old room into a gym for myself. I love having my own space to be able to workout whenever I want to. I learned over the years that I could not go very long without a workout. Missing one day was okay, two days was manageable, but if I got to the third day and hadn't had a chance to workout, it affected my mental health. Realizing this for yourself is very important. So many of us would benefit from the six best doctors in the world: sunshine, water, rest, air, exercise, and a clean diet.

I have learned a lot through the years and I continue to learn as I go forward. I want to be the best version of myself that I can possibly be. Strong and capable, not weak and always sitting on the couch. I have a strong determination to keep me going, and to never give up.

My Aunt Thelma had always been a part of my life. From visiting her cottage in the summer, going to Apple Blossom parades together, hanging out with her daughter Lori, and her coming to visit with Mom. I knew her better than any of my other aunts it seemed. While Mom was in the Villa, she made the effort to visit her. During one visit she told me to be prepared and to expect a breakdown once Mom was gone. I had put so much of my time and effort into Mom's well-being that she expected me to crash. I brushed it off thinking no, I am strong, and was just doing what I needed to do.

I guess time would tell if I had anything to worry about.

Around this time, I decided to get another pet cat for the house from a rescue shelter I had heard about. I was completely drawn to one particular cat—as always, an orange cat stood out to me. I had one when I was a little girl and those have been the only type of cat I have ever had.

When we had been at the Nationals that year, there had been a nurse there checking all the drivers' vitals. That was an eye-opening day for Steve. We both decided that we needed to lose some weight. Some of our friends were on the ideal protein diet so we decided to give it a try. The Christmas season seemed to be the best time for us to try it. Why pack on another five to ten pounds before starting? We only had our Christmas dinner as a treat. The rest of the time we followed the program and did great. When you set your mind to do something, be strong and just do it. It is also easier if you have the family's support. Clear all the temptations out of the house and give it one hundred and ten per cent to achieve your success.

CHAPTER 39

Through The Years: 2017

S teve, Shay, and I were all doing the ideal protein diet and were doing really well. The weight falls off males easier than it does for females. The more muscle in your body, the more fat it needs to burn. Steve lost about 50 pounds. I got well under a weight of 200 pounds, promising myself that I would never go back over 200 pounds again.

Weight was something I had always struggled with, and I knew I always would. Shay was young. It's way easier to lose weight when you're young. He did a great job, and he felt wonderful. His confidence and walking around the house singing were what made me the happiest. I knew he was happy in his body.

Coming from the place of many years of never being happy in my own body I was very pleased for his progress. We stayed on the diet until April, and slowly started the maintenance phase. Common sense is if you go back to all your old eating habits, you will gain the weight back. It's not that hard to make good choices, if that's what you surround yourself with.

In saying that, we were soon heading out on a cruise, where we all fell off the wagon and enjoyed the delicious food. Everything was included. It was too hard to pass it up. But I fit into the smallest size I could ever remember fitting into. What an amazing feeling that was.

When we returned home, I remained on a low carb, high protein, healthy eating plan. Steve mainly did the same, but Shay was a teenager, so he was eating all sorts of things. It took quite a few months before it caught up with him. I was heartbroken, knowing he was going to struggle with this for his entire life. Sugar is very addictive, and the more you eat of it, the more you crave it. I had heard many times it is just as addictive as cocaine. I do believe this, as I've struggled with it so much myself.

Some of us love food. I definitely do! I also love to cook. The kids accuse me of always trying to make foods healthier, instead of just going by the recipe. I figure some better choices are better than none at all. And I always try to help us all out by making healthier versions of things. Over the years they have called me a health fanatic, instead of just appreciating what I was trying to do for each of us.

I was doing my best, but even Steve at times would make me feel like I was doing something wrong. The attitude at the supper table was not always what I wished for—especially since cooking and feeding everyone was my sole responsibility. Again, I had always struggled with my weight, so I didn't wish to see my family do the same. I taught them the best way I could. They know how to make good choices and how to make healthy food. The rest is up to them.

When we got home from the cruise Shay asked for a ride over to a girl's house. He had never showed any prior interest in dating. But suddenly, our little boy went from building stuff in the garage to now wanting to spend time with a girl. Apparently, she had pursued him. We were also surprised to find out that she was two years older. Why would an older girl want to date our younger son? Shay didn't even have his licence. He did, however, have a dirt bike.

Shay learned how strict I was when he got caught taking the dirt bike into town and up the sidewalks to visit his new girlfriend. First love, and our first real challenge in parenting him.

Things might have been more relaxed if they were the same age. Shay was smitten quite quickly. He had been good with money up to that point, but that sure changed when he had a girl to impress. I wasn't allowing my sixteen-year-old son to have a girl in his room. I at least wanted them to be together for a while before I became more lenient with the rules. Overnight, I went from not worrying about my boy because he was always in the garage creating things to now worrying because he had a girlfriend. There were a lot of adjustments to get used to. He let his marks slide, but soon picked them up after I grounded him. I was the meanest mom around for a while. Tough love is always rough.

After the cruise we had planned a family trip to meet Tristan and Sam in Winnipeg. Sam had moved home from Thailand in the spring and after a few weeks she had moved in with Tristan in Thompson. I hadn't seen Tristan at Christmas, so I was determined to get there to see him.

You wouldn't think April weather would be a problem, but the fog delayed us, and our trip took fifty-six hours just to get to Winnipeg. It was ridiculous. But we did make it there and we made some funny memories.

That year Steve won the provincial truck driving competition once again. However, funding for Nationals fell through, so we knew we wouldn't be going on that free trip in the fall.

JJ graduated from Grade 8. Now both boys would be in high school the following year. My baby JJ was fourteen. He wanted to go out to Thompson, Manitoba, to see Tristan for a couple of weeks. This was a great idea until it came time to drop him off at the airport. He had never flown alone, but I was confident I had taught him well. Still, as a parent it was hard to drop off a fourteen-year-old off on his own at the airport.

He had a direct flight to Winnipeg and had to wait for his connecting flight to Thompson. But he made it. They had a great time during his visit. They went fishing, and he hung out with Sam when Tristan was working. Some friends of Tristan's in Thompson (who I met when I was there) ended up flying from Thompson to Winnipeg the same day JJ did on his return trip. To everyone's surprise they were on the same flight. This was perfect because he had a long wait for his flight back home and they entertained him until it was time to drop him back off at the airport. I was so thankful for great friends.

It was Steve's idea that Shay should start racing that year at sixteen years old. My idea was to wait until he was at least eighteen, but I didn't win that argument. Shay took over my car and Steve built me a new one. I wasn't impressed that he had put me into an automatic that first year since I wasn't winning. Why had he set me up for failure? Once I got the standard transmission car, I started to see a lot more trophies and checkered flags. Shay won Rookie of the year and of course, he fell in love with racing.

It was fun, I'm not going to lie. But it still wasn't necessarily my first choice of what I wanted to be doing in the summer. I would do my yoga breathing once I was strapped into the car. It was usually hot waiting to go out on the track and doing this would relax me. I would also be asking myself, *What the hell am I doing this for?* Often, I would have rather been at the beach, but there I was impressing my husband, I guess.

Racing seemed to consume all our family time. If we weren't racing they were working on the cars in the garage. Not me. I went for walks and bike rides by myself in the evenings, worked in my gardens, and enjoyed my sunsets while they were all in the garage. All the time. It was kind of lonely, but I loved nature and the outdoors.

Shay and his dad had been working on a special project—rebuilding an old truck. After Shay had built the lawn mower, he felt that he was ready for a big project. We had purchased two different trucks. One for the motor, and one for the body. They were busy putting them together to make one truck. The deal was Shay would never be able to sell the truck. It would be put into both Steve and Shay's names for that very reason.

JJ got to go on an amazing trip to Europe, playing more competitive hockey, and enjoyed hours and hours of fishing. He had different interests then Shay. My boys were all different from each other.

I didn't tally up the cost or really know what this truck was going to cost in the long run. But I felt it was still a great opportunity for Shay to have that experience with his father. Tristan's father was always starting projects with him but, unfortunately, I never saw many of them completed. It broke my heart because I know if his grandfather were still around, things would have been very different for him.

His grandfather was the most patient man and would have loved to build an antique car with Tristan. Tristan had inherited his grandfather's red truck, which was the last one he had built before he passed away. That was really special. Tristan was out west during the car show that year. But we did manage to get Shay's truck into town even though it wasn't yet completed. Steve and I also had our cars there. I loved doing things as a family and keeping our kids close to us.

And that was Steve's main argument when it came to racing. We would do it as a family! Family fun time. I can tell you I had to remind him of that fact many of times at the track when he would get all worked up, and angry over something not going right. It soon took the fun out of it for me. The drama at the track can be overwhelming and I'd be asking myself, *why am I here?* I also wondered if Shay's truck project would ever be completed. As it would slide to the background with each new racing project.

Racing took priority over our business, over all the regular life stuff, and now the truck was sliding down the list too. I did come to some sort of terms with Steve's racing obsession when a spiritual reader told me it was his thing, and that I should be letting him do it. He needed it and he would resent me if I was the one who forced him to stop. So, I waited patiently for the day when he would come to his senses and see that it was too much. It was too much time. It was too much money. We had to plan for our retirement, and without saving for a rainy day we would have nothing. He wasn't agreeing with me that things had to change. It was our main topic to argue about and it was affecting our relationship.

We had always talked about everything and tried to compromise the best we could. Racing was just above and beyond anything I thought I would ever have to deal with. Our kids were getting a huge privilege, since our company was sponsoring their hobbies. I could see how unrealistic this was; however, Steve could not. I believed we were setting them up for failure. They needed to learn life's lessons and pave their own paths in life. Hard work does pay off but would they ever get to learn that lesson for themselves.

I enjoyed biking a lot that summer, since with my knee problems I really shouldn't be running anymore. Picking blueberries was another favourite thing to do and I had a lot of them growing around the camp.

Mom would have loved this activity but, unfortunately, she was confined to a wheelchair and in a nursing home.

I planned a Tedford reunion for my mother at the camp. It was difficult to get her there in her wheelchair. We had to use plywood to be able to move her around on the gravel. But the look on her face when she arrived and when she could see the lake was priceless. She knew where she was, and she loved being there. She got to see many of her family. My heart was filled with these memories for her.

Since there were no Nationals that year we planned our own trip, and we picked Old Quebec to visit, flying into Montreal and driving. I love to travel and explore and we had a beautiful time. That year we got to travel again because when Steve asked me what I wanted for Christmas, I replied that all I wanted was to experience New York with him. It was a completely magical trip, and I cannot wait to go back. New York has this feeling, and it's so special to experience. While we were there, New York had its first snowfall of the season. Watching people experience their first snow ever was priceless.

CHAPTER 40

Through The Years: 2018

The year 2018 would be one for the books. My good friend Trina whom I had been friends with since we were teenagers lost the most precious person in her life just days into the year.

Trina was the grandmother of a beautiful boy named Mason. One day as I got up to head to my gym, one of my kids mentioned that there was a terrible fire thirty minutes from our home. I knew a lot of people in the area, and I immediately felt that I was going to know the people. I remember thinking, *I don't wanna know!*

After that I must have looked at Facebook because I found out it was Trina's grandson and three other beautiful children who had died in the fire. I immediately called my friend Trina and we talked.

How had this had happened? Life is so unfair, and nobody could make sense of this tragedy. We cried and cried. It was unimaginable. Trina's daughter Megan had lost her only son. This was one of our truck driver's grandsons as well.

I'm not sure if I even pedalled my bike that morning in the gym. I was lost in my thoughts. Mason was the sweetest boy who lit up the lives of everyone who knew him on this earth and had made a tremendous impact in his short years. How could the family ever move on from this tragic loss? All the families actually. Four children. Simply lost.

In February, I took a trip to Cuba with my cousin Dolores. We met another friend Tanya there, with her people. This was a very fun trip and Dolores was very thankful to get away. She hadn't travelled in a while. Beach fun, Cuban sun, and ice-cold champagne. Some of my favourite things to enjoy.

More tragedy struck in April when there was a terrible bus accident out west. The bus was transporting the Humboldt Broncos Junior A hockey team, so this especially hit close to home. At times we were that bus filled with a hockey team with my husband driving. A truck had collided with the bus; many lives were lost, and many people were injured. It rocked the entire country as we are a huge hockey playing nation. Communities were putting hockey sticks out on their porches in memory of the lives lost. We did this with our own boys. It was very touching.

In May, Steve and I took a trip to Cuba to mark our twenty years of marriage. I wanted to go to Cuba with my wedding dress and redo our pictures just for fun.

In Shediac, New Brunswick, I met an angel. Raymond is her last name.

I was searching for a seamstress on the internet. One place I called sent me to the mall because this lady had a booth there. I went as I needed my wedding dress to be altered so I could take it to Cuba for our twentieth anniversary pictures.

I'd had a crazy week and only tried it on the night before leaving town for a hockey tournament. I couldn't believe it. It was too big and loose, but with shortening the straps I would be able to wear it and get my dream pictures.

This lady was almost finished for the day but jumped right in to help me out. Even when she found out that I pretty much needed it right on the spot. She smiled and went to work on it.

She had a lot of wise words for me about life and tending my mom. I could have talked to her for hours, but I had to get back for JJ's hockey game. It all fell into place so nicely and all for a hug. She wouldn't let me pay her at all, even though I was ready to pay her double. What a nice soul. I was so glad I got to meet her. I was in her town again for hockey not long after my Cuban trip so I left her a picture and a thank you note.

We met some new friends while in Cuba, and they helped to take the pictures that day. We had fun and even danced on the beach, with the maintenance guy's music. Steve didn't look like he was having as much fun as me, but he was a good sport and put up with it.

I wasn't sure if we would be able to get away in November when it was actually our twentieth anniversary, so that was why we went in May. Just in case. When we got back Steve built me a small fenced in garden. Again, it was against his wishes because he hated doing anything with carpentry. I had to put up with a lot of attitude for a couple days just to get my fence completed.

Why he had to hate doing things for me, I'll never know. Every time it tore my heart out when he acted so hateful. Of course, as soon as he was done the task he was fine. It was just during the task that it was painful. Maybe one day I will learn not to ask him for things. But he was capable, so why should I have to pay someone?

I love building projects and creating things myself. Obviously, he doesn't share in my joy.

I hired a lady to do family photos again. It was in June, and we decided to do them at the racetrack with our three race cars. That was definitely for Steve's benefit. I would hopefully get a good family picture against the trees, and I did, but the car ones were for him. They turned out great and captured our racing family moments. Tristan was home and despite the black flies he participated. I was a happy Momma with everyone in the pictures.

Lots of things happened in 2018. We got the chance to go to the big Cavendish Music Festival in PEI. Me, JJ, and Steve went. However, Steve left early and missed the best part of the show. After all, he didn't want to miss racing. It was another time when my heart was broken, as one of our favourite songs was played without him there. The artist was there singing our song, and Steve had already left and gone home. I stood on my chair, singing at the top of my lungs, and he missed it.

Steve's Uncle Doug and Aunt Gail were there, along with my cousin Dolores and my friend Tammy. Lots of JJ's friends were there from school, including his girlfriend at the time. My sister Bev and her husband were also there. They showed us the ropes. This was probably one of the most fun times I had that was with them.

The weather was beautiful except for a few rain showers on one day, but that didn't stop us from having a good time. I would definitely be going back another year for this concert.

On the way home I got some surprising news from my sister. My pregnant niece had ended up in the hospital with high blood pressure. They were going to deliver the baby early. Luke's little brother, Liam, was born in July. Now my niece had two sons to take care of as a single mom. Of course, I helped and supported her as much as I could. The baby was in the IWK for several weeks before he was able to go home. My niece ended up being fine and everything worked out well. The baby was healthy, and that was so important.

Somehow, I agreed to let JJ get a Beagle dog to live with us. I didn't need any more responsibilities, but JJ was supposed to be the one taking care of this dog. I was dead set against getting another pet until one day Shay said, "Mom, you know how much he likes hunting, so why don't you let him get a dog?" I'm not sure why Shay was sticking up for JJ, but it was cute for him to do so. I softened and decided to let him get the dog.

We were heading off for our second trip to Europe so the dog would have to wait until we got home. She was about eight weeks old when we picked her up and she was so sweet. Everyone loved her. Steve didn't want another dog either, but he immediately fell in love with Zoey. I got to pick her name. It just suited her perfectly. It wasn't long before she became just as much our dog as JJ's.

During the long weekend in September, Shay's older friend Darrell was having an outdoor party. We had gone before but only for a few hours. This year we were letting Shay stay overnight in a tent. It would be his first big drinking event with friends. JJ was there and ended up being the bartender. We all had a pretty good time. I believed in letting the kids drink around us, in a controlled environment, so that they would be more responsible. This worked out for the most part until Shay got a bit older.

At the racetrack, things were getting worse. Steve was doing excellent, but his biggest hater was determined not to let Steve win. This guy was pathetic, trying to pay the other drivers to take Steve out. Anything to ruin his chances.

He openly told people that there was no way a MacPhee would be winning. He was so consumed by jealousy.

He rammed into the side of Steve's car, forcing Steve out of the race, and ruined his standings. Steve was always upset, however, he never went to the source of the problem and dealt with it. For me, I got a shitty deal. I was in the women's race, going around a corner, when a car was pushing into me, forcing me toward the dreaded wall. Of course, I was cutting hard and pushing back, which from the tower looked like I was trying to wreck her. I ended up being black flagged.

I couldn't understand why she had been pushing on me. She should have held her line. However, as the story unfolded later, she blew a tire in the corner and didn't have any control. This didn't come out though until after I was dragged through the fire as the bad guy. This fellow racer could have publicly let everyone know what had happened but she didn't. She enjoyed me taking the heat and being the bad guy.

This event ruined me for racing. I didn't care if I ever went back out on the track. I hated the feeling of being close to the wall. I had flashbacks of her pushing me toward it.

I finished the year, but my enjoyment of the sport was long gone. The less I had to do with the racetrack drama, the better my life would be. I had a spiritual reading around this time, where Kelley told me my light was being crushed. The racetrack was creating a darkness all around me and I needed to be free from there. The negativity, jealousy, hatred, envy, and evilness were draining my radiant glow. It was time to rethink where I wanted to channel my energies.

Shay won most every race he was in and was the grand champion overall in points. The highest level he could achieve. As I always taught them, you can do anything when you put your heart and soul into it. Shay was mechanically smart; therefore, he had learned everything he could about building a winning race car. Again, hard work pays off.

My favourite type of racing was with my sister Sharon. Sunset, sunrise, five-kilometre runs; we signed up for them all. Running alongside the ocean can't be beat. Just finishing was always my goal, with a combination of walking and running. I signed up for the Valley Harvest Run, as did Steve, Shay, JJ, and a family friend LJ. Well, I may have insisted.

We stayed at Aunt Thelma's cottage. What a trip down memory lane staying there was again. We hadn't been there in years. I love any beach, but exploring that shoreline was always a treat.

When we were running the race, the boys were determined their dad was not beating them. No one had practiced so we all struggled a bit, but we got the medals for completing the race and it was a nice family accomplishment.

Deer hunting soon started for JJ. Muzzleloader guns were allowed to be used in October. Since that first year he had got a deer, he always was able to get one each year. It was great to have the meat in the freezer.

Shay was in Grade 12 and turning eighteen on December 28th. He had plans to become a welder. He was already pretty good at welding. Previously, he had been welding for a man named Wade. Back at that time he didn't have his full driver's licence and I had to pick him up. My proud Momma moment was when Wade came out to my truck in a snowstorm to tell me my son could weld better than most thirty-year-olds. Wade was very impressed with Shay's patient demeanour and said he had a talent for details.

Our official twentieth anniversary was upon us. We were fortunate enough to be able to travel so I booked a Princess Cruise, and we were off on our next adventure. Cruise ships always have photographers, so of course I brought my wedding dress along to wear on our anniversary. We got tons of pictures. I had said we would be celebrating the entire year and we sure did. On the cruise we went to visit the island of Saint Thomas. The town was full of jewellery stores and it's one of my favourite shiny places on earth. I barter well so we bought an anniversary gold diamond band and a heart diamond necklace. After all, who doesn't like diamonds? And hell, I am worth it!

We were happy. My travel agent said she was impressed as many couples were not doing as well as we were. We still enjoyed each other's company. I planned things for us to do (in the off-racing season) and we stayed connected. Every relationship takes work by both parties. If you let things go, they will slip away. My motto was always to fix things right away if they were broken. I was a people pleaser, always putting my deep feelings aside and concentrating on making everyone else happy. I don't recommend that as a plan though.

Being really busy raising kids takes a lot out of us mommas. I always say take care of yourself to be able to take care of others. And I did some, but I later learned I should have done even more for myself.

Steve was very good at saying sorry; however, his strength was not correcting the problem so it would not be repeated. Therefore, "sorry" can get old and repetitive. We definitely had our struggles as every couple does. But I considered us to be written in stone, and seriously, "until death do us part!"

Every spiritual reading that I had prior to this had said that I was married to the right man. We were meant to be together and fit together like two puzzle pieces. I knew the angels had brought us together and higher powers were at work. We had a path to travel on that was manifested for us, and we were living it well.

Tristan and Sam were frantically looking to buy a house at that time. I can't stress enough for people not to rush when buying a house. Something better always comes along. Don't just settle for anything. Always push the limits to get what you deserve. While being patient. Just make sure you know your worth. Finally, they had a house lined up for January.

Christmas that year was beautiful, as usual. I had Mom brought over to our house in her wheelchair. Every year I kept thinking, maybe this is the last one. Will she be here next year?

New Year's Eve we had a party at our house. Just a small gathering with friends and family. It was so nice to have all three boys under one roof.

CHAPTER 41

Through The Years: 2019

This year we were privileged to have Shay and JJ playing on the same hockey team. High School hockey at its best. It sure beat running in two different directions and to different rinks.

Tristan and Sam were staying at his grandmother's house. They had moved home in June of 2018, marking three full years having lived away from the family for Tristan. He had missed us so much and wanted to be back at home. I can't blame him for wanting to get out of Manitoba. They stayed with us for a while as well before they had finally found and bought a house. The location shook me a little when Tristan told us it was right off the Glenwood exit. I had to shake it off, telling myself it would be fine. I wouldn't have to drive past my childhood place. At least I could look forward to new memories in Glenwood.

They did have a rocky start in their house, but they were working toward their future together. They started renovating, and bit by bit were making their new place into a home. Tristan worked at YACRO, houses that were the homes of special needs youth and adults, and Sam worked in mental health out of the hospital. When the province decided to hire more jail guards, Tristan switched jobs, did the training, and started working at the correctional centre in Yarmouth. He was finding his own way. I figured he would be set for the future and eventually would get a full-time position. But you just never know what the universe will throw in your path. Life is unpredictable.

I was introduced to CrossFit. My friend Tessa wanted to try it, so I jumped in with both feet and loved it. It was a bit of a drive, but the atmosphere was just what we needed. I hung on to the hope of having a CrossFit gym right in my hometown. Then I'd be at my best and wouldn't that be badass!

Shay was recently single, which was for the best. We went on a trip to Cuba and permitted the boys to each bring a friend. They had a great time. I really didn't expect all the late nights, but they were young and foolish. Steve and I couldn't keep up with them.

Cuba was my favourite place to vacation but for my next trip my cousin Dolores and I chose to go to Mexico. The prices were almost on par, and it was a good opportunity. We both enjoy the beach so much. We are so compatible.

Soon after returning home, I was to have surgery. Not many people knew this, but I had a breast that was disfigured. I suffered through my life up to this point hating my imperfection. I wondered if the molestation had caused one breast to be so much bigger than the other.

The battle in my head about it every day was real. It constantly didn't fit in anything, and I always had to try to even them out. I had wasted so much negativity on this issue. I hated myself deeply and despised my imperfection. I almost didn't include this event in my book. But as I am literally baring my soul in the hopes of helping others, it needed to be written. The doctors did tests to see if there was an underlying condition, but nothing surfaced. While it's true that most people have one breast a little bigger than the other, the doctors were surprised by the size of my difference. They were not used to seeing such different measurements.

I would be covered under the Provincial Health Coverage and my life fears and hate for my deformation would be fixed. I still doubted my decision about having it done. I did talk with a friend years earlier about it, as she had breast implants and had never ever regretted it. She only regretted not doing it sooner. I kept hearing her words and took the leap of faith. I had a reduction on the one side, and they tucked them to become even.

I had been on the waiting list for years. I didn't think they were ever going to call, but it all happened rather quickly. I couldn't do much for a while as I recovered. It was hard to sit in the recliner and watch the family manage without me. I learned a lot and thought that I could never be laid up like that again. Steve struggled to multi-task and it ripped my heart out again. I felt useless, to say the least. But I recovered and never looked back.

What a difference it made, feeling good about myself. I wasn't skinny. I had curves. But I grew to appreciate my shape. I had worked hard to get to this point. I can't ever remember a time when I hadn't wanted to lose weight. But I had lost a huge discomfort that had dragged me into dark places. I was more balanced, more comfortable in my own skin. I would still always be a work in progress, with managing my eating and exercise. That would always be my battle. But I was happier with my image, and thankful I could have the procedure done.

If you have something that bothers you that much, talk to a doctor, and for Canadians I pray your treatment might be covered too. If not, talk to a professional, as hating yourself is pure wasted energy. You can be successful at rechannelling that energy to good uses.

During 2019 I had another spiritual reading with Kelley. I have had several of them over the years, and Kelley has always nailed me to a T. She told me I'd changed a lot over the years and by fifty I would be at my peak. I had five years to go. I'm a survivor. I can go through anything and survive. But I was getting tired and worn out with everything I was trying to accomplish. In the next six years there would be truths that would come out and I would see them.

I was meant to help others, to be on a stage to teach, speak, and motivate people. I had just started writing my book in 2019. She told me to do it, that I was meant to write it. She didn't just see a book, she also saw a movie. I could make this happen; the universe is powerful, and it was listening. Truth needs to be told—the good coming from the process would outweigh the bad. I was to shine a light on things for others. It wouldn't be easy, but I would have no regrets.

The universe needed this book to happen, to help so many people. I was to trust my gut, as it was always right. She told me my sons needed to find their own ways, and that I could not fix everything. I was to let things go and just be supportive.

I loved having my readings done. There was nothing evil or bad about them. It had nothing to do with the Devil. It was about the spirits, energy, light, and angels. Trust in God and the universe. Everyone has a spiritual path; some would follow it, and some will choose to ignore it.

Shay graduated from Grade 12, another proud Momma moment. I had grilled them from the time they were little that there would be no exceptions, and they would need their Grade 12 education. Shay took a friend to the prom, which was another memorable picture opportunity. Steve let him drive the Camaro, despite the twenty-five-year-old driver insurance requirements.

The rest of summer was busy, as usual, with racing.

I enjoyed a trip to Cape Breton. I had not been to my cousin Cheryl's house since Tristan was little. The boys were surprised when they were met by their beautiful cousins. It was a long ride, but a great weekend.

Another weekend, Tristan, Sam, and I toured Peggy's Cove and stopped at The Wild Leek in Halifax for lunch. To our surprise there sat Natasha and her mother Heather. Everything is connected. We had a beautiful day. We also went to Liam's first birthday party as my niece had booked a cottage for a nice family gathering.

Natasha visited to see Tristan's new house. I took all four of my babies out to supper at Rudder's, a local restaurant. When you have all your precious ones in the same spot it does the heart wonders. I brought Luke, who enjoyed being with us, to Yarmouth for a few days for some summer fun. Hopefully, this would become a tradition.

On one of our racing adventures, we took Shay to a bar for his first underage experience. He was timid to order. Somehow that has sure worn off.

Sharon and I ran our sunset, sunrise 5 km races again. We were also hopeful this would become a tradition. We wanted our sister Bev to join us the following year. Time would tell if that would be possible.

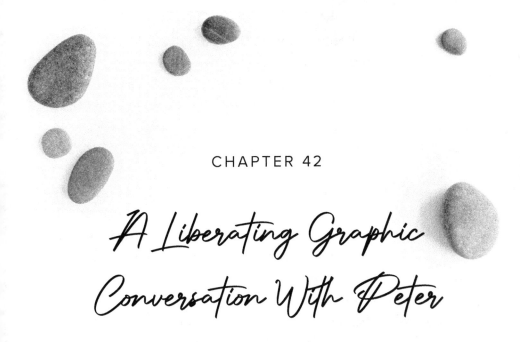

CHAPTER 42

A Liberating Graphic Conversation With Peter

On September 11, 2019, I went for an appointment downtown with Steve. I saw Peter, my biological father, digging in the bins for bottles. If he was still there when my appointment was over, I would have something to say to him.

He was still snooping around when we came out after the appointment. Pulling into the parking lot in my truck, he was bent over and facing away from me. How easy it would have been to just slam into him.

He went about his business until I said, "Are you that poor?"

"Yup, why not collect them," he replied as he approached my truck.

I asked him if he knew who I was. He didn't. I couldn't believe it.

"You seriously don't know who I am?" I said in disbelief.

"Who are you?" he asked.

"I'm Tam," I told him. I wouldn't give him the satisfaction of saying I was his daughter. I did not feel he was ever a father to me.

"Oh, you're Tam?" he said.

"Yup," I said. "Are you still the rotten pig I remember you to be?"

I held myself together and I had my say. I wish I had thought to record the conversation. He called me and my siblings liars. He still blamed everything on Mom, like he had when I was a kid. I remembered how everything was always her fault. He still believed Bev loved him. I wasn't scared as I confronted him. He had no control over me. I cursed him up and down.

After thirty-two years of never speaking to Peter, I finally confronted him because I had learned from my sister that she was almost sixteen when he had betrayed her soul. I had always thought it was just before she was eighteen since she had the baby when she was eighteen.

Peter was sick, sick, sick.

He was thirty-seven when he started raping an almost sixteen-year-old girl. The Bastard!

He swore he never touched us, or beat us, or beat Mom. He said Bev came after him and wanted him. If he really believed that, then he was even sicker than I had remembered.

"You are a sick fucking pig!" I told him.

He turned the conversation back on me, saying I had run around with everyone. That wasn't true. He brought up that I had run around with a guy up the road that owned a restaurant. Well, I had been with him for four years.

"I've been with the same man for over twenty years and thank God he is nothing like you," I told him.

He responded that I was going to hell, but I told him if anyone should be worried about that, it was him.

"You beat us, touched us inappropriately. You were a fucking pig all my life! You raped Bev before she was sixteen and continued to for years."

Again, he claimed it wasn't true. He said he'd never touched any of us and said he had waited until my sister was old enough and wanted him.

"She put my hands on her," he claimed.

I reminded him she was his daughter. However, he disagreed about who his children were.

"Norma tricked me into adopting them. She was not my daughter," he said.

He accused us of lying in court and then told me I had been a mistake. He had wanted a son instead and he wished I had never been born.

"Thank God I was born, or you would still be abusing them!" I spat back.

I told him how I had wished he was home the day they had come to take Bev and the baby away; it would have been a better day if the cops had a reason to have shot him.

He even had the nerve to ask about the baby. He wanted to know where she was. I sure as hell wasn't going to tell him as it was none of his fucking business. Back when I was twelve, I hadn't known what was going on until Bev started showing. Then I grew up really quickly.

He had become pretty worked up, spitting on my truck as he talked and slamming his hand on my door handle. I told him to never touch my truck again or I'd drop him right there. He backed up and never touched it again. Man, that felt good. I had been waiting for this moment, for this confrontation since I had talked with Bev.

I had walked past him many times over the years, giving him a hateful look. Wanting to spit in his face. Had he really not known it was me all those years? I thought for sure that he knew the "Sinclair look."

Peter remembered things, but in his own sick way. And he hated Mom for taking him somewhere on the day they had come to take the baby and Bev away.

I eventually drove off. It had felt liberating to tell him off. Getting rid of that negative energy was rewarding for my spirit and soul.

I had let go of the hate I felt for him years before. I was at peace with everything until my sister had highlighted a few things that I hadn't known. Then I had boiled over.

Now, once and for all, I felt that I was free of my biological piece of shit father.

Years earlier I had sent him anonymously a winter coat. I had asked the pastor at the church to deliver the coat to him. The only other person who knew I had done this was my husband. I did it to free my energy. It had cleared my heart and made me feel good about where I was in my healing journey.

He was just another bum around town with nothing. Well, except for a coat. He never had any idea the coat had come from me, which was just the way I had wanted it. Finding a way to heal is one of the most important things. You must do for yourself.

Hate eats you up.

Let it go.

Peacefulness is bliss.

CHAPTER 43

Through The Years: Fall 2019

Tristan started hunting again now that he was home. He got his first deer, putting meat in the freezer for him and Sam. Around this time he started his new job, at the jail.

Steve and I toured the Volvo truck factory during an all-expense paid trip to Virginia. We have bought many trucks from MacKay's in Truro, Nova Scotia and they took us on the trip as we are one of their favourite customers. I got to the beach, and he got to visit the big race shops.

Marriage is all about compromises, right?

The last truck driving provincial competition was held in October. Steve had lost his touch and placed third. He was discouraged and the funding for such events was dwindling away. I didn't figure we would ever get to go to another one. Again, though, time would tell, as with everything.

Steve and I escaped for our anniversary trip to Mexico this time. I might have mentioned how much I like to travel. Well, I absolutely do.

My big dream started to unfold in November of that year. We dug ground at our camp for our retirement home. I personally designed every detail and had Shane Campbell draw up the building plans.

I put my heart and soul into this project. Steve wanted beams in the big open concept room, a loft, and he wanted a tin roof. He left everything else to me. He had some input, but he could not see the same vision as me. We originally had wanted a small 24' x 24' camp house. But as time went on, with the thoughts of grandchildren and moving there permanently, I decided we were going to have everything we wanted. Getting a builder's mortgage was challenging. They would hand us the money to buy whatever we wanted, but the building process had totally different rules.

I had been picking out design pieces as part of the puzzle for years. I saved Pinterest pictures, which showed what I wanted. I incorporated so many elements into my design. I was pumped. Back when I was a little girl, I wanted to someday have a swimming pool. I had made that happen. Then I started dreaming of this cottage on our lake. Dreams do come true if you have the determination to make them happen. Here I was proving it once again.

CHAPTER 44

A December Curve Ball

Steve was on the phone with his aunt. His mother had fallen, broken her hip and was in surgery. This would be followed by months of recovery. At the time of her surgery Steve had mentioned how it would have been nice to have a brother or sister to share the dealing with his mother.

The reply he got was overwhelming.

His aunt said that he technically did have one. His father had got a girl pregnant before he had met Steve's mother. The girl had moved away to Sydney, had the baby, and gave him or her up for adoption. Steve's father had driven to Sydney to try and work things out while she was pregnant. He told his family he seen her pregnant, but that she hadn't wanted anything to do with him. Steve's aunt was young at the time so that was all she could remembered. The child had been born around 1969 she thought.

I couldn't imagine why his mother would not have told him this story. All these years he thought he was alone, especially since his dad had died when he was seven years old. Many times, he had asked his mother why she hadn't had another child. He'd also mentioned so many times how he would have loved to have had a sibling. She should have told him about the possibility.

I knew I would try every avenue to help find his sibling. I believed one hundred per cent this person existed. The person would be about fifty-three years old in 2020–21 and would have been born at the hospital in Sydney, Nova Scotia. The mother's name was Sherry Harnish.

At the time of writing this book I have not been able to reach her yet. I do know things would have been very hush hush in 1969. Families hid the truth and swept things under the rug.

I don't believe the person probably knows they were adopted, so therefore, they would not be looking for any siblings, biological parents, or any history. Ancestry.com did not give me any leads. But again, I believe that is because the person doesn't know they were adopted and is not looking.

Once again, Christmas was upon us. Steve and I cut down a Christmas tree in our back field. We had no time for the 4-wheeler trip this year, and no kids joined us. Of course, I brought Mom home in her wheelchair again. She slept a fair bit, but she still seemed to enjoy her time with us. We can only tell by her smile, but that is enough.

Tristan, Sam, Sharon, my brother, Tina, and everyone got to see Mom outside of the nursing home, which was a treat. My famous Christmas dinner was delicious as usual. Everyone raved over it. I don't cut corners to make it healthy; I just make it like it should be. It's all real food though, made from scratch.

Shay's nineteenth birthday was here on December 28th. I insisted Steve and I go out to the bar with him. We needed to make sure our baby would be alright. I never expected to see Steve double fisting, or myself polishing off two ice wines. I don't know what they put in them, but I was feeling it.

We had a blast, dancing and being foolish. Shay said he had never seen his mother that tipsy. I hardly drink. I have never been drunk and never to this day have I been sick from drinking. I have only ever had a headache the next day. I never understood why anyone would drink enough to make themselves sick. Hopefully, I'll make it through JJ's nineteenth birthday in the same condition.

I laughed pretty hard about it. We went out to keep Shay safe and ended up too tipsy. Steve was sick on the way home. I thought he was buying to share and had no idea they were all for himself.

Three days later it was New Year's Eve. I hardly felt like drinking again, but we did have a little party. Tammy, Allan, some of the racing crew, Sharon, and my favourite neighbours John and Judy attended. They are special people to my whole family. We think very highly of them.

JJ got his official driver's licence on December 30, 2019. Now everyone was licensed and had freedom. JJ got the hand-me-down Kia. We had originally bought it for travelling to hockey games. Instead of selling it we had said Shay could drive it for two years, and then JJ could drive it for two years. But we laid down the law. They paid for the gas, insurance, and kept the car clean for the privilege of driving a "free" vehicle. I repeat they were privileged to have this car to drive. They might not have realized it yet, however, they would when they were much older.

CHAPTER 45

My Travels By Plane 1996-2020

I love to travel. Once you start, if you love it you get the travel bug. Always dreaming of a new adventure.

I can't put all my trips in this book. It would be a book itself to write about all my travel adventures. I will highlight some because it is a huge part of who I am.

My travels started in 1996. My first ever plane trip was to Toronto with Fred. I loved exploring the city, Niagara Falls, dining out, and shopping. I was in awe.

For my next adventure I saved and planned it all on my own. In 1998, I paid cash for Tristan and me to go to Australia. Tristan was four. I had just met Steve and we had been dating for a few months. I still went. I actually said to myself, *If I miss Steve, I'll know he's the one!* The trip was wonderful, and I did miss him.

My cousin had help entertaining us. Her in-laws took us to see caves, penguins, and on the most beautiful scenic drives. We stopped at many playgrounds to try out some of the biggest slides I've ever seen. We all played on them, and Tristan had lots of fun.

Another lady let us stay with her in the city; she had a lovely pool, and she took us shopping for my opal ring. Twila, my cousin, took us out to explore the many little towns and communities around her home as well as the beach, the farm, and the culture. I even took her truck out a couple times to go exploring by ourselves. Driving on the opposite side of the road from Canada was different. Tristan doesn't remember much, but we have some wonderful pictures, and I will never forget that trip.

My next adventure was our honeymoon. (Turns out I did miss Steve; he was the one.) In November of 1998, our first trip was down south. I immediately loved the beaches, the warmth, and the people. Cuba is one of my favourite places to visit. We renewed our vows and met some lovely new friends from Nova Scotia in Cuba on that trip.

My next trip was when Trina, Megan, Tristan, and I went to Florida. That was a fun-filled trip visiting water parks, theme parks, and International Drive. The hardest part was leaving my little ones at home to go solo with Tristan.

During another trip to Florida, Steve and I took Shay and JJ in March of 2005 when JJ turned two. We rented a car and drove all over exploring. We did the beaches and water parks on that trip.

I collect so many Air Miles by filtering company bills through my credit cards. I used these for our family trips. I've travelled a lot, and I have lost track of which ones I paid for out of pocket, and which ones were from Air Miles. I do know that Air Miles saved us a lot throughout the years.

I'm not sure I'd be able to recount all my trips in their proper order as there have been so many.

I went on another trip to Florida with my friend Gayna and her children and my three boys. This trip was for more of the same fun water parks, International Drive, shopping, and sightseeing. I also took my three boys to Florida on my own on another occasion. Steve didn't like to travel as much as I did and he didn't feel he could just leave our business to run itself. I always believed there was more to life than just working.

We stayed in a huge time-share unit that I had found online. Lots of memories were made and we had a good trip. We went to a basketball game for Tristan. All the boys got matching jerseys because it was a fan appreciation night. Ten days of just me and my boys.

Once Steve and I took a long weekend and went to Tampa, Florida for a getaway. Mom babysat for us. I also believe it makes you better parents if you take a little bit a time for yourselves, to enjoy life, get away from the kids, and come back refreshed to face all the trials and errors of being parents. Every smart, successful person out there is learning something new each day. It is how life works.

I loved to travel both with and without the kids. I have even travelled a few times solo. I got a free flight for signing up for a particular account at my bank. I jumped on that opportunity. I booked an out-of-the-way hotel on the Miami Beach. No, it wasn't the fanciest place, but I could walk for miles. The truckers had 10–4 phones back then. I remember sitting on the beach talking like it was a walkie-talkie with Steve a lot of the time. And as crazy as this sounds, we reconnected.

With our busy lives at home, I found we were not taking the time just to connect. No marriage is perfect, and they all take work. Sometimes it takes the rarest of moments to make you realize you need to make some positive changes. Steve hated when I was away. He liked everything to always be the same routine, but I didn't. I needed to mix things up. We compromised, talked, and things were better when I got home. Maybe it is true that absence makes the heart grow fonder!

Never be afraid to travel solo. You get to experience time with yourself, and you may just learn a thing or two. It's wonderful.

Our most challenging trip would have to be our trip to the Dominican with Shay and JJ in 2008. Thankfully, we met a nice couple from New Brunswick as soon as we got there. The first few days were amazing. The kids loved the beach, and this was their first all-inclusive resort. There was a lot to do. We booked a dune buggy trip, and that was the roughest trip imaginable. We beat over the terrain, in the dust and the dirt with bandanas wrapped around our faces so we could breathe. We stopped at a gorgeous beach, and we also stopped at an underwater spring cave. There, people could swim. I didn't jump in, but I did manage to get in and cool off. I wanted to experience swimming in the cave. It was an interesting day. Not sure I would book one again though.

That night Steve woke up in pain thinking he had gas. He was on his hands and knees rocking, wanting pop to help him burp. He really wasn't sure what to do. The next morning, I sent him to see the nurse. He explained he thought he was having gas pains from something he'd eaten so she gave him some medication. The meds did nothing. I sent him back to the nurse and she gave him a shot for pain. Again, it did nothing, and he had another terrible night.

The pains would come and go. He'd have spells and then be okay for a while. I knew he wasn't okay so the next time he went to see the nurse I went with him. She was surprised the shot had not help him. She said she'd never had a patient that it didn't help. She recommended that we go to the hospital. She couldn't feel any broken ribs, but he was definitely in agony over something. We were a day and a half from going home and Steve did not want to go to the hospital in a foreign country. Knowing what I know now, if we had to do it all over again, I definitely would've taken him to the hospital, in any country.

We struggled through the rest of our vacation. He felt good in the pool except for the time he got in and had to stay in. He had a spell, and it took two hours of trying to get him back out. He had pains in his side that felt like terrible knots. He hadn't drank a lot, but he did have a few.

And it turned out that was a good thing. He didn't feel like eating, especially if he was having a spell. I was so worried. What if he got worse and had to go to the hospital? I considered sending the kids home with the new people we had met and staying behind if things got worse. I just had to have a backup plan. I took care of packing us up and getting us ready to go home, as well as the kids. I did everything. He was miserable. We managed to get to the airport and even onto the plane without him having a spell. Thankfully!

When we landed, he felt good; so, we set out on the three-and-a-half-hour drive home with the kids, instead of going to the hospital in Halifax. On the way home he had a terrible spell. He was holding onto the dash, saying he was not going to make it. The kids were in the back seat, and I had no idea what to do but to keep driving.

This was only one of the many spells he'd experienced over the past four days. When the spell passed, we continued and took the kids home to my mother. We stopped to talk to her for a few minutes, before continuing to the Yarmouth hospital.

We were not there long before they got his blood work back. They walked in and told us that he would not be going anywhere for a while. He was showing signs of having blood clots in his system. They believed that he must have developed them on the plane ride down. They figured it had started in his legs, before dislodging on our rough dune buggy ride. Then the clots travelled to his lungs where they were aggravating an area within his lung. He had one in each lung but no pain on the one side. The doctors we saw told us we had been very lucky not to have brought him home in the bottom of the plane. The alcohol he had consumed must have helped to thin his blood enough for him to get through the last days of our vacation and home.

He was still young. Only thirty-three years old. Blood clots usually form in older people and on longer flights. The only explanation they had was that he was dehydrated. We had woken up, driven to the airport, sat while waiting to board, and then sat on the plane again. He hadn't drank much at all, and he hadn't got up to walk on the plane. It was a champagne flight where everyone toasts to going on a vacation, but Steve hadn't even drank that one. I had both. No fluids thicken your blood.

After we got home Steve spent a week in the hospital. He had never been in a hospital overnight before. He was scared and this was serious. The thought that we had almost lost him. Wow! Our guardian angels were at work once again. It was not his time to go.

He hadn't wanted me to leave the hospital. But I had to go home to the kids. We were all exhausted. I stayed strong, as usual. I knew I had to for his sake. Leaving the hospital with all that information and what ifs running through my mind was hard.

He was off work another three weeks while they got his blood thinners regulated. He now regularly drinks more water every day. As for the rest of his life, he will be at high risk for this to happen again.

Every spring there would be trucking competitions and we started attending them in 2006. Steve went with high hopes the first year, but he had no idea what he was getting into. They hadn't even sent him an outline. He had to do a truck pre-trip, a written test, and an obstacle course. He is competitive; however, he was unprepared so he never even placed. We chalked it up as a learning experience. The following year he couldn't compete because of a speeding ticket he received on his personal time.

We went again in 2008 and Steve won first place. What an awesome day that was. Bragging rights and we got to be part of the Atlantic Team heading to Ottawa in the fall. We met so many great friends along the way. The National's trip was an all-expenses-paid mini vacation. We loved every minute of it. Meeting and competing against the top drivers of the country. That was quite the experience.

In future years, we got to do this trip five more times with Steve winning first place six times at the provincials in total. He also placed second a couple of times. Some years there were spousal competitions. Between me and another lady we would take turns winning that title. I guess I have a competitive streak as well.

One year JJ won first place in the kids' remote-control contest. I won the ladies competition and Steve won his division. That was an especially fun day. We always had a banquet, followed by after parties in the hotel rooms. It was so much fun; with such nice friends we'd made. What lovely memories that I have to cherish. Winning once might be luck but winning six times and always placing was pure skill. Steve is definitely good at handling trucks. It's his thing!

Our National trips took us to Ottawa, Winnipeg, Calgary, Moncton, Regina, and Brantford, Ontario. They were all special, but I'd have to say the first one was the best. Steve did not place first at the Nationals. But he did place second at least twice and third a time or two. The competition was tough, with all the participants being winners just to get there. I'm a strong believer that the energy surrounding you must be in your favour the day of a competition. Sometimes you could just feel the awesomeness in the air.

One year I took Shay to Edmonton. We stayed at my friend Julie's house. He loved all the army stuff and the huge shopping centre. Another time I took Shay to New York. That trip was amazing. Early December in New York is the best and prettiest time to visit. Trying new foods, Christmas lights, walking all over while sightseeing, and Radio City Hall were the highlights.

JJ and I visited my friend Diane in Regina for our first solo trip together. We stayed a couple of nights at a mineral spa hotel, toured the city and farms. Another trip we went on together was to both North and South Carolina. He loved fishing off the pier, Myrtle Beach, monster trucks, and just exploring.

Did I mention I love to travel? This world is huge, and I always have wanted to explore it.

One year, Mom decided to go with me on a plane. She had always said she wasn't into flying. Then when she was diagnosed with Alzheimer's she said there was nothing to lose now, so where were we going? She soon got the opportunity to go with us when I booked a trip for Steve, me, Shay, and JJ to go to Niagara Falls in 2010. Because of work, Steve ended up not being able to go. So, Mom offered to go in his place. I did lose the money I had paid for Steve's ticket. However, Mom had a great time. There was an indoor water park that the kids loved. We were there in December when it was very pretty. Niagara Falls has lots of touristy things to do around there. I treated Mom to that trip, and I am very thankful we have those memories.

I knew Mom's good years were running out. So, I planned another trip to Newfoundland in 2012. We stayed at Melanie's. She was one of Mom's favourite boarders from back in the day of running her own boarding house. During this visit, Mom still remembered who everyone was, however, she had a hard time getting all her thoughts out. We toured around all the scenic routes and had a lovely visit.

I rented a car on a lot of trips. The only problem I ever had was in Toronto. We got T-boned by a van. I saw it coming and sped up so it wouldn't directly hit JJ's door. No one was hurt. It was completely the van driver's fault, and the lady was immensely sorry. She even paid the deductible for the insurance bill. So, it all worked out.

My first time to New York was with friends. Sherry, Lynne, and I walked our butts off all over that city. We were stiff each night, but I wanted to see and do as much as possible. There was no time to waste. Nothing like freaking Lynne out by buying purses in a back alley. Oh, such fun!

Our first cruise was in 2011 and was on the Oasis. We were invited along with eight other people. It was a very cool experience. A huge ship, like a city on the water. The most fun we had was shopping in St. Thomas. They served you alcohol while you shopped, and everything was so pretty. I love to barter, and we got some great deals there. We did a Jeep Safari in Saint Martin where you got to drive your own Jeep. We toured the island and saw the culture. I always pushed the limits by being the last back to the ship.

Steve's more cautious than me. I live on the edge occasionally. Life's too short. Just take chances and make sure you have room on your credit card for the unexpected occurrences.

In March of 2013 we did a family trip to Boston where we watched hockey games and toured the city, including the Boston Duck Tours, which was half on the land and half on the ocean. Steve and Shay's team was Toronto and JJ's team was Boston. They all played that weekend so it worked out perfectly.

I was not gluten-free at the time and I remember going to the best pasta restaurant ever. Oh, my alfredo. More memories on the Boston trip included walking the city and going to the aquarium, which was close to our hotel.

I started out the year of 2014 by meeting my cousin Jessica in Miami. I loved Miami and was excited to go back there. Jessica has her own blog, Turquoise Compass. She was just starting out on a year of travelling, backpacking, and exploring. We did a Florida Keys bus tour, an airboat alligator tour, and just explored Miami together. It was a beautiful start to my year.

Mine and Steve's first time to Mexico was in 2014, and we took the kids. We had a great time that trip. No excursions, just family fun at the resort. Lots of crazy pool time. The kids were a perfect age.

I always want to go to Cuba. You can say I'm addicted to the sun, sand, ocean, oh heck, all of it. I talked my friend Tanya into going with me. After all, this was the year I was turning forty and I was pretty sure no one was having a party. So, I planned a party for two on the beach. We were very much compatible travellers. Beach, beach, and more beach, sunsets, and running in the torrential rain. They have the most gorgeous beaches in Cayo Santa Maria, and Iberostar Ensenachos. Not to mention the coldest champagne! I hope to go back there again someday. I treasured those memories as we bared our souls and recharged in the sun. I had the best tan ever. I came home a better person, mom, wife, and friend.

I am constantly planning my next trip, even before I get home from the one I'm on. Natasha was studying in Toronto during her first year of university in February of 2015. I flew up to spend a weekend with her. We stayed at a brand-new hotel downtown. A perfect location, and, ironically, they put us on the twenty-second floor. (Be sure to read my chapter on my relationship with the number 22).

She met me there and showed me her tattoo, which is a Roman symbol for 22. As it turns out 22 is symbolic in her life as well. Natasha went home on December 22nd to her parents. I believe I was guided by my angels, and it was so very special to me. We had a nice time, but she did come down with a cold and did not feel like doing much toward the end of that trip. Again, I am forever thankful for any time I get to spend with Natasha. I cherish every moment.

In 2016, I took a solo trip to Cuba where I sunbathed, read books, people watched, and completely relaxed. It was a very much needed downtime after always taking care of everyone else.

Natasha and I were also able to squeeze in a trip to Cuba during 2016. Again, Cayo Santa Maria has the best beaches. This is where she took a picture of me setting the girls free. She had done this herself previously and said it was fun. So off we went, to get to the part of the beach where I could have my freeing moment. It really was memorable.

I do have a free-spirited type of personality. I am always up for a trip to Cuba. Hopefully, she will come with me again one day.

That same year JJ and I went to Jamaica. The four of us were supposed to go, but Steve was not comfortable going with his broken ankle from a few months prior. Shay chose to stay home to keep Dad company.

Another huge trip was JJ's European hockey trip in August of 2016. I will say it was a moms' trip. A once in a lifetime deal, so we thought. We were all over it, and it sounded like fun. We were not going with the top players. It was simply whoever thought their kid was good enough and could pay for the trip. I'm in, but truthfully Steve was the one who'd insisted I go. I was having second thoughts, but he didn't want to go, and neither did Shay. It was too long of a flight for them. I have no regrets, Europe was amazing. Our trip was planned for us, so there was no stress from planning anything. We had walking tours of cities, huge meals, bus tours, beautiful hotels, and wine as we watched the hockey practices. We had high expectations for the hockey games, but not everything went according to plan. Still, we made the best of our trip.

The trains over there are silent. The ones used to get around in the cities or the trams I guess they are called. We were on tour, looking at a Michael Jackson memorial outside of an apartment where he used to stay while in the city. The kids were looking at the fancy cars that were also parked in the area. People were walking everywhere; and these trains come through the same streets.

One mom I noticed was gazing at something and she had no idea a train was coming since it was so quiet. I rushed toward her, yelling to get out of its way. She was forever thankful. That was an extremely close call because they were moving pretty fast. I will never forget it. It still makes my skin crawl when I remember that moment. Melinda is a friend of mine on Facebook and such a beautiful soul.

In 2017 we chose to use some of those Air Miles for a family cruise. At the time Tristan lived in Thompson, Manitoba, so he didn't get to go. Shay and JJ got to miss school. I always believed trips were an important learning experience, and this family time was important. The boys got to see us not stressed out from work and life's chores. We were on the Harmony Allure, a sister ship to the Oasis. The boys liked it but to our surprise preferred the resorts. JJ said the pools were too small. We still had a good time and ate way too much cheesecake.

Tristan had not been home for Christmas because he had gone to Thailand to see Sam. Therefore, I planned a family trip in May to Winnipeg and Tristan and Sam would meet us there. I missed him; he was off learning what life was all about. I think we were fifty-six hours in total getting there due to delays, fog cancellations, and waiting around Halifax to leave. The boys were stressed. Let's just go home they kept saying. I remember saying I was going even if it was just to hug my son and turn around to fly back. We ended up getting there eventually. We all stayed in an Airbnb. The most fun thing we did was riding bikes in the park. We were in a buggy with everyone peddling, laughing our asses off with the kids driving. We still have a video clip of that day, which brings smiles to our faces when it is viewed. It was a nice, shortened visit with lots of laughter.

Steve had won the provincials that year, but it turned out there was no funding for the Nationals. So, I decided we would go on our own fall trip. We went to Old Quebec, flying in and out of Montreal. Old Quebec reminded me of Europe. The cobblestone streets, buildings, and the peacefulness. All of it was amazing. Steve didn't like downtown Montreal, but I'm game to explore anywhere.

We often got away just for a weekend when we could. We loved to spend quality time together. I always regret not dancing more, as we both loved to dance. We went to the Quarterdeck for our anniversary, which is a beautiful place on a Nova Scotian beach. It was November but not even cold yet.

Steve always complained about how hard I was to buy for. What to get me for Christmas? I had been asking him to go to New York for years. So, I threw that out there again during our anniversary supper. Just take me to New York, I said, then you don't have to buy me anything for Christmas. He actually said yes. So just over two weeks later we were on our way.

The first week of December is the best in New York. We walked everywhere, saw all the local attractions, and took a bus tour of the Christmas lights. You get to see the city as well as the snazzy houses all decked out. Brooklyn Bridge is a stop along the way. The whole weekend was magical. There is a feeling in New York. If you don't get there, you're truly missing out.

Our last day there was the first snowfall of the season. We were walking in Central Park. Love, love, loved it! Watching people experience snow for the first time is magical on its own. Our flight got cancelled and they put us on a later flight, flying directly home. The most perfect last-minute spontaneous Christmas present ever! I'll go again, I just know it.

My cousin Dolores wanted to go on a trip. I'll take you, no problem I told her. It was 2018. We ended up being able to meet my friend Tanya in Cuba. We had tons of fun in the sun. Another great travel companion, no drama, just beach, ocean, sand, walks, talks, and fun.

In May, Steve and I went to Cuba. I wanted to do wedding dress photos on the beach. We would be married twenty years soon and I didn't think we would get away in November. We had a fabulous time, met new friends from Nova Scotia, and the beach was amazing. There is no such thing as too much sun to me.

That August brought about my second trip to Europe. Hockey being a great excuse. JJ was fifteen and we had a great time. Only three out of the five local friends went this time, but we flew directly to Paris. We went a couple of days early to explore on our own before meeting up with the tour. No regrets, as Paris was amazing. Train rides into the mountains were spectacular. The Eiffel Tower during the day was magnificent. However, before we went home, we went back there at night and that was truly magical. Paris has a unique feeling too and if you don't feel it, you are missing out on the experience.

Another great feeling was standing on top of Chamonix-Mont-Blanc, doing my famous mountain pose. It just fills your soul. The town is exquisite. I pray I will get to visit there once again, but who knows if that will ever happen. I'm already on my second trip to Europe, and I never expected to go even once. I know I am blessed. I also know it didn't come without working hard.

Fall came and we decided we would go on an anniversary cruise. Why not? Off we went again with my wedding dress. I got loads of twentieth anniversary photos. The one I liked the best was with Steve in his ball cap because it's just not him without his hat. Twenty years together and we still enjoyed spending time together. I believe that's pretty special. The cruise went to St. Thomas, where we bought an anniversary band and a heart necklace for me. We had so much fun shopping that day; because they feed you rum punch while you're shopping. We laughed and were silly all day.

For 2019 I planned a trip to Cuba. Shay and JJ were each bringing a friend. At first Shay was bringing his girlfriend, but since they broke up after Christmas, he ended up bringing a guy friend, which worked out much better. LJ and Denver joined us. Denver has a special place in mine and Steve's heart. He's been around since Timbits hockey when they were four or five years old. Shay would be eighteen later that year. I knew he would drink down there. However, I had no idea how much he was going to drink. Quite the experience. Tristan and Sam had just bought a house, so the timing was not right for them, and they decided not to come with us. I had offered to pay for Tristan's flight, but he thought he should get stuff for the house instead. It was okay with me. I understood and I plan on there being many more family trips in the future. Nothing makes me happier than to have all my babies in the same place or under the same roof.

Usually, Mexico is always more expensive than Cuba, but for some reason in 2019 they were equal in price. My cousin and I were planning another trip and we decided to take the plunge and go to Mexico. It had its pluses and minuses. The beach was not as nice as a Cuban beach, but the food was better. We could have guacamole there every day. Yum, yum. The gym was much better equipped, and they had classes that I could attend. I loved that. Our resort was a four-in-one so we could explore a bit, and it was attached to a shopping complex. It was all good and we had a great time. Price does matter to me because I love getting the best deal.

Dolores and I travel well together. We do our own thing in the morning. Beach all day, a mudslide for cocktail hour and getting ready for our evening out. Glamming it up and spoiling ourselves.

Finally, that fall our Volvo dealer came through with an all-expense paid trip to their plant in Virginia. Our salesperson was kind enough to take us along, with another customer for the trip. Steve and I went early and did some exploring of our own. I went to Myrtle Beach and taught Steve how to hunt for shark teeth. He got to do racing stuff. There are lots of race car shops in the area and we got to tour some of them. Once we met up with our people, we were treated very well.

At the plant they were launching new trucks with new features. Dynamic steering, so they pretty much drove themselves. I was the first lady on the track (with a guide) to experience driving one. Ladies first; it was a great experience. Some things you will never forget in life, and this was one of those moments.

I wasn't finished travelling for the year; I planned a trip to Mexico for our twenty-first anniversary. With all the racing Steve got to do, we compromised and did as much travelling as possible because that's what I love to do. I had finally got Steve to the point of enjoying it. He knew I was going whether he went or not, so, he decided he wanted to be part of what makes me happy. After all, I have supported his racing on many a day when I'd much rather be at the beach.

As I've explained many times, I want him with me, but I don't need him with me. That's just who I am.

Well, he loved Mexico. We met a nice couple from Newfoundland. She loved the sun as much as me. We took the introductory tour to become members. They suck you in with the free chocolate massages. I love free so sure, we went. They want us to buy in and become members but I wasn't convinced that I wanted to. I liked to explore new places and I never go to same place twice. They offered to upgrade us so we could experience what members get. Well, we loved that. There was a private beach, buffet, pools, and service. I wouldn't have to carry a towel anywhere. They were there to move your chairs, put out towels, and wait on you as much as you wanted. The beach club had a nice menu as well as ready to go items. We loved being part of this little beach family. So, we did it; we became members. We got nicer rooms, locations, as many a la carte's as we wanted, private check-in, and everything else to make you feel spoiled. I was a happy camper.

Steve wanted to travel more, and we were going to do it in the most spoiled of ways. Plus, the membership we bought could transfer to the boys should we not get to use it in time. We booked again for January of 2020 and we had another great time, just the two of us. We planned a trip for end of March as well. With this membership we can also go to a few other countries. We will be exploring them in our future travels.

Unexpectedly, I also got the chance to go with my friend Tina on a last-minute trip to the Dominican. Her husband had a health issue and couldn't go, so off I went again. We had a few room issues, but we managed to have a good time on the beach there. Little did we know this would be our last trip for a long time. My March trip didn't happen as planned.

COVID changed the world.

CHAPTER 46

Through The Years: 2020

Things in January of 2020 got off to a very different start. Some relatively young people had died and things just didn't feel right. The weather wasn't that bad and we didn't have that much snow.

We did have some icy nights, which resulted in a driver putting one of our trucks off the road. He was not seriously hurt but the accident was deemed preventable. He had a lot of strikes against his record, so we had no choice but to let him go. He was no longer insurable.

Two weeks later he died due to heart problems. We were shocked. Our company has over twenty employees. We were bound to experience loss sooner or later. The truck was in the shop for seven weeks. The insurance covered the damages, except for the five-thousand-dollar deductible, which came out of mine and Steve's pocket.

We did escape to Mexico on the nineteenth of January. Just Steve and me. He wanted to go twice that year so I had booked us back in November on the Black Friday deals. Despite being on the phone a lot dealing with the accident, we managed to have a good time. The driver passed away shortly after we got back from our vacation. It still was hard for it to sink in.

February had to be better. Right? Nope. Things continued to be odd. We started hearing about the coronavirus that mysteriously had popped up in Wuhan, China. It was hitting the city hard and spreading into the country. We never paid too much attention because it was across the ocean.

However, it was only a plane ride away.

We had a trip booked for the twenty-eighth of March to Mexico with JJ. We thought we would be going, no big deal. I had also been to the Dominican in the later part of February on a last-minute deal with Tina. Her husband couldn't go and she desperately needed someone to go with her. I probably shouldn't have agreed to go, but I did. Things just kept happening, before and after that trip.

On the seventeenth of February, another truck had an accident. We only had one out that night because Monday was a holiday. He'd almost made it home but hit black ice and totalled our truck that was only four months old. He was okay; he just suffered minor injuries. We were overwhelmed as we knew the impact from the last time this had happened to one of our new trucks. We'd lost a lot of money. Insurance covers depreciated value and not what your loan says you owe. What a mess.

The driver was deemed at fault. He was speeding according to the computer in the truck. He knew it was slippery and was still going too fast. Not to mention the fact that when roads are treacherous our drivers are supposed to park and wait for better weather conditions. We had to let him go. I one hundred per cent didn't wish to keep him anyway. If ever there were red flags about a driver, it was him. He had made many mistakes and there were numerous incidents. Steve had kept him on, even though the kids and I had said he had to go. We live in a world where it is hard to find workers. We need people that will work hard, but also can pass a drug test, which is seemingly harder and harder to come by. This was one of the many times that Steve had wished he had followed my gut feeling. Waiting to find out how bad the numbers were going to be was a big headache, as was trying to hire two drivers to cover the runs. Steve was driving every day and the stress was piling up.

I heard about a lady that does readings. I made an appointment and went right in. Her name was Bethany. She is brilliant. Likely the best possible thing I had done so far that year. I didn't know this lady and we had never met.

I was skeptical at first. She could easily see on Facebook how close I am to my mom. That was what she started with and it didn't take long for me to choke up. Mom knows I'm there and everything that is said to her, but she has no way of communicating. She's trapped inside her head. Nonetheless, we are strongly connected.

It was reassuring to hear Mom was not alone. She had spirits around her and angels. I have known this for some time. If you've watched Mom interact with the blank air, usually the floor or off to the side of me, it was evident she was not alone. The reader went on to tell me lots of things that could not be found on Facebook.

My daughter was working on her Masters, studying hard. She was very determined and focused. Natasha is an amazing student. These were things not found on my Facebook page. My husband likes to go fast. Really fast and dangerously so. She saw trucks and cars and that he needed to be careful. Something happens, something serious, but he doesn't die. Not surprising because we are a racing family. He loves his speed. But in the trucks too? My main worry was his road rage. Daily, Steve would call to tell me about people going 80 km on the highway and how it shouldn't be allowed. He gets all worked up because he has a job to do, and these slow people are making his day longer and getting in his way. He tended to waste a lot of energy on things he couldn't control.

She told me I needed to work on myself more. Clear out the regrets and guilt. To let it go; write it down and burn it. To connect to the trees and outdoors. Heal my energy because I gave so much of it away. To rest and take more time for me.

The biggest thing that helped was her telling me not to worry about money. The accident was costing us money, but our business would replenish itself. I needed to hear that, and to remember it when things were not looking good.

I can't dwell on things I can't change. It is a waste of energy. Keep working hard and moving forward.

We were still building our camp—more like our retirement home—on the lake. She said I would get what I wanted. I had my plans drawn up and I was determined to get our dream home out of it. My energy around that project was right on target. At this point we couldn't wait, but we were falling into a difficult time to build anything. My reading gave me some things to work on and overall, a sense of peace for some of my worries.

I headed out on my trip a few days later. The trip was good. More sun and fresh air. I soaked up the sun as it gives me energy. I crave it and thrive off it, just like the ocean and trees. They ground me.

When we arrived home, things were getting crazy over in China. Many people had died. Cases were popping up in Europe. The news was all about the COVID-19 virus. When we came home, I went to see Mom the following day. She was supposed to be bathed at 9:30 a.m. However, when I arrived, it was already done. They claimed they didn't know that I was back. I still fed her, dried and curled her hair, brushed her teeth, cut her nails, cleaned her nose, and did a few other things for her. On the following days I continued to go in to feed her breakfast and do her care routine every day as normal.

On Thursday, I noticed after I got home that Shay had seemed tired, but continued about his day, which included bringing his girlfriend's little brother over to meet us. He was three. He clung to Shay the entire time. My kids have always been good with younger kids. Hopefully, they will be naturally good parents.

On Friday Shay didn't look very good. He came home from school, and I asked if he wanted me to contact the doctor. He said he just wanted to go and rest as he had to go to work in three hours. I opened his door later to check on him and he said he was still going to go to work. That didn't last too long. He was miserable and left work early, driving past our house and going over to his girlfriend's. I was home and had allowed JJ to have the hockey team over for a party. Steve had gone to a hockey game with a buddy. Shay called me at 8:45 p.m. feeling so sick, and said he was finding it hard to breath. He didn't know how high his fever was, but he was starting to scare me.

I could have driven over there but I knew I couldn't carry him, and it didn't sound like he could carry himself. Shay was scared, and I could hear it in his voice. I told him I was calling an ambulance. He texted me the address. He also texted me to tell me that he was spitting up blood. I called Steve to get his ass home.

My plan was I was going to be at the hospital when the ambulance got there. The paramedics had tried to get an IV in with no luck. Shay's temperature was extremely high and was dangerous. He was pretty much delirious. They had given him medication for his fever. I met him at the hospital and he was so sick. The hospital was seriously busy with wall-to- wall people. We waited at the desk for twenty minutes before he even got checked-in. We were put in a room with three patient chairs. Shay soon started throwing up and his fever wasn't breaking. I kept asking for him to have an IV. They finally decided to put one in but had a hard time getting it in again. But they still couldn't hook it up until the doctor ordered something for it.

They gave him Advil as his fever was still 39.6 Celsius, or almost 103 Fahrenheit.

He was suffering and I felt so helpless.

If he moved or took a sip of liquid, he would just vomit. Finally, at 5:30 a.m. we saw the doctor. They got the IV going and gave him something for the nausea. His fever broke around 8 a.m. and he went for X-rays. It showed spots on his lungs. Later that day they swabbed him for influenza and he had to be isolated. It turned out he had Influenza B and pneumonia. No wonder he was so sick.

He had gone in Friday night and was released Sunday night. It was Monday before I noticed the medication had kicked in. The doctors told me if I got through the next two to four days without any symptoms that I would be okay. Ironically, no one in our house or his girlfriend's house got sick. I figured someone would, but we were lucky.

I was at Mom's all that week. People were joking about the full moon, Friday the 13th, and a time change all falling within the same week.

Little did they know the storm that was brewing.

Shit literally hit the fan when the government started recommending that anyone coming home from travel had to self-isolate for fourteen days. This was on Friday the thirteenth of March. I had a call from the Villa asking me to stay away until it was fourteen days past our return from vacation, despite being home for over a week already and having been at the nursing home multiple times.

Seriously? When the order went out it was intended for moving forward and wasn't meant to be retroactive. Regardless I stayed away.

I planned on going back in on Monday for Mom's next bath but that didn't happen. On Sunday I got another call from the Villa. All long-term senior homes would be imposing restrictions. No visitors. No exceptions.

I don't just go to visit; I do a ton of Mom's care. She has no voice and I was her legal guardian. She cannot ask for a single thing. She was completely confined to her bed and chair. How could this inhumane act be legal?

In other provinces and in Halifax, senior homes were a deadly environment for spreading COVID. The homes with wards and not private rooms were seeing so many deaths.

Yarmouth, the town I live in was still free and clear but we were locked out as a precaution. I reached out to every government office I could call, fax, or email. Some of them got back to me. But no one with any good news. Nothing could be done.

I cringed because I knew what gets done and what doesn't for my mother. I knew just by hearing who was working.

Did I mention how short staffed they were for the entire year of 2019? Sometimes Mom was being cared for by complete strangers when the casuals or aids worked on her floor. They did their best, but seriously how could they possibly know the routines? But it didn't matter. My hands were tied, and I couldn't do a damn thing about Mom's rights or about her being alone. She was so scared she would end up alone.

I had promised she wouldn't ever be alone. I went every day. My brother fed her at supper frequently. I hired Donna, a lady I knew, to be there on days when I couldn't be. I didn't want her to be left staring at the walls 24/7. Sure, they tried to feed her and do her basic care. But other than that, she was on her own. Cold, hot, hungry, thirsty, uncomfortable, maybe an itch she couldn't scratch. Just let that sink in. She couldn't ring a buzzer or ask for anything.

Every nurse had a different idea of what was best for her. Some were great but some needed to just follow her care plan.

Things were changing daily. It was time to start listening to the news every night at 11 p.m. Hearing the official updated numbers. There were no cases down south. Just China, Europe, etc. Then it hit the United States, British Columbia, and Toronto.

Many people were heading out that week or had just left on vacation, thinking it was all being blown out of proportion. But shit continued to hit the fan. Italy was losing 400 to 600 people a day. The kids were on March Break. Little did anyone realize it was going to be the longest March Break ever.

Canada was taking more and more precautions every day. The news hype kept growing. People needed to come home now. Some cancelled their trips. The ones that had left before the 13th didn't have great trips because they were a ball of anxiety. They had just reached their destinations when things began to spiral out of control.

What if they didn't get home?

There was talk of shutting the borders.

The rules and laws continued to increase daily. On the twenty-second of March, a state of emergency for Nova Scotia was issued. More enforcement became mandatory. We were down to staying home and only going out for essentials or working if you were in the essential category. We had to limit ourselves to meeting with just five people in our households unless our family was bigger. No socializing and we had to stay two metres apart from other people if we were in a public place. And again, only if you needed to be there.

One person was allowed to go shopping; not the whole family. They closed all parks, beaches, and government-owned playgrounds. Gas was cheap at sixty-five to seventy cents a litre. So far, we were still allowed to drive around.

The next step would be a provincial lockdown.

We had JJ's birthday supper on the twenty-seventh of March. We just had the family of course. His seventeenth birthday "Corona no beer" celebration was lobster and a big crazy cake.

By the thirty-first of March, New York, and the US were exploding with COVID cases. Italy and Spain were also devastated. They hadn't taken as tight of precautions as Canada had.

A lockdown hadn't happened yet, but we had 147 confirmed cases in Nova Scotia. This virus spread like wildfire through the droplets in the air. It survived on surfaces way too long. Wash your hands like crazy was the rule. You couldn't buy hand sanitizer, toilet paper, bleach, Lysol wipes, etc. The shelves were bare beyond the purchase limitations that were put into place. If you were out and someone heard you cough or sneeze, look out, as you might get stoned.

On April 19, 2020, we had 600 cases in Nova Scotia. Things had become worse. You were not allowed to drive around for no reason. If you were caught with other people in your vehicle, without the same home address, you would each get an eight hundred dollar fine. We had to stay six feet away from other people on sidewalks or in stores—anywhere. There was to be no contact.

School was all being done online. I kept telling JJ these will be your easiest three credits ever. He was working full-time, learning what life was about. Although he hated doing the school work online. Shay was working at Canadian Tire and doing some of his welding theory online.

On the morning of the nineteenth of April, we were on our way to Lantz to pack up Steve's mother's apartment. She had been in the hospital for months. Hailey, Shay's new girlfriend was also with us. Shay had to work. We got near Bedford when my cousin who was meeting us there started texting me. She lived in Sackville, so she hadn't left her house yet. There had been a shooting near Debert, Nova Scotia. The details were scarce and being updated on Twitter by the RCMP.

As we neared the city, we started seeing more and more cop cars. We had just got on the 102 heading north when we got the message that the shooter was on the same highway headed south.

We were not far from our exit. We had a big trailer with us. We couldn't just stop so we continued. I mentioned he was not going to randomly shoot us. I had no idea that he was indeed shooting people randomly.

The police presence was unlike anything I'd ever seen. Every exit and overpass were covered with RCMP who were packing assault rifles. We had no idea the extreme seriousness of the situation we were in the middle of. Taking our exit with cops flying through the stop lights we encountered a roadblock. We pulled over. Great, we were sitting ducks. Finally, the cop waved us through.

We arrived at the apartment at approximately 11:55 a.m. My cousin texted me that they had got the shooter in Enfield, just down the road from where we were. In fact, we would have passed that exit close to the time they shot him.

He had killed a lot of people. Including an RCMP officer in Shubenacadie. Lantz, where we were, was in the middle of Shubie and Enfield. What a day to pick for this much needed road trip.

Steve's mom had been in the hospital for over four months. She was paying rent for nothing, and we needed to get the job done. But what a crazy day.

We didn't know the full extent of the tragedy until we watched the news that night. The killer was crazy—shooting people and burning down homes in Portapique, Nova Scotia. Posing as a police officer with a real looking cop car. Hauling people over and shooting them. Shooting neighbours that would come to help at the burning houses. He was on a path of destruction until he was killed at the Enfield gas station in a stolen SUV.

The entire province, country, and world felt this one. It was the biggest mass murder to ever happen in Canada. Had we had clearer details at the time, we would not have continued into the area. I really thought my cousin was exaggerating when she didn't even have near enough information. She wasn't leaving her house with him on the loose. We were already three hours from home in a state of emergency because of COVID-19 with nowhere to go except our destination.

I had even felt with all the police around that we should surely be safe. But he had killed twenty-two people, including a pregnant mom, during his shooting spree. I strongly believe an alert on our phones would have saved lives. I don't use Twitter at all. They knew early in the morning he was posing as an RCMP officer, with a replica cop car. We likely wouldn't have even left our house at 8:20 a.m. that morning if we'd known. Even on the way home we passed so many police vehicles heading back to their home bases. We got home at 10 p.m. as things were still unfolding on the news. There were thirteen dead on Sunday, but the number climbed to twenty-three by the time all the details were sorted out in the fires and shootings from the night before.

It was a terrible tragedy. My heart went out to all the families.

On the twenty-nineth of April, Nova Scotia suffered another tragedy. We lost a Cyclone helicopter with six Canadian Armed Forces members on it.

They were on a practice exercise off the coast of Greece. They had not been there long because just a week earlier, the female crew member who lost her life had played her bagpipes in honour of the tragic Nova Scotian shooting victims. Then eleven days later she met a tragic ending of her own.

Enough is enough, 2020 was already one for the books.

May 2, 2020, we had 960 confirmed COVID cases in the province. The numbers were only going down by ten to fifteen a day. The cases were mostly in the city and in nursing homes. The Yarmouth area had not been greatly affected yet.

A day earlier the Nova Scotian Government had allowed sport fishing to start. They also relaxed the outdoor rules. We could now go to trails, parks, cottages, and outdoor places, as long as we stayed six feet apart. And only interacted within our immediate family.

There were still no social gatherings of more than five individuals allowed. If the numbers stayed low, we'd be good. If they spiked, we would be back to being confined and under restrictions.

I was a member of CrossFit and belonged to a yoga studio. Thankfully, I was doing both classes online. There was no way I was gaining fifty pounds because we were in a lockdown. My mental health would not have survived if I wasn't doing those classes.

Some people were scared to go outside. I wasn't, and no way was I not getting my fresh air and sunshine.

Our work didn't slow down, and in fact we got busier because everyone was ordering online.

By the May long weekend, we were allowed to bubble with another family. Beaches were opened but the state of emergency was extended. School was officially over—no more in-person classes—but kids were still expected to do online work. We had over 1,000 cases in Nova Scotia. Prince Edward Island and New Brunswick barely had any and were doing better than us. Most restaurants opened to do takeout. Thankfully, the green houses were open because I was playing in the dirt.

Our trucks were getting busier as things start to open up. We bought two new trucks and were back to full staffing. I worked out a lot. I had not been bored at all.

The biggest change was not being able to tend Mom. She was all alone. It had been sixty-four days since I had last been there to visit. Her rights were stripped from her. If the government could do this to her, I could only imagine what else was to come.

A week ago, had been the worst day. Mom had seizures. I got called but was completely helpless. I checked in on her before bed. I had a good conversation with the nurse. I asked who would be with her, checking on her throughout the night? I was told it was confidential.

How could that be with the day Mom had? I couldn't be told who was with her?

I cried for hours. I was so mad that these people could be so cruel. I couldn't be by her side like I normally would have been. Damn COVID-19. I was so sick of seniors not having any rights. Especially the ones who were completely dependent on their power of attorney being their voice.

I was down all week. Tears like never before. Poor Mom. I even asked for legal advice. There was nothing much anyone could do. Even the courts were impacted by COVID. The lawyer told me to keep advocating for seniors. They needed me.

All I could wonder was this. How long was this COVID crap going to keep me from Mom?

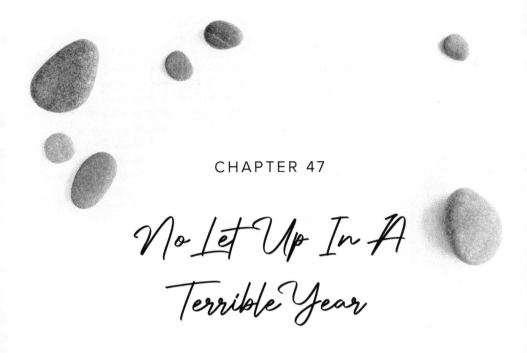

CHAPTER 47

No Let Up In A Terrible Year

Nova Scotia continued to see tragedy in 2020. This time, it was a three-year-old boy who went missing in Truro. I didn't know what had happened. Did he fall into the river? They searched for days. Now he was listed as a missing person. It was so sad. The parents were dragged through the mud. It didn't make sense. I didn't know what to believe.

By June of 2020 things were busy. The town was crazy, especially on cheque days. Some people were wearing a mask to go out. Some stores required masks while others didn't. Staying six feet apart was the new normal.

In every public place, and for most appointments you were required to wear a mask and use sanitizer. At the end of May the government announced beauty salons, physio, massage therapists, gyms, etc. could reopen but they had to follow the requirements as set out by the government. Restaurants could open at half capacity. We were in Halifax and took Tristan and Sam out for supper. It was so weird being allowed in a public place. Tristan turned twenty-seven that year. Some things were starting to feel more normal.

Toward the end of June, we were allowed to have bigger gatherings, as long as everyone stayed six feet apart. For weddings, funerals, etc. you were still supposed to only bubble with one other family, but I saw a lot more than that happening when people gathered.

Racing was starting to open again. They would only allow so many spectators in to the races. While I was looking forward to having the year off from the crazy race season, it would be good to see the kids race.

In the US, the COVID numbers were skyrocketing. It appeared like people didn't care. There was no control. Our province was free and clear for over two weeks, then travellers for business or summer homes arrived and we were right back in the game. PEI had two months in the clear, then five cases popped up just over the long weekend in early July—right at the same time they allowed our Atlantic provinces to bubble. The big question was what was happening with the schools? They had not announced anything for certain.

Not that I'd want to go to the US, but you could not travel abroad anywhere. What would happen to the big airlines? So many small businesses were folding too.

June was no better than the previous months for our business. Another driver hit a pole in a parking lot and cost us another five-thousand-dollar deductible. This seemed to be the trend for 2020. Then we received a letter from a lawyer in Quebec stating that we needed to stop using our TST company name immediately. We were said to be breaching a trademark agreement and they would take us to court if needed.

We were a little company in Nova Scotia. We did not travel anywhere the other company did. We were not in competition because we worked for other companies under contract. We didn't own trailers, dispatch ourselves or do anything along the lines of the other company. I hired a lawyer to communicate these things in response and we waited to see if we would need to change our name to JTST, which was just our family's first initials. We had been TST since 2000 and we had been a registered limited company since 2004. Now we had a problem?

The other big news in June was they allowed seniors homes to have short outdoor visits with their loved ones. I was not that excited about this news. Mom could not focus on a face six feet apart from her. I didn't know if she would even be awake for our visit. But I made an appointment for the fifteenth of June. We were allowed two people, so I got my brother to meet me there.

Mom was awake and did respond to my voice. I was so surprised to have her respond. I explained the best I could about how strange the world was right now, and that we could not visit her, hug her, or come closer than six feet. If we did, she would have to be in quarantine for two weeks. Such bullshit.

I needed to be able to care for her. Life was cruel and unfair. Now this took the cake. Seniors had become prisoners. They now had to be alone during the ending of their life. Sure, if they knew Mom was on her last two or three days, I would be allowed to sit with her, but by then it would be too late.

So many of the little things were not getting done for her. Did they notice her glasses were broken and the little foot pad was digging into her? No, but I did from six feet apart and they were all shocked when I pointed it out. When your glasses hang on the end of your nose there is a problem. I took them a couple days later to get them fixed. They handed them to me over the fence.

I couldn't stand not being able to wipe her face, hold her hand, or kiss her cheek. She did move her hand and respond with facial expressions when I explained the circumstances to her. I didn't care what the others said; I knew she heard and understood me. I also knew she couldn't respond. But that didn't mean that she didn't understand. Stop thinking there is no point visiting them, because they don't know who you are. Bullshit excuse. Go see your elderly family often. Higher powers are watching over us.

My best advice? Do what you can live with and sleep with. If it keeps you up at night, then there is a problem. Deep down you know right from wrong.

When my mind won't shut off at night because something is bothering me, I act on it. I am different. I know that. I am a doer. I don't slack in life. I try to do more than I can fit into a day. I try to help people. That's how I was made. I have many purposes on this earth, and I plan to fulfill them. I got to see Mom two more times that month. Once with Sharon and once with Bev. Mom was okay for all the visits and somewhat awake. But she had responded best at my first visit.

In July, the weather was good. Very hot most of the time. We were busy with work and building the camp. Which was not done but should have been. Very frustrating. We were camping in the chalet for now.

My gardens were doing great. I loved getting stuff to eat out of them. I was doing tons of landscaping at the camp and around the house. People were wearing masks shopping and around town. It was recommended in a lot of places and was becoming more common and even mandatory in some places. We still had no cases around here, so people were not being too cautious. I had relaxed a lot.

I could now visit Mom once a week, still outdoors, and staying six feet apart. It was so hard. I just wanted to take care of her. Hold her hand so she could feel I was there. Four months and I still couldn't help her in any way. It was driving me crazy.

The government had relaxed things a little bit more. On the twenty-second of July, which was also my birthday, we were supposed to be able to give a quick hug and have outside visits with five people, up from the two people that had been allowed previously. However, seniors' homes were able to decide how to proceed with the new rules. Of course, they announced they would only start on the twenty-seventh.

What right did they have to keep us from our family? They sat around in meetings and decided they needed more time. For what? Put a mask on us and let us hug our family. It was not that hard! I'd had enough of Mom being alone, and me not being there for her.

Hailey, Shay's girlfriend got to spend lots of time with us through COVID lockdowns. I really like her, in fact she kind of reminds me of me! She hasn't had an easy childhood and doesn't have parents looking out for her. Very sad as she has a heart of gold and common sense for most things. It was nice to have a female around and someone that appreciated my everyday efforts.

The government announced the kids would be going back to school. I was grateful they would get to go. JJ would be in Grade 12. He had worked the entire time, from the sixteenth of March all through the summer, starting at 7 a.m. every morning, five days a week.

We also got word there would be racing, starting on the nineteenth of July. I was so annoyed with the family. For months I had tried to get them motivated and ready. Instead, we had two weeks of rushing around trying to get the cars ready. Once again racing had taken over our summer.

If they had listened to me, in all our locked-down time we could had got the cars ready so we could have been enjoying this nice weather and some family time. I did not enjoy the stress of getting ready. Everyone was cranky.

The biggest news during July was provided on my birthday. I was handed a card stating, "Happy Birthday Grandma." When I finally figured it out, I was so emotional. A Grandma. How sweet and I was so excited. We all were. The first grandbaby on the way.

Tristan and Sam were going to be parents.

CHAPTER 48

Back At The Racetrack

August started with some of the best summer weather we'd had in years. I was enjoying the pool. The gardens were producing nice veggies. Construction on the camp was still going slow. We should have signed a contract with penalties as we felt our builder was not making us a priority. The garage was busy again, working on the race cars. My friend Gayna was around, ever since we had a hot tub night back in May. It had been nice to have her around. We introduced her to the racing world.

The first race day went well. JJ drove my car and did well considering the car was having issues. For the second race day, Shay decided to build another car to race. They each had two cars to drive in the different classes. I might go crazy with six cars to worry about. Sometimes they couldn't handle one each, and now they were trying to keep two working right and on the track. Oh boy.

Steve's "parts car" was working well and winning races. He wanted it for parts to keep Shay and JJ's cars on the track. However, he decided to play with it, and it was a little rocket. We had a short race season this year because of COVID. Steve managed to win checkered flags frequently in both of his classes. Shay and JJ won a few in the Cavaliers. Steve was a champion in the Sportsman Class as well as the Civic Class.

Businesswise we were busy. Thankful for our blessings. Glad we'd chosen the right profession.

September brought school again. We had our first COVID case in the region in Clare at the university. Let's see how many by the end of the month was the word. We took JJ to race at Scotia Speedworld in Halifax. He did amazing in his father's car. JJ's car would have needed a different transmission for that track, so it was easier to just take Steve's parts car. They had fun and we were planning more trips.

I wrote a poem for my racing family.

ON THE TRACK

SOME GO LOW
SOME GO HIGH
WHATEVER IT TAKES
TO GET YOU BY

CARS GET CLOSE
CARS GO 3 WIDE
CARS CLIP AND
CARS COLLIDE

HIT THE DOOR
HIT THE SIDE
SOMEHOW
I'M GETTING BY

DRIVE IT IN HARD
KISS THE WALL
WHATEVER YOU DO
JUST DON'T STALL
HOLD YOUR BREATH
OR SAY IT ALL!

Masks were now required almost everywhere. I was allowed to go in to care for Mom for a few hours, Monday to Friday. Better that than nothing at all. It had been six long months of not being able to help her. I still couldn't believe seniors were caged up and kept from their family. Only a few got to have their caregivers in. The rules were so strict.

Mom's condition had deteriorated—most of which was normal, but without a doubt COVID had rushed her along.

The hours and hours spent alone sitting in her chair.

So unfair. It broke my heart.

We had a short but good race season. We went for Funday, the last race of the year where they gave out the trophies. It was the worst race day ever by far. JJ got threatened. None of us took that very well.

I wrote a letter to another driver, a couple days later, a person who I had actually respected before that day happened. I let her know how disgusted I was with her behaviour, and the behaviour of some of the others. Threatening JJ, a seventeen-year-old competitive driver was over the line. It's racing. Shit happens. And he didn't do anything wrong. But she and the others sure did. Their over-the-top reaction was uncalled for.

I still cannot believe how that day went down. Everyone perceives things in their own way, but this got spun out of control by two people. It never should have happened. We packed up and left before the features and trophy presentations. I have no regrets for leaving. It was by far the best thing for our family and team.

Being in a brawl would not have been good for any of us.

The rest of September was good. We went on a couple out of town racing road trips. Steve turned forty-five and we had a small get-together for him. So many campfires and fun all summer.

It was October and fall was in the air. I hated to see winter coming as there would be no trips or ways to escape the cold because of COVID.

JJ was muzzleloader hunting. He did well as usual. We were busy with work, and I was settling back into the routine of taking care of Mom again. She was not doing great. COVID had definitely played a part in her going downhill quickly.

In November, Nova Scotia was doing okay with COVID, but the rest of the country was getting hit hard. Even higher numbers than when it had all started. Toward the end of November, Halifax had an outbreak. We were forbidden to go shopping there. Due to the new restrictions, schools were not allowed to play sports anymore. JJ was in Grade 12 and being robbed of how things should be for the graduates. The last weekend we had been to see him play hockey was our twenty-third anniversary.

I was at Mom's as much as possible. She didn't eat very much, often forgetting how to swallow and chew. I wasn't surprised on the sixteenth of November when the doctor called me in and said she didn't have that long. Still, it was hard to hear. Slowly it sank in. All I wanted to do was to be with her.

Thankfully, I had got my Christmas decorations up early because by December I was trying to be with Mom every hour possible. No one could say how many days she had left. She was eating two servings of applesauce a day and was hanging on. I remember feeding her the last time on fourteenth of December. She ate like a little bird eagerly opening her mouth. The next day there was no interest.

She held on until the 22nd of December.

I wasn't surprised she picked that day. The number 22 is significant in my life. I hope she has as many angels and spirits with her as I believe she does. I felt her leave her body, and I knew she was at peace. No more suffering.

We spent Christmas at the camp, which was not one hundred per cent completed but was still truly a dream come true. My designs and planning had come together before my eyes. Everyone was there, which made my heart so full. I pulled off a big surprise of getting Steve a side-by-side. Being busy sure helped me cope. I could be sitting around depressed and sad, but Mom would not have wanted that. I was never bored. I can always find things to do. I actually never have enough time in the day to do what I want to do! Ever!

I indulged with baking and eating more than usual throughout the season. I was comforted by cooking as it was always Mom's thing. I saw and felt her presence on the 23rd as I was making the pies and cookies in my new pantry. I loved my new space; it was almost perfect!

The year ended much the way it had started—in tragedy. On the fifteenth of December a scallop fishing vessel, the Chief William Saulis, sank with six local fishermen on it, devastating the local communities. It was heartbreaking for so many families right before Christmas and one more thing that truly broke my heart in 2020.

New Year's was celebrated calmly with a few friends at the camp. I had bought 2020 underwear back in December of 2019 thinking it would be a great year. I burned them at the party. We were all hopeful for the best in 2021.

It had to be better, right?

CHAPTER 49

2021: A Good Start

C OVID was still a factor as 2021 got under way. There were still a lot of
restrictions.

On the seventh of February we all watched JJ's hockey game but had to do
it online. No spectators were allowed in the arena. The YCMHS Vikings beat
the PEB Sharks 4–1. There is a long-time rivalry between the two Yarmouth
County high schools. The Vikings also beat PEB on the twelfth of February.
We were allowed back in the arena to watch that game. The COVID rules
were forever changing.

JJ would be graduating that year and minor and high school hockey
would be finished for our family. The best way to end our season was by
defeating PEB twice.

After the game on the seventh, Sam and Tristan went to stay at the
hospital. There was a big blizzard coming in overnight. They had an early
morning appointment for a C-section.

On Monday, February 8, 2021, my life blossomed and I became a
Grammie. I'd always thought I'd want to be called Grandmom. (My kids
called my mom that.) However, as the time drew closer, I just kept thinking
about who was really special to me. It was my Grammie, although I never
got to spend much of my childhood with her. I do remember her pantry. I
liked to go in it looking for baked goods. I loved her laugh. I feel her with me
to this day.

Kelly John Hubbard, my first-born grandson arrived at 8:45 a.m. A perfectly beautiful baby. Because of COVID I only got to meet him on his second day in this world. That was hard when I just want to see him every single day. To hold him and love him. Sam's mother got the first day and I got the second. I did get a FaceTime call to see our newest sweet little person.

They got to bring Kelly home on Friday, the twelfth of February. I will enjoy every moment of being a Grammie. Time is the most precious gift. I want to read him books, bake with him, play outside, go exploring for treasures, and teach him all about nature. Grammie and Papa are so excited for this new chapter of our life to unfold. I couldn't be happier to embrace all its glory. I was truly blessed and thankful.

CHAPTER 50

My Mom, Norma Tedford

I loved my mom, Norma Tedford.

I considered her to be the only parent that I ever had. Mom had such a hard life. She endured too much suffering, although I believe her childhood was good. She was brought up on a farm, with no shortage of chores to be done. Her stories of the rocky beach, cranberry fields, back pasture, hayfields, and gardens are treasures I hope to always remember.

She married young, having her first two children with Charles K. He wasn't much help in the raising of the children and they parted ways early on.

Her next marriage was to Peter Sinclair, my biological piece of shit father. She didn't know he was a very sick man. His sickness (a chemical imbalance of the brain, I'm sure) grew worse over the years as I fully described in my previous chapters. After that nightmare she eventually married Charles d'Eon. Her best years were spent with him.

She did divorce him though after many years of marriage. We never understood why, but we figured she knew he wouldn't be able to take care of her and she knew she had the signs of early Alzheimer's. They remained friends and he continued to be Grandpére to my children.

She lived many years on her own in her apartment. She was very social and loved to help the less fortunate that she encountered. As the signs of Alzheimer's increased, things needed to change.

Throughout the journey with my mother and her Alzheimer's, the one thing that always stood out in my mind is how alone she felt.

Our journey started in 2005 when we were travelling to the Valley to see a doctor who studied the disease. Mom was still herself, but we knew she was heading down the path of Alzheimer's. We didn't need to be told the diagnosis, however, I continued to take her in the hope she would qualify for an experimental drug treatment.

She had nothing to lose.

Our future years together were numbered.

Here is her story of her journey with Alzheimer's as I remember it.

In the beginning I wrote letters to every government official I could think of. I pleaded for help. Getting Mom on the "The List" was just the first challenge. The list grew so many branches along the way, and around every corner there was a new issue to be resolved. Mom's story was one of the many.

I'm including as much information as possible. I could not just write about all the good parts, I had to share the true struggles as well. There were many nurses who I thank from the bottom of my heart for their gentle care. You can sure tell the ones that are in the right profession.

To anyone reading this that is going through a similar experience, I feel for you with my whole heart. Most of my struggles with my mother happened before COVID. Only her last year was tarnished by COVID. The homes were already short staffed before the pandemic. I can only imagine how much worse things became for all seniors during and since the pandemic. I believe, *all seniors deserve more.*

I sent my letters to the mayor, government officials, and any address I could find that I thought might have been helpful. My need to advocate for seniors ran deep, and I had to speak up as they could not. I followed the procedures that were outlined for me to care for my mother Norma Tedford. My siblings pushed for me to have her assessed and have her put on the waiting list. I agreed and after three assessments over a period of fourteen months she finally met the requirements to be put on the list. Most would say this should have happened sooner, but according to the guidelines she could not at sixty-seven get on "The List." This finally happened in February of 2014.

I was told to pick three places that she would like to go and live in. Her first choice was Meadows, second choice was the Villa in Dayton, and her third choice was Nakile. All of these were close by in my area. I did all the work on my own. Mom's worker projected her wait time would be within one year. By the end of March of 2014, Norma was locking herself outside in the cold, and I had to move her immediately out of her apartment. I found a senior's boarding home for her. This worked for a while until they finally said she was beyond their care level. She needed one-on-one care to keep her safe and they had other seniors to care for. They said they couldn't watch her every minute. She was busy, walking all day, picking everything up, and no longer knew what was harmful or dangerous. She was a classic Alzheimer's patient—ninety per cent of the time she was happy and joking with the staff, and ten per cent of the time she had crying and confused spells, asking what was happening to her? If the care person did not have experience with the upsets in these patients, they would not know how to manage them. If someone was bossy or pushy with her, she might rebel and become more agitated. Patience, love, hugs, and kindness were what she needed when she was confused or upset.

I had only ten days to figure out what to do next and I had three choices.

First was to put her on the Nova Scotia-wide list and hopefully she would be placed in a home quickly. However, she could be placed anywhere within the province and this could rob her of her last months of knowing her family's faces. She still knew us but could not call us by name. Also, she could not have been brought back to the Yarmouth area until a bed became available within her normal wait time period and no sooner. So, she might jump the queue to have a bed, but it could be a long wait to move her closer to home.

Secondly, we could put her in the hospital to wait out the time until her placement. The doctor's exact words to us were, "that is for people without any family and nowhere else to go, and it is not pretty there."

Third, we could move her into my home for a few months to wait for a placement. Norma's worker, Jennifer, felt Mom would be placed by the end of the year, possibly by October.

Therefore, on the thirtieth of June, I moved her into my home. My very busy home where we have three active sons and owned and operated our own trucking company. Jennifer had been very supportive. Norma qualified for one hour of personal care a day (where I had to be home), ten hours a week of respite care, which I could use on days I chose, and I could leave the house. We also would get a program supplement of $500, plus one of $400. One would pay for me to tend her, and the other to hire extra care for her. Extra care cost, at the time $15–20 per hour.

When the family is taking care of a senior, they are also entitled to sixty days per calendar year of respite vacation beds in a seniors' homes. I immediately booked her in for our vacations and as the fall drew near, I booked her for every other weekend almost until Christmas as we travelled with our boys for rep hockey. I also used most of Norma's money to hire care for when I could not be home. For example, two days of forty-eight hours of care, cost me a minimum of $550. Vacation bed government supplemented (low income) required that she only pay $22 per day.

That was an overview of the program and I felt I could manage with the vacation bed option as a break and the rest of the time hire people to tend her.

In July she went to Kentville for ten days. They found her to be very busy, but they managed without any one-on-one care for her. In August she went to Lunenburg for five days. Again, they were surprised by how busy she was, but they managed again with no one-on-one care. The end of September she went to Nakile while my husband and I went on vacation to Newfoundland. I checked on her several times by phone and had other people check on her as well. I also knew some of the workers there. They found her to be very busy and took it upon themselves to hire one-on-one care for her. (I had been told there was no one-on-one budget available.) I thought things had gone well on each of the visits.

The day after I picked her up from Nakile, I received a phone call from her worker saying that Nakile did not feel they could take her again as she had played with the windows and doors, and they felt she was not safe there. She was a flight risk? They had coded locked doors as do all the nursing homes. There was also supposedly no budget for one-on-one care? I felt very discouraged as I knew this meant that for a future permanent placement she would also be refused.

Shortly after that call Jennifer had called again to say that Norma would be up on the list to get one of the twenty new beds opening at Nakile, but she would, "not be safe enough there." Nakile was to be removed from her list of options. This did not settle well but what more could I do?

Two weeks later Norma was scheduled for respite at the Meadows for five days. Our family was excited for the break, and I was happy to have her only a few minutes away where I could stop in and make sure she was eating and check on her, but still get a rest. I took a detailed list about Mom with me, which I had faxed over the day before. I stayed for over two hours and gave the nurses lots of tips about her care and personality. I left feeling good and was shocked when three hours later I received the call that I would have to pick her up immediately. Norma's worker called Meadows and offered to find money for one-on-one care, however, Meadows claimed without even leaving the phone to check that they had no extra staff to call in, and she needed to be picked up right away. I went to get her (I was a complete mess) taking my aunt with me and was shocked again when no one approached us or talked to us.

A nurse handed me her pills and walked away. No one spoke to us at all.

The following week I called for a meeting as being Norma's legal guardian I needed to know why she had been sent home. As well, I wished to have more answers provided about how this could happen. Norma was said to have been agitated and upset for two hours when they decided they could not care for her, and she had to go. Yes, she was taking everyone's stuff. Yes, she had slapped a worker, and yes, she had pulled on a bathroom door trying to get out and it came off its track. However, they had never called and described her condition or asked if she needed meds to calm down. She did have a prescription for this if needed. Which had never been needed in the past. Just she had to go, and it was another door slamming in her (our) face again.

I found it hard to believe that in our care system that homes could pick and choose who they could help. We all pay taxes and I believe all seniors should have the same opportunities on their journey to their last home. I was hurt by the actions and the unprofessionalism of this care home. The way I was spoken to on the phone and how, when I went to collect my mother, no one had talked to us at all. Facing reality, which was what this all boiled down to, seniors like my mom (and their families) are the ones who lose in this system. It is sad really as they should be there to help the families who need help the most. As should all nursing homes.

Two days prior to the meeting, Meteghan did call and say they would take her at the end of October with one-on-one care (which with the circumstances they had found it in the budget somewhere) and I would get a break. They did great with her in Meteghan. Knowing with all the recent refusals that Norma's paperwork was going to be needed to change to state a secure unit was needed I added Meteghan to her list.

I discovered that the Villa in Dayton had to be removed from her list. She could not go there because they didn't have a secured unit. Meadows did have a secured unit, but they had over a two-year wait for a regular bed and were not sure of the timeline for the secured unit. I could not get a timeline on Meteghan's secured unit except for knowing it would be months.

To top matters off, my private care workers were busy with their regular jobs, school, and family. They kept cutting back on what they could handle for extra shifts. She was awake for eighteen hours (needing one-on-one care to be safe) and if I was lucky slept for six hours, usually between 12–6 a.m. Occasionally she slept for seven hours. I was trying to give Norma the level of care she deserved, with what was available to seniors. But I found out the neediest seniors and families could not use all the help that has been put into place. We were left feeling Mom had been labelled as "a bad senior," too much work, and too busy.

I'm not sure people know that just because you may be on "The List" and your name comes up that a nursing home can still refuse you care (I had no idea). Seniors can be refused because they need too much care. And not all seniors living with family members can use the respite care, which is supposed to be available for sixty days in a calendar year. There is no one-on-one care budget and seniors are therefore drugged and restrained more frequently and sooner than they would be if they had access to one-on-one care. (Once they get into a home.) Families are forced to send their loved ones away (using the emergency list) because there are not enough local beds in secure units available near them.

My mother ate the best for me, and she had lost 40 pounds in her last year of life. When I was away from her, she lost weight. How was I supposed to send her far away to be drugged and to lose more weight? She would have been skin and bones when I did get to drive to wherever to see her. I had tried to do everything I could and needed to be able to live with my choices. I sacrificed months of my life to give my mother all of what she deserved as her life came to a sad, disease-driven end.

My eyes had been opened to see what all seniors were concerned with, and I'm sure there are many more in similar situations. I cannot just sit back and accept there is not more that can be done. When you see these seniors staring at the four walls, waiting for their end to come, there must be more that can be done. When you see families struggling to try and do all they can to care for a family member, and to get so many doors slammed in their faces, you understand why people give up. I am known as the strong one, and even I was pushed to my limits.

For the record, Pam our local mayor did communicate with me a few times. Then she never did get back to me. I know she has a lot on her plate; however, her platform is bigger than mine and I was counting on reaching as many people as possible to bring about an awareness of our seniors and their struggles. Like everything in life, you really don't know about the state of things until you have lived through it yourself.

After a year of waiting, I was forced to expand Norma's options as her care began to take a toll on my health and family life. I added North Queens to Norma's list in early June of 2015. A few weeks later in June Norma received her call to be placed in Caledonia at North Queen's Nursing Home. Although it was two hours away, I agreed to place her since with the new rules, to turn down the bed meant Norma would fall back to the bottom of "The List" and I would have to start the waiting period again.

So, I packed Norma up and made the two-hour drive to her temporary home and travelled as much as possible to see her over the next three months. In this home Norma would have a roommate and share a bathroom with a stranger. Trying to teach the nurses about her individual needs and to prevent her from losing weight were my biggest concerns with her being so far away. I was feeling guilty over the four hours spent driving instead of tending to my mother's needs. She was isolated from her family that she was used to seeing every day. It was a very long and sad three months.

In September Norma's name came up for a transfer to Meteghan. Knowing that it was another temporary placement, I transferred her so she would be a little closer to home. Keep in mind that every move robs these seniors of what precious memory and abilities they have left. It robs them of their quality of life in their last years, instead of placing them in their hometown and dealing with the new surroundings only once. I traded a two-hour drive for a twenty-five-minute drive and brought her to another new home with strangers who didn't know her once again.

The nurses in each of these homes are great, however, they never seem to have enough time to meet everyone's basic needs. Norma would again be sharing a room with another resident and a bathroom with three others. I spent the next two weeks driving there every day trying to teach the nurses all the little tricks to take care of Norma as she couldn't tell them anything for herself. Norma was described as the busiest senior some of these nurses had ever seen. Many commented they had no idea how I had managed to keep her home for the year that I did. She was always on the move, getting into everything, hardly sitting still for a moment, and unable to follow directions. If you told her, "No, you will get hurt," she couldn't understand and would do it anyway. Her comprehension of right and wrong was gone and she could easily hurt herself.

The first day I stayed home was in October. I decided my home and family needed some attention. However, I received the call that uprooted and drastically changed everything. Norma had become tangled in a chair leg, had fallen, and had broken her hip. I was off to meet the ambulance at the hospital and spent the next six days by my mother's side as she waited for and finally underwent a hip replacement.

In different homes Norma had been described as the busiest resident by many of the nurses before breaking her hip. But her life and care needs changed dramatically as she was now confined to a chair or a bed after the operation. Norma would need a lot of physiotherapy in the weeks to come. She did receive some but not as much as what was required for her full recovery. In Meteghan they only had a physio aid for so many hours per week who was required to see all the residents who required care. Norma's post operation instructions were to have range of motion exercises done three to four times a day and to walk assisted if she could tolerate it as often as possible. Some days were better than others, but normally Norma only received her exercises once per day, plus whatever I could do while I was there. The nurses had very little time to help while trying to provide for the basic needs of fifteen others on that wing.

I was constantly having to ask the nurses to help me. Norma's care was time-consuming. To meet her basic needs takes more time than what can be provided to her on a wing of thirteen to sixteen residents. You might ask, "How can it be that two nurses cannot meet all their needs?" I have spent many hours in these homes and can plainly see that the nurses are run off their feet. Norma was not the only one who had to wait her turn as many are told, "I will be there as soon as I can." How are seniors expected to wait for help in the washroom or to get to a washroom? When you need to go, you need to go. And then you have all the ones who cannot speak for themselves and need to go. Their schedules must be viewed as important too.

My heart goes out to these nurses, and I was torn when I had to bother them to assist me with toileting Norma or walking her (it took three people for safety reasons). Feeding her took at least one hour per meal, bathing her took three people and about forty-five minutes and she only got one per week. Taking Norma to the bathroom took between fifteen to thirty minutes each time with a special sit-to-stand lift, and she could not be left alone even for a moment. So what happens to the others while the nurses were with her? What happened to her when they were with the others? They had to wait alone.

Earlier in my struggles, our local government representative Zach made some calls and it turned out that the Villa in Dayton was built and equipped to make any unit safe and lockable, despite the fact I had been told I would have to remove her off that list. Finally, there was some good news. So, I had a meeting with the Director, and they actually accepted Mom into her new home. Thank you, Zach. If I had settled for Mom being removed from the list for placement at the Villa, she would have never made it closer to home. In November of 2015 Norma's name finally came up on the list to come home and be placed in the Villa St Joseph in Yarmouth. Finally, she would be within five minutes from her family who could assist with all her time-consuming needs. Her grandchildren could visit and we could see her face light up on a daily basis as she smiled at us while we fed and talked to her. Norma could finally have a private room where I knew her sleeping patterns would be better (she slept all night every night).

She was now in a gorgeous bright new facility but once again I faced the challenge of teaching all the nurses about my mother who could not speak for herself. Some could not get Norma to eat. I had many little pointers for this task. Therefore, we tried to be there for as many meals as possible. I went every day as Mom waited longer and sometimes went without what I considered to be her basic needs fulfilled. If I miss a day, I would ask for Norma to have two to three, fifteen-minute walks per day for exercise and regaining strength after her hip replacement (as was recommended). Also, her meals, drinks, snacks, of course would require assistance to try to get her to eat. And I asked for her to have between five-to-six-bathroom visits as close to the right times for her schedule as possible. Believe it or not sometimes this was not possible as there were twelve others in Norma's Villa and only two Continuing Care Assistant's to take care of them all. Plus, there were breaks for the staff that had to be covered.

On weekends and holidays Norma might not get even one walk, let alone three per day if I didn't stop in often and wait for the nurses to be able to help me. Plus, if Norma had to wait for too long for toileting, it forced her to wet in her Depends. I really didn't want that for her or for the other seniors before it became absolutely necessary. How many other seniors in these homes are forced to give up on their dignity earlier than what they should have to? I have never blamed the nurses, but I still felt that I must ask for what I felt my mother needed and deserved. I certainly had learned her schedule with the many hours I had given my mother as there was no greater gift than one's time. Many nurses had never seen a family member do as much for a resident in a home as I did. I couldn't just visit and see Mom in need and not do everything that I could to help. The nurses sure appreciated the hours I spent feeding Mom as they had others that needed to be fed. My brother also fed Norma as often as he could. She would eat very well for us, but it was still time-consuming.

I am only asking for basic needs such as feeding, toileting, and walking to be covered. The extras I did as much as I could, such as washing Mom's hair, brushing her teeth, doing her nails, rubbing on lotion, and giving her extra snacks and drinks. I spent time with her watching TV, taking her to the live music events when they were available, listening to music in her room and touring the building so she was not left staring at the walls for hours while they were tending to the other residents. Don't these seniors deserve at least one more set of hands to assist with the busy times and to help cover the breaks so there are always at least two nurses on the floor?

I have spent a lot of time in a few of these homes and I can clearly see the need. Why can't the government see it too? Absolutely you need to have a RN on duty, however, it is the CCAs who are the ones with the more hands-on, day-to-day care for the residents. This is where we need to increase the staffing ratios. The population is aging and the studies show the disease, Alzheimer's, is expected to double in the next twenty years. What are we waiting for? Much more training needs to take place if the CCAs are going to be able to deal with the behaviours and individual care needs of these seniors.

I have done much research on the topic, and I have learned a lot along the way, as my grandmother also suffered from this disease and spent her last years confined to a bed. I wish the health officials sitting in the offices making these decisions and guidelines would follow the nurses around for a day to see what level of care their time currently allows. Spending a day with someone like me as I tended to Norma's needs would help them to see what families would want for their loved ones. I mean it is necessary for them to do more than to simply take a guided tour of a beautiful new facility. They need to be in the real working environment to see the effects of their decisions.

Taking care of Norma consumed my life but what could I do? Turn my back and ignore her needs? Settle and say, "that's just the way it is?" Too many are turning a blind eye to what really needs to be done. I find many people assume everything gets done. That is not the case. I'm not saying the nurses don't try and of course they do their best. But reality is much more can—and should—be getting done for these seniors. I don't envy others for having lots of money, but I certainly think they are very lucky if they have enough money to pay for private care should they ever need to have it provided in their senior years. To me that would be like winning the lottery—I would have had a private nurse for Mom daily as she so deserved to have one.

All I knew at this point was that I was thankful for her forever home being the Villa Saint Joseph du Lac.

She was there until the day she died.

CHAPTER 51

Life Goes On At The Villa

Things were great at the Villa in Dayton, however, as with any care facility, there were always issues. Not every nurse followed the care plans the family helped to make. They all have their own ideas of what was best.

I struggled many times to be Norma's voice. I tried my best to give Mom the best ending to her life. As I have said many times, seniors deserve more. Early on one of the LPNs was not very welcoming. The nurses were not used to a family member being so hands-on and involved with their family member's care. I did write a complaint letter to the Director. And to my surprise the nurse completely admitted how she had been treating us. She also completely changed her attitude and became one of my favourites, once she accepted that we were always going to be there. Of course, there would always be others who were not as friendly as they should have been. But I couldn't write letters about everything. At times it was overwhelming, and I shed many tears in my mom's room when I'd experience these unprofessional moments.

I was always a strong advocate for my mom and all seniors. I felt she, and they, deserved more. I always went to Mom's care plan meetings, but the information discussed in the meeting rarely made it back to the nurses doing Mom's care. Time after time they didn't know about the changes to her care.

I always asked them to talk to Norma as they did her care and to explain everything being done.

An open letter to my mom's nurses:

> *Life is not perfect, and I realize that. I really do. However, when you are in the position of totally losing control of your own world as Alzheimer's patients have, please tell me that someone, everyone, is watching out for them.*
>
> *Their dignity is just as important as the senior who can still walk and talk. Their rights and their voice need to be heard over the routines and chores that get done every day.*
>
> *Sometimes things become routine, and some routines are really important. But with the daily needs changing with good days and bad days, the people around seniors need to be ever changing as well. They need to be flexible. They need to realize that these people stuck in chairs have nothing—surrounded by four walls, three meals a day is all they have to look forward to. And some don't eat very often.*
>
> *They are lonely in their heads even if they can't speak their thoughts. They are extremely lonely. The little things make all the difference in the world to Alzheimer's patients and it is all they have left.*

March 10, 2019

> *Some topics no one wants to talk about. This topic is pretty crappy, but we are all human and we all do this. I want to share my knowledge and experience to help others.*
>
> *I'll refer to a bowel movement as a BM. Most of us take them for granted and do this in the privacy of our homes. We toilet train our toddlers at an early age. It is installed in the brain's memory as a daily function.*
>
> *As we become seniors, we would like to retain our dignity and still do our BMs. This won't always be possible if we develop diseases or sicknesses, such as Alzheimer's.*

As it progresses, sometimes we do not know how to find a bathroom or ask for help. But we can still be successful if someone is watching out for us and guides us to the bathroom often enough.

In other circumstances, when we make it to a seniors home (the wait list is long), we may have to wear Depends, even if we didn't before. And you are then depending on a group of strangers to guide and help you. The problem is some seniors who can still ask to go to the bathroom are being denied this right. There is not always enough staff to help and in some cases two staff are required to assist.

I have spent the last four years observing seniors being denied their right to dignity and being able to go to a bathroom. I have witnessed seniors being told, « It's okay," and to just go in their briefs. I have watched puddles form under chairs. I have noticed an odour and had to alert nurses that a resident needed to be cleaned up. The problem is not confined to just one home. It is in the whole country's system.

I have noticed residents and nurses would benefit from an extra set of hands. When a resident needs to go they shouldn't have to wait because another nurse is on a break. Even if you have no voice, your body still knows when it is sitting on a toilet or commode. Should you be put on a schedule to have this right, or should you be given laxatives and expected to fill your pants?

I understand not every senior, especially ones with dementia, are willing to be put on a toilet. Some are aggressive and violent as they are confused and upset with changes that they don't understand. Some are too fragile, and cleanup is hard on them. Especially being rolled and moved around.

I have first-hand experience with a seventy-two-year-old family member who was confined to a wheelchair. She was unable to communicate her needs, but her body still knew when it was put on a commode, and she was able to have her BM without strong laxatives. Should there be a time limit on sitting on a commode chair? She was cut down to a ten-minute timeframe and then the use of a bedpan. I had insisted that she be given twenty minutes and she was when I was present. If it took twenty to thirty minutes what was the harm? At least she would not be sitting in feces.

Wouldn't you be causing more problems by having them spill out of their Depends and requiring a lot of time to clean them up and wash their chair? And how does your skin handle that?

She did receive a natural stimulant which would help her along and if not the doctor started her on an every-third day suppository and an hour later she was put on the commode safe chair, which had a belt and a bar for support.

Twice daily she was put on a bedpan which was not comfortable. I had received permission for her to use the safe commode chair instead. I had to push for this. I believed it was her best option for her level of care. Physio did an assessment and deemed this process to be safe for her. We had been doing that routine for weeks. I was very thankful as it was easier on her than the bedpan method and had worked quickly and productively.

But on the sixth of March, I received a phone call that changed everything. The chair with the safe bar and belt could not be used for her BMs any longer because the manufacturer's directions deem the chair not safe for that practice. We had been using the chair and the family felt the chair was safe. There had not been any incident while using the chair. She had been having great success. I feared without the use of the chair she would end up sitting in feces for extended periods of time.

I would like to think that would not happen, but I knew from experience if she was just changed and put back in her wheelchair while staff tended to others, and she were to have a BM it might very well be a long time before it was her turn for care again. Not to mention if one nurse was on break, then she would have to wait until the two were available.

Many people do not realize the circumstances involved in nursing homes until they have a loved one residing in a home or worse, when they end up in a home themselves. A lot of families visit for short amounts of time, and everything may appear comforting. I urge you to pay close attention to the routines and care plans of your loved ones and strive for their best care.

More people need to speak up if we are going to make a difference. Contact your MLAs, send letters to every government office. Changes need to take place in the best interest of everyone's future.

More nurses are needed. Better procedures need to be in place to insure the dignity of our aging family members.

You must be their voice.

I have never felt the homes have nearly enough staff to provide a dignified existence during the last stage of our beloved seniors' lives. I have always said, "Our Seniors Deserve More."

*　　　*　　　*

Seniors have a right to have a proper bath. Here are the details from my personal experience in fighting for Norma's right, which I shared in many letters and discussions.

My mother Norma lived with my family for a year while she waited for a long-term care bed. During that year home care did scheduled visits including a bath every other evening. Norma was not a difficult client, and she enjoyed her baths.

Norma was first offered a bed in Caledonia, and later transferred to Meteghan and finally in November of 2015 arrived in Yarmouth her hometown. As she was admitted into her forever home, we were given the grand tour of the beautifully built facility. The tub room was of special interest being one of the last few things in life Norma could enjoy. We were told she could possibly have two baths a week if the nurses could fit it in as one per week was the regular practice. I remained hopeful and asked many times if she could have two baths but was always being told it wasn't possible.

Her first scheduled bath was on Monday a few days after getting settled. I always arrived in time to feed Norma her dinner and was looking forward to her bath. I was told by a full-time CCA that my mother had a sponge bath that morning. I immediately said she was to have a whirlpool bath in the afternoon and was promptly told she was not a good candidate for a tub bath. This was the first roadblock of many when dealing with Mom's care, but I finally got it sorted out with management and she was able to have her tub bath. For those who do not know Norma had Alzheimer's and could not speak for herself. She was completely dependent on others for every aspect of her care and she was confined to a wheelchair.

Going forward Norma enjoyed her one bath per week for over three years in this facility. As her condition deteriorated her left side became weaker. She often was unable to hold her head up and leaned to the left a lot. Her wheelchair was specially designed to support her needs. We had the use of a bath chair with a belt, bar, and side support, which worked perfectly to support her weak side to bath her. I was always present as the third person for her baths. Norma was not aggressive; she was no trouble to bath other than the time needed to complete her bath which was thirty minutes. As her POA I felt she was one hundred per cent safe, and the nurses did not have to strain in any way to complete her baths.

In November of 2018 Norma lost the use of the other equipment in her care plan but could continue to have her supported baths with the lift chair. I immediately requested two baths per week as an alternative because she would be sitting in soiled Depends more often. I remember this meeting well as I was devastated and teary-eyed. Norma was finally granted the right to have two baths per week as the other parts of her care had changed. This continued until March of 2019 when a worker researched the manufacturer guidelines for this particular chair and brought them to management's attention. Despite the chair working for Norma and there being no incidents it was removed from her care plan. We tried a regular sling bath, which I knew wouldn't work due to her weak side and it was not at all safe. My mother's condition was agreeably changing but surely there could still be a safe way to give her a proper bath. Paralyzed people get baths! Norma was weak on one side and needed support. Yes, I agree it needed to be done in a safe environment for everyone involved. Unfortunately, I was just promptly told they were no longer bathing her. It was very hard to accept that she would be even more confined to her chair and bed and never getting into the tub again.

I requested the use of the same chair but with it already placed in the tub and using the ceiling lift sling to set her onto the chair and leaving her hooked up. It would be safe for everyone, but I was denied the use of both devices together even though logically it would work and support her. I couldn't imagine everything being followed one hundred per cent by the manufacturer's directions in any facility and I voiced this to management. If something worked and was clearly safe when viewed why not give the resident what they needed? I had not given up on Norma getting her RIGHT to have a bath back and had asked management to look further into a safe way to bath her. As the fact is paralyzed people get baths why can't our seniors. I always said I am a voice for all seniors and, "Our Seniors Deserve More."

Following up on this summary, it took months, but Norma did get her baths back. A support chair was ordered, which worked with a supportive sling. Mom had her warm peaceful baths once again. I can't stress enough the need to be involved with your loved one's care, and to ask for what you believe in.

*　　　*　　　*

What I really want the Nurses at the Villa to understand is I only ever wanted what I felt was best for Norma, my mother. After all, I knew her best. I just wanted less resistance when it came to her care and schedule.

What really stopped them from wanting to follow her schedule of care? I'm not talking about when there was a true emergency, and something needed their attention. I'm just talking about their average every day of work. Was it really that hard to take her to the commode on the scheduled time and to give her fifteen to twenty minutes? I don't think they or I had the right to take her dignity away because she had no voice. I struggled every day watching the nurses make the decision that she only deserved to be changed.

Furthermore, at times they wrote on her chart about things that were done when they weren't. I was told there were times that information was filled out on the chart to "keep me happy!" Yup, imagine how I felt being told such things.

I had heard all the stories that some nurses were writing what I wanted to hear without actually doing it. And sometimes a nurse decided to do it the way they wanted to, and not according to Norma's care plan. I have tons of proof but where would it get me to argue with the nurses that would be continuing to provide Norma's care for an undetermined amount of time?

I couldn't possibly be there to do all of Mom's care as much as I would have loved to be. But I believed she deserved to be given her dignity.

The resistance against her care plan on some days was overwhelming. Then I wondered how much inappropriate talking went on in Mom's presence. Yup, I had heard lots of conversations happen in Mom's room. Ask yourself, just because she can't respond or you may think she didn't hear or understand, can you be one hundred per cent sure she hadn't heard you disrespecting her daughter? Only God knows the answer to that. And I do believe God was watching.

I had said to my sisters many times to do whatever they could to close their eyes and feel at peace with. If it didn't feel right, then it wasn't. I hope the nurses can live with every decision they had made when it came to Norma Tedford.

Stereotyping all seniors as to whether they should be fed three meals a day or to be changed two or three times is not right. I'm not sorry that I insisted Norma be changed four times a day. I have spent way too many hours there witnessing all sorts of things. I was not there to watch out for the others, but some have no voice and could surely use someone to speak up on their behalf.

If they were trained about the Alzheimer's disease, they would know that you are not supposed to argue with them, scold them, correct them, belittle them by saying what they are doing is gross, disgusting, or they should know better, or they shouldn't be doing that, etc.

I heard these things being said every day. If they knew better, they wouldn't be doing it. It was common for them to pee and poop in odd places, strip off and be naked, swear, spit, bite, hit, put their hands in places they didn't belong, etc. Their brains were not working properly. Read any info on Alzheimer's and start treating them the way they deserve to be treated. Kindness goes a long way.

October 2, 2019

In my continued struggle to determine what was best for my mother on a daily basis I often heard and saw nurses who wanted to do things their way. I cannot possibly listen to approximately thirty different nurses that cared for my mother. I relied on what I knew and believed to be what my mother would have wanted. I consulted with Dr. Julie Chandler and trusted her judgment in pointing me in the right direction. She is truly an angel on earth.

Here is an example of what took place way too often in the homes.

Norma's had two seizures on the twenty-fourth of September on the same day. I always asked the LPN to hold her meds that day but when I left, I figured she was just going to sleep through the afternoon and supper, and I forgot to ask. I did get her up in her chair before I had to leave, and I put her by the TV for the music but turned her so the nurses could observe her. At 4:45 p.m. she was given her meds and at 5:10 p.m. when my brother arrived, they were drooling out of her mouth. He got a face cloth and cleaned her up. I find it hard to believe the LPN woke her enough to get her to swallow. But this was what she claimed and that she had woken her up. At this point her meds were not doing all that much and I did not feel giving them to her on a seizure day was a good idea.

She had her second seizure at about 6:40 p.m. in her chair as they took her back to her room. I was called but the LPN had not seen Mom yet. I asked her to check on her and call me back. She stated it was a shift change in fifteen minutes and someone else would have to call me. I asked again because I wanted to know how she was after the seizure. No one called so I decided to go down at 8:15 p.m. to see for myself. When I arrived the CCA said the LPN had asked her to call me when she got a chance. I said that's funny as I thought you were not allowed to do so. Mom looked pale and her feet and legs were cold. I got her a warm blanket for the lower half and sat with her for a while.

I don't always come in during the early mornings, but I did the following morning to see how Mom was. I found her in the dark shortly after 10 a.m. and proceeded to open the blind. I noticed her mouth was extremely dry and her lips were stuck together. I got a face cloth and washed her up. An RN had said not to get her up I was told. I said she was getting up and I wanted to talk to the RN.

We have never left her in bed the following day after a seizure. I didn't understand why Norma's routine was changed, and no one had even called me. I got the mouth swabs and cleaned her mouth out. I sat the bed up and she opened her eyes as I got some water, and she had a half a glass. She didn't have anything the previous day, so I knew she needed liquids. She's always tired and she was no different than any other day. The RN and LPN came in telling me that she should be in bed resting in case she had another seizure. The RN also said they were going to try later today to get fluids into her and a meal, so she didn't get dehydrated. If they knew anything about my mother's chart, she had never had seizures on back-to-back days. I explained that and noted she probably wouldn't take in much unless she was up, as it stimulated her.

I often wondered why any nurse in the building would think they knew more about Norma's condition than I did. I had followed every detail of Mom's life with this disease every day. They saw her periodically. They said they never thought to call. I said after four years and numerous meetings and documentation about notifying me of any changes, I again was not called. If I hadn't shown up, how long would Mom have been in the dark with a dry mouth? No music or anything. Just alone. It was truly sad.

*   *   *

My COVID crisis letter was sent to everyone that I could think of. I couldn't handle Mom being alone. It felt like they were in prison. Families were forbidden to visit or care for their loved ones during this lockdown.

May 10, 2020

I write to you today with a serious request. I will take any precautions necessary to be able to enter my mother's nursing home. My mother had two severe seizures on Friday, the eighth of May. I was in contact with the nurses but unable to visit because she was not in palliative care.

Any one of her seizures could be her end, with severe Alzheimer's. Being kept from attending to her needs is devastating. It is not humane. I have done a lot of her care for the past five years she has been in homes. I am talking daily feedings, baths, hair, nail clippings, teeth brushing, and there is nothing I have not done for her. I do not just visit.

I communicated with a lady in Halifax who now gets to see her mother in a nursing home. In fact, it is Northwood. She is in a pilot project where all she had to do was become a volunteer. She gets to spend forty-five minutes with her mother and forty-five minutes with other residents Monday to Friday daily from 1:30-3p.m. This started on the twenty-nineth of

April and has been continuing. All seniors in the province should have the right to see their family.

To my understanding the legislation is the same for all of Nova Scotia. But here you have special exceptions being made for the most dangerous COVID place in Nova Scotia. The laws were put in place to protect seniors, yes, I'm fully aware. However, if all of Nova Scotia is to be under the same laws, we must be able to have a similar pilot project here as well. I find it hard to understand why Northwood would be the exception to the rules. And furthermore, to limit this privilege to only homes with outbreaks is taking away the rights of all our seniors. Treat all Nova Scotians equally, especially our seniors who have been locked away without even the freedom of choice. We need to see our seniors. I'm not saying open the doors wide. Make the first step being a volunteer status. One family member absolutely. We can sign wavers, be tested before entry, or just simply wear protective gear. Whatever it takes for the ones who desperately want to be there and help with their family member and being able to do so. Time is running out for many. Please do not take your time making these necessary changes.

Nova Scotia Strong,
Tam MacPhee

September 11, 2020
I received this response from the home finally.

Nice hearing from you. We will be notifying the families who fit the criteria set out by the Chief Medical Officer later today. Your mother certainly is one.

We were on a Zoom meeting with other homes in the province earlier this week and at the outset, there will definitely be timelines for the visits. Most who were on the meeting are going with 11 a.m. to 2 p.m. time frame only. We will be offering 11 a.m.–2 p.m. and 4–7 p.m. Initially visits will be Monday–Friday. Only two people per resident can be caregivers and only one at a time can be in the building.

The program will begin on Wednesday, the sixteenth of September. Training/orientation will be provided to the caregiver before the initial visit. This training/orientation will occur on Wednesday, Thursday, and Friday of next week. We should be able to see everyone in those three days. The training/ orientation will be provided at 10:40 a.m. and 3:40 p.m. on all three days and should take about twenty minutes. The training/orientation will include instruction on proper hand washing, use of hand sanitizer, social distancing, etc.

A waiver and assumption of risk document will be presented to the caregivers and will require them being signed before the initial visit.

*   *   *

November 30, 2020: Time is running out.

I am writing this just to let you know. On Saturday Amy came to see me to discuss Mom's condition. I was thankful to have a caring nurse to be having the discussion with. The world needs more nurses like Amy.

We discussed medications available and that I want to be on board with every change and notified if a nurse feels she needs something. (When I'm not here.) I also expressed my concerns if Mom was to have a seizure while I'm not here. Amy said when Mom is palliative, they wouldn't have to do her vitals. She is on comfort measures only. This sounded good as I expressed sometimes they don't call me until a half hour later and I want to know right away. In her condition I'm worried a bad seizure will take her. I want to be here for her. Amy definitely understood my concerns.

Amy said she wrote it all up in two places for LPNs and CCAs. Leaving Saturday, I felt I would get that call should need be. Sunday, a nurse called me at 9:05 a.m. Mom had had a seizure; all her vitals were fine, and it had happened forty minutes previously. Norma was into her deep sleep. Once again (as many others) she had not seen the write up and neither had the CCAs in their book. I shouldn't be surprised as I can't count how many times this exact same thing has happened in the last five years. As much as I communicate with staff, communication between staff shift changes and such doesn't seem to happen. All care is important, but I thought with palliative care, communication would certainly happen.

I not writing to blame any nurse, the one who called is also a very good nurse. She made a note and stuck it on Mom's wall for next time. There probably won't be a next time as Mom goes weeks between seizure days. When I asked why she did Mom's vitals, she said it's procedure for seizures. I reminded her of Mom's palliative condition and no need for vitals, comfort measures only, and to notify me immediately of any meds needed and changes to her condition.

One thing that is clear after five years, getting all the nurses on the same page with family requests and in-house procedures is never going to happen. Hopefully writing this will help someone in the future have a better experience. But as some of the nurses have said, "I'm rare." They are not used to having a family member be this hands-on when caring for a loved one.

Well, I definitely took that as a compliment and saw the need for residents to have a family that is present in their care.

CHAPTER 52

A Story Of A Mother And Daughter

I n January of 2015, Tina Comeau wrote a story about Mom and me for publication in the Tri-County Vanguard. It was called "Yes Norma, you're my mom" and detailed the impact of Alzheimer's on a family and the need for changes within the long-term care homes.

Tina has provided her permission for me to include this article in my book.

> *Her laugh is endearing.*
>
> *Her smile, when she shares it, infectious, as it causes you to smile back.*
>
> *She looks at the woman seated across from her, at times with so much curiosity etched on her face that you can't help but wonder what she's thinking about.*
>
> *Or, likely, what she is struggling to remember.*
>
> *The woman seated beside her at the table refers to her by her first name.*
>
> *"Norma, look at me."*
>
> *"Norma, it's time for lunch."*

"Norma, let's have some soup."

Sometimes Norma will respond. Sometimes not.

When asked why she calls Norma by her first name, Tam MacPhee—the woman feeding Norma her lunch—looks into the woman's eyes and says, "Because if I call her Mom, she doesn't always remember she's my mother."

And then she might not get any response at all.

CHANGED ROLES

For Tam MacPhee and her mother Norma Tedford, their relationship has changed.

Because so much has been taken away, it makes the rewards, in their infinite simplicity, mean so much.

"I don't look for rewards, but I find them when she thanks me for tucking her in at night and says, 'I love you too,' uses my name sometimes, gets out a couple of thoughts that make sense, walks by and hugs and squeezes me for no reason," Tam says.

It is one of a countless number of situations where the child becomes the parent.

And the parent becomes the child.

For these two women their roles have been reversed not by choice, but by Alzheimer's.

Alzheimer's has robbed Norma of her memory. Robbed her of her common sense. Robbed her of the way she used to behave.

It has stolen things from her daughter as well. The meaningful conversations between a mother and daughter are gone. The weekly lunches at a restaurant have stopped. The trips they used to take are a thing of the past.

As the family waits for a nursing home placement for Norma, who is 68, Tam (one of Norma's four children) has taken her mother into her home.

And it's a busy home at that.

Living here are a husband and wife who own and operate a trucking company. Two boys at home—one a teenager, the other almost a teenager—who both play rep hockey. An older son studying elsewhere. Two dogs that bark when someone new comes to the door.

The first thought was it would be temporary.

Norma has been here since last June.

Tam could sign a paper that would expand a nursing home search to anywhere in the province, instead of just locally. It might speed up the process of finding a placement.

But what if Norma was placed in a home in Sydney? In Halifax?

That's too far from Yarmouth, her daughter says.

"I at least want to be there once every day to feed her," says Tam, who worries otherwise her mother might fade away to nothing.

Once when Norma had come back from a respite, she had lost eight pounds.

FIGURING OUT NORMA

Tam MacPhee calls them her tricks of the trade. The ways she can get Norma to eat.

First there is the hand holding so her mother doesn't swat the food away. Then there are the heaping spoonfuls to maximize every bite of food she takes into her mouth.

There is the eye contact to keep her from becoming distracted.

Calling her by her name so she focuses on the person who is feeding her.

"She could try to get up and leave 10 or 20 times during her meal," says Tam. "And rarely does she pick something up and eat it. She just plays with it. She can't make her own decisions that I need more food to survive."

It is hard and at times exhausting to be caring for an Alzheimer's patient.

In a sense it is like looking after a toddler.

A gate blocks off a set of stairs in the MacPhee home and stools are strategically placed at the entrance to a hallway to prevent Norma from wandering. A doorbell is attached to the door of Norma's room that rings in Tam's bedroom so she knows when her mother wakes up in the morning.

Because Tam can't stay at home full-time due to her job, home care workers come in for shifts. The family receives seven hours of personal home care, which Tam has to be home for, and 10 hours of respite. She spreads those ten respite hours out so she can go to work and do errands. Still, sometimes it takes a long time to leave the house.

If someone new is coming in Tam has to go over four pages of notes on ways to make tending Norma easier.

IN NEED OF RESPITE

Because her children are very active in sports and travel a lot for games, there are weekends when Tam needs—and wants—to be with her children.

On these weekends she hires people to look after her mother, although sometimes such scheduling doesn't always work out. Sometimes there are last-minute cancellations.

"One time I had to leave on a Friday, and I came back on Sunday. My brother did one shift, but it was still $500 for me to be gone for the other people I had to hire for shifts."

The more weekends she's gone with her kids, the more costly it becomes, even with government funding help.

The family has got respite beds in the past, but they've also been denied.

One seniors' facility is concerned Norma is a flight risk. At another facility she was very agitated and difficult to control.

Both facilities say Norma's needs are greater than what they are equipped to handle with the size staff they have. So, these respite options are no longer available.

The last respite Norma qualified was in Caledonia in a secure Alzheimer's unit. That is a two-hour drive away.

Tam says because some local facilities feel they aren't able to cope with her mother's needs when it comes to a respite bed, they're also not going to be able to take her in when her turn comes up on the waiting list for a long-term bed, unless it is in a secure Alzheimer's unit, which is the type of care Norma requires.

Not all facilities have such units and for those that do the wait may be a few months, or it could be a year or longer.

"I didn't know seniors could be refused because they require too much care," Tam says. This has all been a learning curve.

Her mother does take medication to help calm her down and while at times she is agitated or upset, she's not always like this, says Tam. A lot of the time her mother is happy.

Very busy, admittedly, but content.

"But we are left feeling that Mom is labelled as a bad senior," Tam says. "Patience, love, hugs and kindness is what they need when they are confused and upset."

And families need to feel supported too.

SHE'S STILL MOM

Sometimes Tam will use the word mom.

"She'll look at me, 'Mom?' and I'll say, 'Yes, you're my mom,' and she'll say, 'Oh, okay.'"

Other times she won't react at all.

Still, Tam is always on the lookout for those glimpses of her mom.

In a way Tam knew what to expect. When she was a teenager, her grandmother—Norma's mother—also developed Alzheimer's and lived in the home with them.

Tam's children also use Norma's first name a lot.

"They don't use Grandmom a lot anymore, which is kind of sad," Tam says. "They use Norma because she responds and answers to it, whereas they could say 'Grandmom' and she doesn't know that anymore, except for once in a while."

But they hug her, they dance with her—Norma loves her 50s and 60s music—and most importantly they love her.

Tam says having her mother in their home has taught her children a lot about compassion.

Tam, meanwhile, admits that she worries for her own future.

Will Alzheimer's lay claim to her as well?

All she knows for now is that she'll never give up on her mom.

Even though she says words that totally don't make any sense with the conversation, I know she's still in there trying to connect the pieces.

Sometimes she'll walk up to you and say, 'Can I tell you something?' and you're like, 'Yes!' but then she says, 'Oh never mind,' because she can't remember what it was. You want so bad to know what she's thinking."

Other times she may get out three thoughts in a row that make some sense.

Not quite a meaningful conversation, but for Tam close enough.

"She's 80 per cent the patient, and 20 per cent of the time my mom," says Tam, referring to the circumstance life has dealt them.

Except for when hugs are traded. It's then that the percentage sways the other way.

During those tight embraces, when Norma holds Tam in her arms, it feels like she hasn't forgotten that she's her mom.

Because no mother could forget how to hug like this.

Chapter 53

More Of Mom's Story

Since many people were asking me about Mom after a story about us had been in the local paper, in August of 2016 I wrote an update letter and sent it to the newspaper.

My letter was published under the headline: "Yes Norma, you're still my mom."

This is what I shared with readers.

> *My mom Norma Tedford has always been a strong woman. She never had an easy life.*
>
> *She worked hard to raise us and for everything she ever had.*
>
> *She lived as simple as possible.*
>
> *Norma is 70 years old, and Alzheimer's has robbed her of her senior life. I spent over a year helping her in her apartment daily. She also spent a year living in my home.*
>
> *She has spent the last year living in three different long-term care facilities.*
>
> *The road has been long, but I can say she is finally close to home and settled into Villa St. Joseph du Lac. Her days consist of sitting in a chair with a seatbelt, unable to walk on*

her own since she fractured her hip back in October of 2015. She is confined to the "safe chair."

She is happy most days and I love to see her smile. Often, she stares at me with a look of appreciation, other days she stares at the wall or empty space as I wonder what she is thinking of or trying to figure out.

She still talks and although most of the words are jumbled together, occasionally she says something that I can understand, and she may even ask a question. I cherish those days when she has these clear moments.

Before this journey when Mom was healthy, I never realized how residents of seniors' homes actually lived. Sure, I knew the basics. But now that I am there every day with my mom, I see their lives so much clearer and it's sad.

Norma's days consist of three meals, toileting times, two walks per day when three of us—physio people and family members—can assist, which is not always possible.

She watches TV, plays with an activity blanket and a toy Elmo, watches more TV, and has an evening snack. On nice days I take her outside in her chair for some fresh air.

Occasionally there may be an hour of music where a band plays music. Norma enjoys being taken to the chosen area in the building to listen. There are other activities and outings, but they are not always suited to all residents.

We need to remember there are 24 hours in a day and the amount of time Norma (and all residents) are on their own to stare at a TV or walls weighs heavily on my mind.

Norma cannot ask for what she needs.

She cannot ring a buzzer.

She can't holler to a nurse because she has forgotten how to ask for anything.

For three years I have been her voice, trying to advocate for what I feel she needs and deserves. I just try to cover her basic needs.

I am there daily with my mom for hours. I often do-little extras for her. My brother is often there too. Most residents barely get a visitor and if they do it tends to be for a short visit.

I often ask myself, are we really putting our loved ones in these homes and assuming all is well? The nurses are awesome, and Mom is quite comfortable with most of them, but their time is spread between thirteen residents on Norma's wing. There are two CCAs doing the hands-on care. One, when the other is on break.

They are busy most days and one-on-one time with residents rarely happens.

I want more for mother and all seniors. They are lonely and the best gift anyone can ever give them is their time. Maybe to talk. Maybe just to listen. Possibly to read them a book, show them pictures, walk with them through the halls, go along with their stories whether it makes sense or not, and just be there to hold their hands.

We all need to remember their days are long. Time is precious and spending time with them is rewarding to our hearts and souls.

A doctor once told me Alzheimer's causes the longest funeral grieving period of all diseases.

I have come to see what she meant as I say goodbye to little pieces of my mother each day, week, month, and year.

Memories of how she used to be are cherished.

Thankfully, she still has her beautiful smile and laugh.

CHAPTER 54

Norma's Last Ride

While sitting with Mom during her last days, I wrote one more letter to our local newspaper about her final weeks. It was important for me to encourage others to make memories with their loved ones before it's too late. This is what I shared.

> **Norma's Last Ride: Make memories with those you love...**
>
> *My mother Norma Tedford's journey was first published in the Vanguard in January of 2015—" Yes Norma, you're my mom"—with a few updates in the years since.*
>
> *In 2015 she lived with myself and my family. I called her Norma, instead of Mom, because she didn't respond to "Mom."*
>
> *Norma was diagnosed with Alzheimer's at the age of sixty. The specialist told us most patients live seven to ten years with this disease. We knew what was happening. We had travelled the same journey with my grandmother. The disease slowly shrinks the brain, disabling its ability to take care of yourself mentally first and eventually physically.*
>
> *Norma went from living on her own with home care and myself there nearly every day, to a private seniors' home.*

When that didn't work out, I brought her to live with my family. The only alternative was letting her go in a nursing home anywhere in Nova Scotia, via the emergency list. I couldn't let that happen and risk her being alone. I needed her to be close. But eventually she needed to be in a seniors' facility.

The first was in Caledonia. Being two hours away was hard. She lived there for three months. Then she was transferred to Meteghan. Two weeks later she broke her hip. Her mobility was limited. Her walking never returned fully.

On the 30th of November, 2015, Norma was transferred to her forever home: Villa St. Joseph du Lac. Finally, a private room, as I believe every senior deserves.

Five years later and I still did her personal care and visited every day when I could.

Lost time in 2020

COVID restrictions were hard when no visitors were permitted in the building. That was a circumstance I could have never imagined. I called frequently. I struggled on days they were short staffed. There were days she suffered seizures. But unless she was in palliative care, I still could not go be with her.

I live five minutes away.

I was devastated.

When we were first allowed to visit, we had to stay six feet apart and wear a mask. In Norma's condition this proved very difficult for her to know anyone was there.

As the province continued to set guidelines for long-term care homes, they finally permitted a few residents to have caregivers—designated hours set by the home, but better than nothing.

I was able to care for her and be with her once again.

Norma was barely eating compared to pre-COVID. Some of this was the disease progressing. The rest, I believe, was from being alone so much.

Some days were better than others.

Norma's Last Ride

On the 16th of November, I was called for a meeting. Norma's ability to swallow, chew, and remember how to eat was diminishing. The doctor and RN said it would be best to stop all meds and nourishment and to allow nature to take its course.

I was upset to hear the words, but also relieved to end her suffering.

I did not feel right to deny her a drink to quench her thirst. They agreed to put her on comfort feeding if she was able to swallow.

When I asked, does she have days or weeks left, I was told, "Don't count on weeks."

I immediately planned to take her home that weekend if she was able to go.

I wanted to show her our camp we have built. I wanted to take her for "Norma's Last Ride."

I called HOPE as their van is equipped for her wheelchair. They informed me they don't work weekends. I explained the situation and they were able to find a driver willing to help me out. Our community is amazing. I am forever grateful.

We saw our pet goats. She loves animals. She saw our camp. We listened to Christmas music. She had smiles to share. There were private goodbyes with family members. At one point in the van, she was strapped in tight and could see out the window. Her brother pulled up beside us. Neither could get out of their vehicles but I'm sure she heard his voice.

Norma was never one to fly in a plane—until she was diagnosed with Alzheimer's. Then she was eager to go. "What do I have to lose?" she would say.

I was fortunate enough to take Norma and my two youngest sons to Niagara Falls in 2010. Then in 2012 we took a mother-daughter trip to Newfoundland.

Now our journey would be through palliative care, as her life was coming to an end.

I encourage everyone to make memories with family before it is too late.

COVID has made us stop and think about what is truly important to us. Now is the time—or as soon as COVID allows it—for us to act on it.

Memories and time are more special than any purchased gift could ever be.

And take pictures.

On the day of Norma's last ride, I knew that soon photographs are all I would have left of my cherished mother. I will sit in my loft at our camp and look out over the lake— she loved reminiscing through my memories and my pictures.

Norma died on Dec. 22, 2020, with two of her daughters by her side. I was one. I laid next to her and held her. I felt her leave her body, and knew she was finally free.

Her final time was peaceful.

She was surrounded by love.

NORMA TEDFORD—APRIL 16, 1946–DECEMBER 22, 2020

****

CHAPTER 55

Quotes And Advice To Share With You

Best relationship advice for young ones. Compromise is key, however, do not put up with anything now that you are not willing to put up with in five years' time.

*   *   *

Key to success: Give everything 110% or you are wasting your time.

*   *   *

Choices are the #1 thing that will change your life.

*   *   *

If something is broken, fix it in a timely manner, especially your relationships.

*   *   *

Learn from where you came from but strive to be better going forward.

*   *   *

Every smart and successful person continues to learn daily as life goes forward.

*   *   *

Life's pages have yet to be written. Get up and make things happen.

*   *   *

Wear the good clothes, treat yourself, smell the flowers, use the fancy dishes. Life's too short to save these things. ENJOY!!!

*   *   *

Sunshine, oceans, nature's scenic beauty, sunsets, stars, moon, forests: show all of God's creations and Devine power.

*   *   *

I'm telling my story so it can be a survival guide for someone else. Not just one person but many.

*   *   *

I believe life is better when you turn up the music, sing, walk barefoot, lay on the beach, float in the turquoise water, go on adventures, LOVE people, drink the wine, eat the sweet fruit, LOL. Those things won't make life perfect, but they sure make this strange ride more fun!

*   *   *

Life is short, break some rules!

*   *   *

Never regret anything that made you smile! LIVE LOVE LAUGH

*　　　*　　　*

Own your story, own the pain. Learn from it, live past it. Inspire others with your life lessons.

*　　　*　　　*

The life in front of you is far more important than the life behind you.

*　　　*　　　*

Can't! really means I don't want to leave my comfort zone! Just try and amazing things will happen.

*　　　*　　　*

This year I was tested more than ever. I am tired. I lost a lot, but I also won, I failed, I cried, I laughed, I learned, I loved, but most of all I'm still here, I did not break: Tam's 2021

*　　　*　　　*

I don't need a therapist. I just need some time to myself. Time to get away from the chaos, from the anxiety life brought, from all the things that brought out the darkness. Time to rest. That's all I really needed. Time. To recollect, to grow. And somewhere in-between to just find my true self.

*　　　*　　　*

Ask her what she craved, and she'd get a little frantic about the ocean, sunshine, beach, woods, music, plants, and the seasons.

*　　　*　　　*

And when you get to where you're going, turn around and help her too. Because there was a time, not long ago, when she was you.

*   *   *

Love yourself, Conquer your bad habits. I may have one left, but I have overcome many!

*   *   *

One thing I learned through life to avoid disappointment is:
The only expectations you should have are from yourself.

*   *   *

Is there anything the universe throws at her that she can't handle?
She has been broken. 💔
She has been knocked down. 😵
She has been defeated. 😔
She has felt pain that most people couldn't handle. 🥵
She makes mistakes that are steppingstones for her future.
She finds a way to get back up. 🦋
She never gives up. 🧘
Her light is radiant. 😺
Her motivation is unstoppable! 🏇
She is you!

*   *   *

Tam: love, sincerity, affection, and generosity are perfect words to describe you. Your pink aura indicates that you've achieved a perfect balance between your spiritual and material existence. You love to be surrounded by friends and family. You recharge from the elements and soul time.

You take care of your body and spread a positive and healing energy to those around you. The pink aura is very rare, so is the person who has it.

*   *   *

People who journal their thoughts, clear their minds. Self-therapy at its best!

*   *   *

Gut feelings are guardian angels 🐯 Trust them and listen.

*   *   *

Some of the best therapy is writing letters to those who have wronged you. But never send them, burn them, and release them to the universe.

*   *   *

Do you listen to every word of a song? Everybody has a story to tell, and every song is a story. Start listening.

*   *   *

More sleep. More music. More tea. More books. More sunsets. More creating. More long walks. More laughter. More hugs. More dreaming. More road trips. More fun. More love.

*   *   *

It's a different type of pain when you don't cry anymore, you just take a deep breath and accept it.

*   *   *

There are two versions of myself. One when my mother was alive, and one after she passed. The two are joined, and related, but they are completely different beings.

*   *   *

I'm such a
Look at the sky,
Look at the sunset,
Look at the moon,
Stay in the car to listen to
the rest of the song
Kinda person.

*   *   *

If it excites you and scares you at the same time, it probably means you should do it.

*   *   *

Your dream doesn't come with an expiration date. Take a deep breath and try again. Jump!

*   *   *

When someone is not meant for you, the universe will trigger them to mess up, hurt you, or disappoint you, until you get the message to release them.

*   *   *

When you come out of the storm, you won't be the same person that walked in. That's what the storm is all about.

*   *   *

You often feel tired, not because you've done too much, but because you've done too little of what sparks a light in you. Recognize this and change.

*   *   *

There's always a reason why we meet people. Either we need them to change our life, or we're the one changing theirs.

*   *   *

I don't just listen to your words. I listen to your use of words, your tone, your body movements, your eyes, your subtle facial expressions. I interpret your silences. I can hear everything you don't say in words.

*   *   *

Every positive change in your life begins with a clear, unequivocal decision that you are going to either do something or stop doing something.

*   *   *

Some of the best advice you'll ever get will come from your gut instinct. Just be still and listen.

*   *   *

There are two types of tired: one that requires rest, and one that requires peace.

*   *   *

Sometimes a person needs to hear those three words. No, not those words, these. I've got you.

*   *   *

If you truly love her. You will clean your hands before you touch her. You will wash your heart before you give it to her. If you truly love her, you will work on yourself first.

*   *   *

I love words, but I fall in love with actions. They're so much louder.

* * *

Here's the thing about sorry; it's just a word. It doesn't erase what you did, it doesn't fix anything. It's an acknowledgement. It's everything you do after sorry that proves if you really are.

* * *

Yesterday someone said to me, "I would've never guessed you've been through what you have; you carry yourself so well." And that's when I realized, it's not what happens to you, it's how you handle it.

* * *

Health & Energy: Without this you have nothing; must take care of yourself first so you can take care of others.

* * *

Giving: Give without expecting anything in return! Giving your time in many cases is better than money.

* * *

Honesty: Don't lie, be true fully in every aspect of your life, especially your relationship.

* * *

Peace: Enjoy all that brings you peace (for me ocean, sunshine, nature, beach, forest, yoga, meditation, stillness, all water).

* * *

Gratefulness: Be thankful for all you have.

*   *   *

Family: Spend time with them. (Time is the most precious gift.)

*   *   *

Creativity: Be creative in all you do so you can enjoy the beauty of your creations.

*   *   *

Love: Love all things, choose love over hate. (Do not waste energy hating.)

*   *   *

When writing the story of your life, don't let anyone else hold the pen.

CHAPTER 56

My 22 Story

W hen I was in my thirties, I started to notice the number "22."
Yes, it has always been my birthday July 22, 1974, however, if I looked at a clock it always seemed to be 7:22 or 12:22 a.m., often when I went to bed. Or 3:22 a.m. if I got up to use the bathroom. Or I'd be driving and see 2:22, 5:22, etc.

At first, I thought it was all coincidences. But as it continued to show up everywhere in my life, I became more curious. I often smiled, even though I didn't yet know the meaning of it. I would be pumping gas, buying groceries, travelling, just regular everyday things, and there it was 22, 7:22 or multiples of 2s.

Someone told me to research it on the internet because the universe was trying to tell me something. Apparently, people born on 7:22 have an incredible spiritual purpose. In the Bible, 22 is strongly associated in so many areas.

Each 2 represents an angel watching over me. They are there to give me strength and guidance. The more twos I see at a time, the more angels that are present.

I have always felt guided by the angels from the time my sister and I were little, seeing them watching over us in bed. During the time of standing up to the abuse of my father and getting us out of that environment. We had angels overseeing us.

To having the strength to break free from Fred's hold.

Pushing for the right to see my baby girl grow up; even though I was not supposed to be able to find her until she turned eighteen.

To mysteriously meeting my husband and against all odds giving him a chance.

None of these things would have been possible if it were not for my guidance from my angels.

I am forever thankful.

I believe Natasha was my biggest miracle of all. She was meant to be on this earth. To many people she is not supposed to exist. To me she is a blessing and a path I had to take. Somehow, I was strong enough to bring her into this world. Her path is proving to be miraculous in many ways. She is a bright light with a sparkle in her eyes. A true beauty inside and out.

Her first year of university was in Toronto. I went to visit in February of 2015. The 22's that popped up in that trip were abundant. I had price bid for a hotel online and got a beautiful new one downtown. For only seventy-five dollars a night it was amazing. Upon check-in ironically, I got the 22nd floor.

I smiled as I took the elevator up to wait for Natasha's arrival. When she got there, she thought I had asked for the 22nd floor. Nope. Just happened to be where they put us. In the room she said, "Did Tristan tell you I got my first tattoo?" I hadn't heard about it. She showed me and told me it was Roman numerals for the number 22. At that moment I realized she went to be with her family on December 22, 1995.

I mean I always knew, I just had not realized the importance of that number. The number 22 was very important to her as well.

The feeling of how important 22 was in my life grew and grew. I am so fortunate to have angels watching over me and my girl. The warmth it brings me deep inside is an amazing feeling. At times it has felt a little strange, but the more I researched, the more I trust in my angels.

The highway exit to where I grew up was none other than mile marker 22. I didn't realize this until I was about forty years old. So, my entire life I have had the presence of angels.

Why am I so special? I have a greater purpose on this earth that I must fulfill. I must be strong, to take care of so many others. I give freely without expecting anything in return.

One's time is precious. I freely gave my mother many hours and I don't regret being there for her. I have struggled to balance all my expectations, but somehow, I manage to go above and beyond what most would be able to do.

I am truly grateful for the strength and guidance from my angels.

My middle son was born at 7:22 a.m. after a horrific ordeal to get to the IWK hospital in a snow and ice storm. At that time, I had no idea the meaning behind 7:22 was so powerful.

Here is some research I have found.

Angel Number 722 brings a message from your angels that you are to believe in yourself, your intuitive messages, and your inner promptings, as they are direct messages about your life purpose and soul mission.

Your angels encourage you to follow the guidance and directions given and trust that you are fully supported in your spiritual endeavours.

Angel Number 722 is a message of encouragement from your angels. Maintain a positive perspective and outlook and through the spiritual law and attraction you will manifest positive results, rewards, and blessings into your life.

Angel Number 722 brings a message of faith, trust, and self-belief, and the angels encourage you to step forward on your life path, with confidence and grace.

I also sometimes see 11:22. This one gets to me because the 11th is Fred's birthday and the 22nd is mine. Both numbers are powerful, as I have witnessed in my journey. In the universe we were meant to come together and create Natasha. We were meant to experience the connection between us, the birth of Natasha, and the pain of the path that followed. I do believe, my many experiences have made me who I am today.

My friend Tina sees 11:11 as much as I see 2's. We text sometimes as we are always amazed. In 2018–2019, I also noticed seeing 11:11 sometimes and, of course, would always think of Tina. She too is a strong, amazing woman who finds the strength to go above and beyond in this universe. No matter what is thrown in her path. She's a fighter.

My race car had to be number 22. I couldn't imagine being out in my car with any other number on it. I don't do the engine work, but I noticed when the hood was up that the engine is a 2.2 eco tech. How perfect is that?

In September of 2019 while at a trucking competition, Steve and I were talking to another competitor. It was a cold morning waiting for their turns. Steve asked him what his number was. As he turned it over to reveal the number 22, I felt the warmth and stated, "You are going to do well; that's a good number." I showed him my racing sweatshirt with my bright pink number 22 on it. We all laughed, and I pictured an angel on each of his shoulders.

I never gave it anymore thought until that evening at the banquet. He had won first place in his division. As he walked by, I said, "Told you that was a good number." He was so excited and said, "You were right!"

The number 22 continues to amaze me in my life.

I designed our camp and dream retirement home, hiring an architect to draw me the plans, and worked with him to get my details to come to life. I hired a builder and micromanaged every detail to get things the way we wanted them. Without me even trying, the cathedral peak of our ceiling was none other than 22 feet high, so said my builder.

One day during construction my son counted the windows and of course he said, "Mom, you have 22 windows." At that point I had not counted them. We all laughed.

The designer had no idea 22 was so important. At one point I messaged my builder to see how many handles I needed for my kitchenette, and of course he answered 22.

As we were doing the retaining wall we needed more big cement blocks, and the total we ended up with again was 22.

In my kitchen I noticed a shelf was missing and when I went to measure how deep it needed to be, it was 22 inches. I just smile and feel the warmth from my angels.

One day I was getting ready to ride my bike. Standing outside on the ground level patio, I put on my biking app. It told me I was 22 feet above sea-level. That totally amazed me.

This all tells me that my dreams are coming true, and I am on the right path. I was meant to have this amazing retirement home. My creatively divine space.

On Jan. 21, 2021, I was driving down the road. I was early by half an hour for where I needed to be. I was in deep thought when I saw the red and blue lights in my mirror. I pulled over and couldn't believe I was rushing. I had no reason to do so. I was asked for my licence, and he said he'd be right back. What the heck?

Upon his return he said, "You were going 22 km over the speed limit."

I said, "Really, 22?" Yup ninety-two in a seventy zone. He could have given me a ticket where I'd lose my licence for a week. He did not. He pointed out that he had given me a lesser one.

Go figure, my angels were watching over me again.

I drove off and was overcome by the warmth and tears. Momma was with me; I just knew it. I was happy and sad all at once and overcome with emotion.

Later that same day I stopped by a friend's for a few minutes to pick something up. I stayed longer than I had planned. When I left, I immediately saw a truck going slow. He was waving both hands, and it was my husband. He was in a different truck as one of our guys had called in sick. I grabbed my phone to send him a quick message. Snapped a picture on my screen as it was 2:22. Warmth again overcame me.

I have no doubt my angels are with me daily. Since Mom has been gone the number 22 is dominating my days. I love it, they make me so happy.

Many of my special friends are born on the 22nd of their month. My biological grandmother Lillian Tanner was born in 1922. Little Nan who was extremely special to me, was also born in 1922.

The number 22 just resonates with me so much. It's truly special.

I must add on the second day of the second month of 2022, I was coming down a hill a bit too fast. I saw the lights and looking down I was going 122 km.

I said out loud, "I can't be getting a ticket on this special day, can I?" Of course not. The cop came back with a warning as I could see my exit from where I sat. With the warmth overflowing me like a thousand hugs, I drove home all smiles. Continuously 22 guides my way, with light and love from the universe.

Future Books

Watch for my next book—I'm creating a Soul Searching-Inner Peace workbook. It will go hand in hand with "From Under A Rock."

Also in my future "My Spiritual Journey" which has been spinning in my head before this one even went to print, where I will share all my "aww" moments the universe has brought to me and so much more.

Clifton Saulnier
PHOTOS

Acknowledgments:

To my dear friends who read the first drafts, gave advice and gave me the strength to finish this huge project, I thank-you from my whole heart. You know who you are!

To my higher self, thank you for seeing this through. The good outweighs the bad.

Follow me:
tammacphee.com
@tammacphee on socials

CPSIA information can be obtained
at www.ICGtesting.com
Printed in the USA
LVHW082056291222
736096LV00017B/234/J